CONTENTS

CONTENTS

FOREWORD
AMERICAN NIGHTMARE

"My daddy was a blueshirt and my mother a madam
My brother earned his medals at My Lai in Vietnam"
–Shane MacGowan

War as TV spectacle – War as rock and roll death trip – War as cultural phenomenon – War as waking nightmare. The American dream of early success in the Vietnam conflict sooned turned sour in the face of draft-dodging and desertion, violent ant-war demonstrations, mounting casualties and fatalities amongst young US soldiers, the spiralling cost of the war, floods of disillusioned, disgruntled and disabled combat veterans and, finally, the growing realization that this was a war America could not win. And as ever, the non-stop, opportunistic motion picture industry quickly began to mirror every aspect of the Vietnam War and its fall-out, from the anti-draft mumblings of Andy Warhol's **Nude Restaurant** to the gung-ho posturing of John Wayne's **The Green Berets**. *Search And Destroy* is a book about those movies, and the socio-political changes they reflect.

Search And Destroy makes no claims to documenting every Vietnam War-related movie ever made; too many hundreds, or maybe even thousands, of feature films were released betreen 1970 and 1990 alone in which one or more character is some kind of "Vietnam Veteran". The book tries to focus instead on those films which are actually set in Vietnam during the conflict, and on the more interesting of the "Viet vet" films – films in which the main character or characters are vets and where this is the decisive factor in their behaviour, or the more imaginative genre films in which vets figure. The book also includes Jack Stevenson's fascinating summary of documentaries made about the Vietnam war, as well as covering obscure areas such as underground and porno cinema, making its range of film coverage as extensive as it is ultimately varied, and thus hopefully demonstrating how the conflict and its ramifications managed to infiltrate every level of American culture in the late 1960s, 1970s and 1980s, until US success in the Gulf War finally deflected some of the heat.

The release in 2001 of both **Apocalypse Now Redux** and a new documentary, **First Kill**, in which combat veterans are interviewed about their first enemy victims, and in 2002 of the Mel Gibson vehicle **We Were Soldiers** shows that the Vietnam War retains a cultural resonance which may never fade, and which even – or perhaps especially – in the aftermath of September 11 2001, continues to exert its influence over the collective psyche of America. All future war movies – and perhaps all future wars – will be judged by the benchmark of Vietnam.

–Jack Hunter

CHRONOLOGY
THE VIETNAM CONFLICT

1627   French missionary activity in Vietnam.

1820   Captain John White of Salem, Massachusetts, the 1st American in Vietnam.

1847   French forces and Vietnamese Mandarins clash at Tourane (Da Nang).

1861   French capture Saigon.

1862   Tu Duc, who ascended to the throne in 1847, signs a treaty with the French giving religious, economic and political concessions.

1863   French control extends over Cambodia.

1887   France creates the Indochinese Union: Cochinchina, Annam, Tonkin and Cambodia.

1890   Ho Chi Minh born in central Vietnam.

1911   Ho leaves Vietnam.

1918   Ho (aka Nguyen Ai Quoc) in Paris.

1920   Ho joins French Communist party.

1924   Ho goes to Moscow and later China.

1930   Ho and others form the Indochinese Communist Party in Hong Kong.

1932   Bao Dai ascends to the throne under French tutelage.

1940   Sept: Japan occupies Indochina but leaves French administration intact.

1941   Ho returns to Vietnam and forms the nationalist Viet Minh (Vietnam Independence League) against the Japanese and French. The US Office of Strategic Services (OSS) ally with Ho Chi Minh against the Japanese.

1944   Vo Nguyen Giap forms military wing of the Viet Minh.

1945   9 March: Japanese take over French administration.
             11 March: Bao Dai proclaims Vietnamese independence (under the auspices of the Japanese).
             July: Potsdam conference, Germany – British to disarm the Japanese in South Vietnamese while Chinese Nationalists are to do the same north of the 16th parallel. Vietnam, Laos and Cambodia to become, once again, French colonies after the removal of the Japanese.

Summer: Famine in North Vietnam kills 2 million out of 10 million Vietnamese. Political unrest.

18 August: Japanese surrender and transfer power to the Viet Minh.

23 August: Bao Dai abdicates.

29 August: Ho Chi Minh proclaims provisional government in Hanoi (with Bao Dai as Supreme Counsellor).

2 September: Japanese sign official surrender in Tokyo Bay. Ho Chi Minh proclaims independence for the Democratic Republic of Vietnam (quoting the American Declaration of Independence, conveniently supplied by the OSS).

13 September: British Forces, under General Douglas Gracey, arrive in Saigon, while Chinese Nationalists proceed to loot Hanoi.

22 Sept: French soldiers released in South Vietnam attack Viet Minh and other civilians, aided by French civilians.

26 Sept: 1st American killed in Vietnam: OSS officer Lieutenant Colonel A. Peter Dewey mistaken for French.

October: 35 000 French troops arrive under General Jacques Phillippe Leclerc to restore French rule. Viet Minh expelled from Saigon.

1946   March: Ho Chi Minh allows French troops into Hanoi in exchange for recognition of Vietnam as a "free state" within the French Union.

May: Sept: Ho in Fontainbleu negotiating complete independence. Talks fail.

June: Admiral Thierry d'Argenlieu, French High Commissioner for Indochina, announces separate government for southern province, Cochinchina.

23 November: French warships bombard Hai Phong and French take Hanoi.

19 Dec: 30,000 Viet Minh launch offensive against the French in Hanoi. Ho creates a rural base and the First Indochina War begins.

1949   8 March: Bao Dai installed as head of state and Vietnam is designated an "associated state" of the French Union under the Elysée agreement signed with French president, Vincent Auriol.

1950   14 January: Ho declares the Democratic Republic of Vietnam as only legal government. Recognised by the People's Republic of China and the Soviet Union. Military aid from China to the Viet Minh (much of it US made, from the Chinese Nationalists).

February: US and UK recognise Bao Dai's South Vietnamese government. Rise of anti-communist fervour in the States under McCarthy hearings.

30 June: Truman commits US to war in Korea under the auspices of the UN when North Korea invades South Korea on 26 June.

26 July: Truman authorises military aid to French ($15 mil) including weaponry and advisers.

27 September: US Military Assistance Group (MAAG) in Saigon established.

1951   February: Amid increasing casualties for the Viet Minh, Ho Chi Minh creates Lao Dong (The Workers' Party) as a substitute for the Communist Party.

December: General Giap eschews conventional battle and begins hit & run attacks.

1952   4 November: Dwight D. Eisenhower elected president of the USA. Steadily increases aid given to the French, supported by his " Domino Theory" i.e. communist victory in Vietnam would mean inevitable fall of surrounding countries (often used in later years to justify US involvement in Vietnam).

1953   27 July: Armistice signed in Korea.
20 November: Operation Castor – French construct outposts surrounding air base at Dien Bien Phu (NW Vietnam).

1954   13 March: 50 000 Viet Minh attack Bien Dien Phu outposts. Siege ensues after Air Base is crippled by bombardment.
7 May: 10 000 French surrender. France eventually withdraws from Vietnam.
8 May: Geneva Conference on Indochina begins to negotiate solution for SE Asia.
16 June: Bao Dai selects Ngo Dinh Diem as Prime Minister.
21 July: Geneva Accords divide Vietnam into 2 at the 17th parallel. Elections to be held in whole of Vietnam within 2 years. US opposes this, as they fear Ho Chi Minh's victory.
October: After French departure, Ho Chi Minh returns to Hanoi.
9 October: General J. Lawton Collins, Eisenhower's special envoy, arrives in Saigon, supporting Diem with $100 million in aid. Nearly 1 million leave North Vietnam for South Vietnam, with US naval assistance.

1955   Jan: 1st direct US aid shipment to Saigon and begins to train the South Vietnamese army.
April/May: Diem crushes Binh Xuyen, the Vietnamese mafia.
July: Ho Chi Minh is in Moscow and accepts Soviet aid.
23 Oct: Diem defeats Bao Dai in a US-backed referendum.
26 Oct: Proclaims the Republic of South Vietnam with himself as president.
Dec: Radical land reform in North Vietnam results in landlords being tried before "people's tribunals". Diem awards land seized from Buddhist peasants to Catholic supporters.

1956   Jan: Diem cracks down on Viet Minh suspects – torture and execution.
28 April: Last French soldier leaves South Vietnam. French High Command for Indochina dissolved.
16 July: Diem rejects the Geneva Accords and refuses to participate in the general elections.

1957   Jan: USSR suggests that N and S Vietnam be recognised as separate countries. US rejects.
May 8: Diem in Washington. Eisenhower affirms support for the "miracle man" of Asia.
Oct: Communist insurgents in South Vietnam. Over 400 South Vietnamese officials assassinated by the end of the year. Decision made in Hanoi to form 37 armed companies in the Mekong Delta.

1958   22 July: Prince Souvanna Phouma dissolves neutralist government in Laos which is replaced by the anti-communist Phoui Souanikone.

1959   March: Armed revolution begins with Ho Chi Minh declaring a People's War to unite Vietnam: Second Indochina War.
May: North Vietnamese establish the Central Office of South Vietnam. Group 559 formed to move cadres and weapons in South Vietnam via the Ho Chi Minh Trail (which leads through Laos and Cambodia).
8 July: Major Dale Buis and Sergeant Chester Ovnand killed by guerrillas at Bien Hoa (1st Americans to die in the "Vietnam Era").
Dec: Charles de Gaulle takes power in France and forms the Fifth Republic.

1960   April: Universal and indefinite conscription in North Vietnam.

8 Nov: JFK defeats Nixon for presidency.

11 Nov: South Vietnamese army attempt to overthrow Diem's increasingly nepotistic and corrupt government – brings about harsh crackdown and falling popular support.

20 Dec: National Liberation Front for South Vietnam formed in Hanoi – dubbed "Vietcong" by the South Vietnamese, meaning Vietnamese Communists. Ho's forces increasingly infiltrate the South and blend in with the locals.

1961   Jan: Under Kennedy's Secretary of Defense, Robert McNamara, US policy will be to wage a limited war to bring about a political settlement.

May: JFK sends 400 Green Beret Special Advisors to South Vietnam to train the army in counter-insurgency. Organise the Montagnards in the mountains into Civilian Irregular Defense Groups (CIDG).

October: Kennedy Aides, Maxwell Taylor and Walt Rostow, visit Vietnam and recommend US troop intervention. MacNamara wants to send 200,000 troops, but JFK refuses, but sends more equipment, helicopter units and advisors to Diem.

Dec: Viet Cong control much of the South Vietnamese countryside.

1962   6 Feb: Military Assistance Command for Vietnam (MACV) is formed, replacing MAAG (1950).

March: Operation Sunrise (Strategic Hamlet Programme) – rural South Vietnamese are gathered into fortified villages, which are, however, quickly infiltrated by the Viet Cong. Some of these are then bombed, with US help, by Diem – civilian casualties.

1963   3 Jan: 350 Viet Cong defeat heavily armed South Vietnamese at Ap Bac. 3 US helicopter crew are killed.

May: Buddhists riot in South Vietnam when they are denied the right to display religious flags during the celebration of Buddha's birthday.

June–August: Buddhist unrest spreads.

2 Sept: JFK criticises Diem on US TV as being "out of touch with the people".

1 Nov: Duong Van Minh and other generals stage a coup against Diem and General Ngo Dinh Nhu (both are assassinated when they surrender the next day).

22 Nov: JFK assassinated in Dallas and Lyndon B. Johnson is sworn in as president.
End of year: There are 15,000 US advisors in S. Vietnam and $500 m has been given in aid.

1964   30 Jan: General Nguyen Khanh seizes power in Saigon.

6 March: Secretary of Defense, Robert McNamara visits Vietnam and expresses support for Khanh. Advises Johnson to continue providing aid.

17 March: US National Security Council recommends the bombing of North Vietnam.

31 July: Covert South Vietnamese maritime operation against North Vietnamese military bases.

2 Aug: Three North Vietnamese patrol boats attack the U.S.S. Maddox in the Gulf of Tonkin.

7 Aug: Congress passes the Gulf of Tonkin Resolution giving Johnson extraordinary power to act in SE Asia.

Late Aug: US aircraft bomb North Vietnam for the first time.

30 Oct: Vietcong attack Bien hoa airbase – Johnson does not retaliate.

Nov: Protests in Saigon against Khanh.

24 Dec: Vietcong car bomb US billet at the Brinks Hotel in Saigon.

1965   7 Feb: Vietcong attack US installations – Johnson authorises Operation Flaming Dart (air raids in North Vietnam).

18 Feb: Khanh ousted from government and replaced by Dr. Phan Huy Quat.

24 Feb: Operation Rolling Thunder begins the bombing of North Vietnam.

8 March: 2 Marine battalions, the first US combat troops in Vietnam, land at China Beach to defend the airport at Da Nang.

9 March: Johnson authorises the use of napalm.

14–16 November: US forces defeat North Vietnamese troops in their first conventional clash in the Ia Drang valley.

25 Dec: Johnson suspends the bombing of North Vietnam to pursue peace negotiations.

1966   31 Jan: Bombing resumes.

29 June: US aircraft bomb oil depots near Hanoi and Haiphong.

1 Sept: De Gaulle visits Cambodia and calls for US withdrawal from Vietnam.

27 Dec: Large scale US air assault against suspected Vietcong positions in the Mekong Delta.

1967   1 May: Ellsworth Bunker replaces Henry Cabot Lodge as US ambassador in South Vietnam.

Aug: McNamara, testifying before a senate sub-committee, asserts that the bombing of North Vietnam has been ineffective.

3 Sept: National elections in South Vietnam. Nguyen Van Thieu elected president.

29 Sept: Johnson says that the US will stop bombing in exchange for "productive discussions".

29 Dec: North Vietnamese Foreign Minister, Nguyen Duy Trinh, says that talks are only possible when the US stops bombing.

1968   31 Jan: Tet Offensive: North Vietnamese and Vietcong attack 100 South Vietnamese towns and cities.

25 Feb: US and South Vietnamese troops recapture Hue after 26 days.

March: My Lai or "Pinksville" massacre occurs.

31 March: Johnson orders partial halt of bombing.

Mid-May: North Vietnamese diplomats in Paris for talks with US delegation.

31 October: Operation Rolling Thunder ends.

5 Nov: Richard Nixon elected President with Spiro Agnew as his VP.

27 Nov: Henry Kissinger accepts position as National Security Advisor.

1969   25 Jan: Peace talks in Paris with US, South Vietnam, North Vietnam & Vietcong.

23 Feb: Vietcong launch large-scale attack against South Vietnam including Saigon.

17 March: With Operation Menu, Nixon authorises secret bombing of Cambodia.

3 Sept: Ho Chi Minh dies in Hanoi at the age of 79.

16 Nov: First public discussion by the US army of the previous year's massacre at My Lai.

1970   4 May: 4 students killed by National Guard at Kent State University, Ohio.

12 Nov: Lieutenant William Calley on trial at Fort Benning, Georgia, for his part in My Lai.

1971   29 March: Calley convicted of murdering South Vietnamese civilians.

3 October: Thieu re-elected as president of South Vietnam.

1972   25 Jan: Nixon reveals that Kissinger has been in secret negotiations with the North Vietnamese.

30 March: North Vietnam launches offensive across the demilitarised zone.

15 April: Nixon authorises bombing near Hanoi and Haiphong.

1 May: NVA capture Quang Tri City.

1 Aug: Kissinger meets with Le Duc Tho in Paris.

8 Oct: Breakthrough in discussions between Kissinger and Tho: NV troops in SV allowed to stay; Thieu remains in power.

30 Nov: American troop withdrawal from Vietnam is complete. 16,000 advisors and administrators remain.

13 Dec: Peace negotiations collapse in Paris.

18 December: Operation Linebacker II involves severe bombing of Hanoi. These "Christmas bombings" are widely condemned.

1973   8 Jan: Talks resume between Kissinger and Le Duc Tho.

27 Jan: Paris Peace accords are signed.

29 March: Last US troops withdraw from Vietnam.

1 April: Last US POW, Captain Robert White, is released.

16 July: Senate Armed Services Committee begins hearings on the secret bombing of Cambodia.

14 Aug: US stops bombing Cambodia.

1974   Jan: Thieu declares that war has begun again.

9 Aug: Nixon resigns because of Watergate and is replaced by Gerald Ford.

1975   15 March: Thieu orders northern provinces of South Vietnam to be abandoned.

20 May: Reverses his orders and wants Hue to be held. The city falls 5 days later.

23 April: President Ford describes the war as "finished".

25 April: Thieu flees to Taiwan.

27 April: Saigon is surrounded by the NVA.

29 April: Ford orders Operation Frequent Wind – evacuation of Americans from Saigon by helicopter.

30 April: The last Americans, 10 US marines, leave Saigon and the NVA occupy the city. End of the war.

–David Sorfa

INTRODUCTION
IF I SHOULD DIE
IN A COMBAT ZONE

"The Beatles and the Stones/ put the V in Vietnam"
–The House of Love (1991)

"The first rock'n'roll war" the *New York Times* dubbed Vietnam, reviewing reporter Michael Herr's memoir *Dispatches* (1977). The observation's become a cliché, central to the philosophy of the Herr-co-scripted, Doors-scored **Apocalypse Now** (1979), cheapened by the baby-boomer-seducing soundtracks of every Vietnam movie since. But, though Herr undoubtedly filtered the war through his own rock-obsessed perceptions, the underground circuit running between South-East Asia and San Francisco in the Sixties is a clear, complex fact, its repercussions still felt in music, movies and literature today.

Rock'n'roll was part of the American infection in Vietnam, insinuating itself on transistor radios, played even on patrol, its impact warped almost unrecognisably by its surroundings. Trapped in besieged, haunted Khe Sanh in 1968, Herr and the Marine garrison heard The Beatles' "Magical Mystery Tour" as a hideous threat from the surrounding enemy, "waiting to take you away/dy-ing to take you away." The Stones' "2000 Light Years From Home" resonated too, while black GIs, radicalised by riots back home, held Aretha and Hendrix tight. As the war's futility became apparent to its participants, counter-culture attitudes took hold too, dress-codes and discipline collapsing, drug use from marijuana to heroin outpacing even Haight-Ashbury.

And the lines crossed: Vietnam infected rock'n'roll. "On the streets I couldn't tell the Vietnam veterans from the rock and roll veterans," Herr said, back home. "War and music had run power off the same circuit for so long they didn't even have to fuse... rock and roll turned more lurid and dangerous than bullfighting, rock stars started falling like second lieutenants." Sixties rock had grown from the folk-peace movement – Dylan the link – and found its audience radicalised by potential drafting, and so the music's self-conscious social seriousness, its responsibility to rebel, had begun. While movies and literature nervously held back, Vietnam handed rock America's dangerous edge.

As if to prove rock's Siamese twinning to the war, '68 and '69 saw optimism end in My Lai and Tet, Altamont and "hippie" Charles Manson's rampage (the latter noted by a soldier preparing to meet Kurtz in **Apocalypse Now**, madness everywhere, while writer Stanley Booth noted Altamont, where he feared for his life, was "as close to war as makes no odds").

As crowds and raw materials began to bloat rock at decade's end, its unconscious resemblance to Vietnam's self-perpetuating, gargantuan techno-insanity became unavoidable. The **Woodstock** movie emphasised tannoy towers that could have nested machine-guns, restlessly buzzing 'copters, crowds suffering in sludge, "a paddy field of its own making" in Charles Shaar Murray's words, rock'n'roll as a test of endurance (continuing in Glastonbury today). Rock tours became military-style operations, Bob Dylan naming his 1975 roadshow *Rolling Thunder*, after the campaign to bomb North Vietnam; Oliver Stone's **The Doors** (1990) captured how the excessive spectacle of Vietnam-era rock started to replicate fire-fights. More destructively, veterans driven to smack in Vietnam returned to deal it in their own neighbourhoods, contributing to the ghetto meltdown that birthed gangsta-rap.

Songs that directly commented on Vietnam were never more than a steady trickle, and divided almost equally between pro- and anti-, hippie and straight. For every "I Feel Like I'm Fixin' To Die" by Country Joe, there was a "Ballad Of The Green Berets" by Sgt. Sadler; for every "Draft Morning" by The Byrds, a "Universal Coward" by Jan Berry. The war's unspoken centrality to rock was better shown when Dylan's austere 1968 *John Wesley Harding* was agonised over for its absence of comment on Vietnam, seen as comment itself. Meanwhile, urgent bulletins like Crosby, Stills, Nash & Young's "Ohio" and Marvin Gaye's "What's Going On" were encouraged.

Though Hollywood all but ignored the war while it was raging, its influence on Vietnam was insidious too. "Nineteen-year-old Americans, brought up on World War Two movies and Westerns, walking through the jungle, armed to the teeth, searching for an invisible enemy who knew the wilderness better than they did, could hardly miss the connections," reported historian Loren Baritz. "One after another said, 'Hey, this is just like a movie.'" Herr saw soldiers acting for TV cameras while under fire. Hostile terrain was called "Indian country".

The mythic figure behind such thinking was of course John Wayne – specifically Wayne as unstoppable, ultra-patriot Marine Sergeant Stryker in **The Sands Of Iwo Jima** (1949). Responsible for countless Marine recruits, including Ron Kovic who, crippled in Vietnam, would renounce Wayne in **Born On The Fourth Of July**, Stryker's catch-phrases, "Saddle up!" and "Lock and load!" would later be adopted by Tom Berenger's demonic Sergeant in **Platoon**. Wayne himself, after visiting Vietnam in 1966, tried to update this impact with **The Green Berets** (1968), to fit the war's attritional ugliness into World War Two clichés. The only significant 'Nam film of the Sixties, its pro-war intent is sabotaged by the actors willing to appear in it – looking drugged, body-snatched, speaking stilted propaganda. It was Wayne, so it was a hit, but it stood alone (Wayne's Indochina associations, though, continue: Garth Ennis's savagely funny Nineties comic *Preacher* replays his Vietnam visit – a shadowy giant, dispensing "Fuck Communism" lighters).

When wartime Hollywood did acknowledge Vietnam, it did so, inevitably, in Westerns – **The Wild Bunch** (1969)'s Mexico incursion, and a Cavalry patrol's decimation by half-seen, Viet Cong-like Apache in **Ulzana's Raid** (1972). Horror directors also displaced the battle bloodiness becoming familiar on TV news, as in George Romero's **Night Of The Living Dead** (1968). Literature, too, was distanced, World War Two phantasmagorias like Joseph Heller's *Catch-22* and Kurt Vonnegut's *Slaughterhouse-5* filling blackly absurd needs.

1973, when U.S. troops left Vietnam, signalled the war could leave cultural quarantine. Curtis Mayfield's *Back To The World* LP detailed the poverty and confusion black troops returned to, while veteran Tim O'Brien's *If I Die In A Combat Zone* was an exceptional start to what would soon be a flood of soldiers' stories. The "fall" of Saigon in 1975 quietened nerves still more, and fearful reactions to veterans Americans saw on their streets, unavoidable debris of defeat, fuelled the first cycle of Vietnam films. There'd been exploitation precursors – like Bob Clark's **Dead Of Night** (1972), in which a veteran declared missing in action takes vampiric revenge on the small town whose values made him enlist. But it was **Taxi Driver** (1976) that fixed the image of the veteran as damaged death-machine, a walking American nightmare, cut loose from a lost war. Henry Winkler in **Heroes**, William Devane in **Rolling Thunder**, Dennis Hopper in **Tracks** (all 1977) and Bruce Dern in **Coming Home** (1978) were all cracked.

1975 was also the signal for Coppola to start work on **Apocalypse Now**. Its four-year construction from unstable elements including Hopper, hurricanes and Manila dictator Marcos's helicopters saw movie-making replicate the war's chaos, as had already happened with the rock which was its other subject (Michael Herr helping the fusion he'd noted in 'Nam).

By 1977, while Coppola struggled, mainstream Hollywood tentatively tried films about the actual war – Sidney J. Furie's **The Boys In Company C**, a decent, darkly funny platoon movie, and a 1964 skirmish in Ted Post's **Go Tell The Spartans**. *Dispatches*, Philip Caputo's *A Rumor Of War* and Ron Kovic's *Born On The Fourth Of July* were all successfully published the same year, suggesting an awakening appetite.

But it was Michael Cimino's **The Deer Hunter** (1978), as visceral on first viewing in its scenes of home-town hurt as Vietnam violence, which made the war safe for cinema. The **Green Berets**-style machismo of De Niro's gook-blasting, and wild inaccuracies – the Army suggested Cimino "employs a researcher who either knows or is willing to learn something about the VN war" – surfaced later. The presence of John Wayne in his final and bravest performance, insides liquefying from cancer, days from death, to hand Cimino his Best Director Oscar completed some kind of circle.

1982 was another flashpoint, **The Deer Hunter**'s closing chorus of "God Save America" ringing through the Washington Memorial's dedication to U.S. war dead by Wayne wannabe Reagan, letting veterans feel forgiven. A bestselling oral history that year, Mark Baker's *Nam*, gave them back their voices. TV's *Magnum* meanwhile made Tom Selleck's vet an amiable 'tec, soon followed by *The A-Team*'s chirpy vets on the run, and in 1983 Reagan invaded Grenada, announcing the Guilt era's end (no-one informing more than a million Vietnamese dead, or their defoliated nation). Ted Kotcheff's vet-taking-vengeance-on-society Stallone vehicle **First Blood** (1982) may have seemed nothing special (not compared to David Morrell's ambiguous, ironic novel anyway) but subsequent surprise hits – Kotcheff's **Uncommon Valour** (1983) and **Missing In Action** (1984) – fed the country's new mood by reopening hostilities in South-East Asia, rescuing (mythical) U.S. POWs; **Rambo: First Blood II** (1985) resulted.

It was applauded by Reagan, as was a far greater work, Springsteen's "Born In The U.S.A." (1984), a rare statement of the typical veteran's scuffling impotence in Eighties America. Like Ivan Passer's **Cutter's Way** (1981), in which mutilated, embittered veteran John Heard attempts reparation from America's rich, it was a rare dissenting voice. John Milius's **The Flight Of The Intruder**

(1988), where Willem Dafoe single-handedly bombs Hanoi in the war's dying days for a laugh, was a late entry in the decade's status quo – read John Pilger's *Heroes* for such raids' real hideous effects, and revisionism's vileness.

Platoon (1986) completed the war's convalescence, a hit movie set in Vietnam, directed by veteran Oliver Stone. It smashed the floodgates, 1987 alone seeing Kubrick's half-masterpiece **Full Metal Jacket**, Coppola's **Gardens Of Stone**, and John Irvin's neglected **Hamburger Hill**, the true story of a futile 1969 battle, paratroops minced struggling for a ridge. A desolate Washington D.C. at the start, racial tension, anti-hippie speeches, Vietnamese calmly farming, and a man not noticing his arm's been torn off add to the weird perspective.

By 1988, the war was just a backdrop – to detectives tracking a rapist in **Saigon**, and Robin Williams' routines in **Good Morning Vietnam**. Williams' smash hit, about a "subversive" rock DJ on Armed Forces radio, showed one pernicious change from the real Sixties: the ruthless reversal of rock'n'roll's once adversarial presence in the war, its deradicalised reduction to nostalgic jukebox. Sugaring the Vietnam pill with feelgood, familiar music let sagging one-time protesters and their children mourn America's lost "innocence" while dancing to The Doors, let them think rock and protest both belonged in the past. The displacing decade between Saigon's "fall" and the 'Nam movie's rise had done its work. Americans now watched *The Wonder Years* (start: 1989), not the Iran-Contra hearings; **Platoon**, not Stone's **Salvador** the same year. "It made me wish I'd been around to protest things," wrote a reader after *Rolling Stone*'s Sixties special, soon after the Gulf War.

If **Platoon** helped the war's delayed destruction of protest, and neutering of rock'n'roll, Stone at least tried to make amends, with **Born On The Fourth Of July** (1989)'s ruthless evisceration of small-town patriotism, and **Heaven And Earth** (1993), bravely placing the war's Vietnamese victims centre-stage. Seeing the lush landscape and ordered individual lives of peasants ripped apart by American intervention ensured it was a flop, of course, as was Brian De Palma's **Casualties Of War**, reintroducing the spectre of the My Lai massacre. Sidney Lumet's **Running On Empty** (1988), about violent protesters at Vietnam's napalming still being hounded in Reagan's America, was also blanked.

New twists on the war's still half-buried legacy keep coming. Books stumble out like lost jungle patrols, from Neil Sheehan's definitive history *A Bright Shining Lie* (1989) to Stephen King's *Hearts In Atlantis* (2000). The French have at last offered Indochine, and John Woo's **Bullet In The Head** fetishised the infamous picture of a South Vietnamese officer's head-shot to a suspect in an action movie redolent of Asia's unstable Sixties. Tony Liu's **Three Seasons** (1999) proves the ironically layered, changing times; a Vietnamese-American director filming in Ho Chi Minh City, where Harvey Keitel's ex-Marine tourist drinks to forget, at the "Apocalypse Now" bar.

–Nick Hasted

PART ONE

WAR

CHAPTER 1
SEARCH AND DESTROY: VIETNAM COMBAT FILMS

Back in the 1950s and early '60s, when it was the French fighting a war in Vietnam, and the Viet Cong were known as the Viet Minh, Hollywood produced a number of films dramatizing events there, and documenting America's limited – but growing – involvement in aiding the anti-Communist regime. The most notable of these include: **Jump Into Hell** (1955); **China Gate** (1957); **The Quiet American** (1958); **5 Gates To Hell** (1959); **Brushfire** (1961); **The Ugly American** (starring Marlon Brando, 1963); **Year Of The Tiger** (1964); **To The Shores Of Hell** (1965); **Operation CIA** (1965); **Marine Battleground** (1966); and **The Lost Command** (1966). From Spain came **Crucifix In Hell** (aka **Flame Over Vietnam**, José Maria Elorrieta aka Joe Lacy, 1967), a depiction of the travails of missionary nuns in Nam.

America's shift into full-scale conflict had commenced in March 1965 with the inauguration of Operation Rolling Thunder, the sustained bombing of North Vietnam, after Viet Cong fighters had attacked two US Army bases, killing a number of soldiers. It was not until three years later, in 1968, that the first US production purely dealing with America's full military deployment in Vietnam would appear. And, as public opinion turned against the war, it would be the last until a decade later. John Wayne's **The Green Berets** is generally regarded with hindsight as a slice of pure US propaganda, a fascist flag-waving exercise perpetrated by the most right-wing actor in Hollywood in cahoots with the government. Shot in the States and with white extras in yellow make-up portraying the Viet Cong, **The Green Berets** was generally ridiculed and reviled on release as an unrealistic, old-fashioned treatment of a subject which required modern perspicacity and sensitivity to reveal its true complexity. Instead, the Vietnam conflict had become just another arena in which Wayne could stage his tired, nationalistic "heroics".

Physical Assault (aka **Prisoners**, William H Bushnell, 1973), based on the novel *The Prisoners Of Quai Dong* by Victor Kolpacoff, is a claustrophobic independent film which undoubtedly deals with the war in Vietnam, without overtly referring to it or showing men in combat. **Physical Assault** is set instead in a locked interrogation room, where a group of US soldiers are interviewing/ mentally torturing an East Asian (Viet Cong, we infer) prisoner (played by Mako). The monotony and futility of the interrogation, and the conflicts between the various men involved, seem to reflect the futility of the Vietnam War itself, and remind us that the US soldiers are as much prisoners in this situation as their VC captive.

It was not until 1978 that a new wave of Hollywood movies dealing with the troops in Vietnam would appear, **The Boys In Company C** and **Go Tell The**

John Wayne, *The Green Berets*

Spartans preparing the way for **The Deer Hunter**, the film which made such an enormous emotional impact on American audiences [see chapter 2]. **The Boys In Company C**, directed by Sidney J Furie, begins in 1967 with five young recruits in training camp (where their tough drill instructor is played by R. Lee Ermey, who would later reprise the role in **Full Metal Jacket**). Soon they are shipped to Vietnam, where they see action (firefights, mines, booby-traps etc) and also some of the dubious pleasures (dope, indigenous hookers) to be found there. This was a much more negative portrayal of the war than the John Wayne version, but still riddled with enough war film clichés to render it of little interest.

Ted Post's **Go Tell The Spartans**, like **The Green Berets**, starred a Hollywood legend; Burt Lancaster played the role of Major Barker, posted to Vietnam in 1964, when the full-scale conflict was yet to happen. Probably the best of the early Nam combat films, **Go Tell The Spartans** tells of a group of US soldiers sent to establish a forward position deep in enemy territory. The film's title derives from an inscription found above an old cemetery housing the bodies of the French fighters who preceded them. The film builds to its climax with increasing VC activity, attacks and deaths. As they finally try to evacuate, Barker and his group are ambushed and killed. The film underlines the fact that even in 1964, all the futility and absurdity of the Vietnam War was there to see.

1979 was the year of the ultimate Vietnam war movie, Francis Ford Coppola's **Apocalypse Now** [see chapter 3], but also produced the only Australian contribution to the genre, **The Odd Angry Shot** (directed by Tom Jeffrey)[1]. As the film's title suggests, **The Odd Angry Shot** is mostly concerned with the boredom of being in Vietnam; the continuous torrential rain, the

Burt Lancaster, *Go Tell The Spartans*

drinking and gambling, and the moments of male bonding. When combat does occur, most of the deaths are off-camera. The film ends with one full-scale battle, then the wounded are carried off home.

Also that year came David Greene's **Friendly Fire**, a 3-hour TV movie dealing with the accidental death of a young soldier killed by his own troops, and his parents' subsequent investigative crusade to reveal the truth.

1980 produced a rousing and violent exploitational Italian entry, **The Last Hunter** [see chapter 4], and from the USA **A Rumour Of War**, a lengthy TV production based on combat veteran Phil Caputo's autobiography of the same name. **A Rumour Of War** was a strong condemnation of the Vietnam War and the conduct of the American troops who were

How Sleep The Brave

fighting it. **Charlie Bravo**, a rare French entry directed by René Demoulin[2], deals with a band of rescue nurses captured by the Viet Cong. **Search And Destroy** (1981) was one of those films with both in-country and back home action; **How Sleep The Brave** (aka **Once Upon A Time In Vietnam**, also 1981) is notable as being the only British Vietnam War movie. Directed by exploitation film veteran Lindsay Shonteff, it's a tale of fresh-faced recruits arriving in Nam and immediately being sent on a series of hazardous missions, during which many of them die in brutal fashion. The combination of English actors and what looks like English countryside never really make for a convincing film.

    Don't Cry It's Only Thunder (1982) was a Saigon-based melodrama about medical corruption, while **Saigon: Year Of The Cat** (Stephen Frears, 1983) was an examination of events in the South Vietnamese capital in 1975, just before the end of the War and the Communist take-over.

    The late 1980s saw a high concentration of combat or Nam-based movies in the wake of Oliver Stone's mega-hit **Platoon** in 1986 [see chapter 5], most prominent of which was Stanley Kubrick's long-awaited **Full Metal Jacket** (1987 [see chapter 6]). 1987 also saw the release of films ranging from the lousy comedy **Good Morning Vietnam**, a vehicle for kiddies' geek actor Robin Williams, to the savage exploitationer **Hell On The Battleground**, starring William Smith. The two best films that year were **Hamburger Hill** and **Hanoi Hilton**, again two contrasting studies of the conflict. **Hamburger Hill** – a bit like the Korean War-based **Pork Chop Hill** (1959) before it – is another study of the ferocity and Sisyphusian futility of war. Directed by John Irvin, it shows a recreation of an

Hamburger Hill

actual battle, the assault on Dong Ap Bia, that commenced on May 1st, 1969. For 10 days US troops advance up, then retreat back down, the same hill, slowly gaining ground but losing many dead along the way. Finally, they get to the top, achieving – what? Featuring much interplay between its young, shell-shocked characters and insights into the nature of the conflict, **Hamburger Hill** remains one of the better Vietnam War pictures. **Hanoi Hilton**, directed by Lionel Chetwynd, focuses instead on POWs, this time those held in the infamously brutal Hoa Lo Prison, known as the "Hanoi Hilton", where US captives lived in daily fear for their lives – and their balls. The film follows a group of prisoners through several years of captivity to final release, and never flinches from showing the squalid and often violent nature of their incarceration.

1988 saw even more Vietnam-based films released. Most high profile was **BAT 21** (1988), based on a true story and starring Gene Hackman as Colonel Iceal Hambleton, a pilot shot down whilst on a routine reconnaissance mission. The film shows the concerted attempt to rescue Hambleton from the area of jungle he is stranded in (which is marked to be carpet-bombed). Using a makeshift radio code based on golfing terms, the Colonel and his rescuer (played by Danny

Casualties Of War

Glover) manage to avoid the enemy and finally make it out of the burning bush. Three more Nam-based films – all fairly routine – appeared that year: **Saigon Commandos**, directed by Clark Henderson, is the story of a military police officer fighting corruption and drug trafficking in war-time Saigon; **The Siege Of Firebase Gloria** (directed by Brian Smith) is a full-on action film set during the Tet Offensive, with plenty of stock Nam ingredients (including R. Lee Ermey as a grizzled sergeant). And **Platoon Leader**, directed by Aaron Norris, was a low-budget, fast-moving **Platoon** copy featuring William Smith once again.

Brian De Palma's **Casualties Of War** (1989) was the last Vietnam combat picture by a major Hollywood director, and remains one of the better ones. The film stars Sean Penn as the brutal platoon sergeant Meserve, who captures a young Vietnamese woman as a sex slave, and Michael J Fox as Eriksson, the private who reports Meserve and his cohorts for the woman's multiple gang-rape and eventual murder. Like Elia Kazan's **The Visitors** [see chapter 7], **Casualties Of War** was based on a 1969 newspaper article on the rape and murder of a Vietnamese woman by US troops. After being captured and continually abused by Meserve and his buddies, the woman survives a murder attempt only to be shot dead trying to escape. When Eriksson reports the incident, he meets resistance from his superiors and only narrowly survives an assassination attempt. Finally, Meserve and his cohorts are court-martialed and sentenced to several years in the brig. The film ends with a scene of Fox as a vet back in the States, still haunted by his ordeal. 1989 also saw the release of **The Iron Triangle**, directed by Eric Weston, and supposedly based on the war memoir of a VC soldier. Beau Bridges played an American officer captured by the VC in this examination of the "good" and "bad" on both sides of the conflict. **84 Charlie MoPic** (Patrick

84 Charlie MoPic

Duncan, 1989) is one of the most interesting of the lower-budget Nam movies. This stark film is seen from the viewpoint of an army cameraman, who speaks but is seldom glimpsed. Duncan – a Vietnam combat vet himself – shot the film on 16mm, to give a more authentic, grainy feel, and **84 Charlie MoPic** takes on the air of a documentary as the mobile camera follows every explosion, firefight and brutal killing. Explicitly anti-war in tone, **84 Charlie MoPic** ends on a suitably downbeat note: our cameraman stops shooting to aid a soldier under fire, and is shot dead. The film runs out and fades to to black.

After the low-budget **Last Stand At Lang Mei** (1990, based on the battle of Khe Sanh)), the genre fell away sharply in the '90s, with Gulf War movies such as **Heroes Of Desert Storm** and **Desert Shield** (both 1991) taking precedence[3]. Only **The Walking Dead** (Preston A Whitmore II, 1995) was of particular interest, being the story of a predominantly black platoon in Nam, and the racial conflicts and tensions between them and the few white soldiers in evidence. In this sense the film shares an ethos with the Hughes Brothers' **Dead Presidents**, released the same year [see chapter 7], whose central in-country segment ran along the same lines. Both are films by young black film-makers presenting the harsh reality of the black experience in Nam. Though the odd TV movie like **A Bright Shining Lie** (1998) appeared[4], it was only with Randall Wallace's **We Were Soldiers** in 2002 that another major Hollywood production was released. **We Were Soldiers** is a very late, and certainly outdated entry to the Vietnam War film cycle. The film stars Mel Gibson (who had previously starred in the pathetic 1990 CIA-pilots-in-Nam comedy **Air America**) as Colonel Hal Moore, commander of around 400 US troops flown by helicopter into the isolated Ia Drang valley in Vietnam. Based on an actual event in November 1965, the film shows the heroic and bloody struggles of the young US soldiers against an enemy outnumbering them by almost 10 to 1. Later known as Death Valley, this was the first major conflict between US and North Vietnamese troops in the

Mel Gibson, *We Were Soldiers*

Vietnam War. Concentrating on the kinship between the men and Moore's qualities as leader, **We Were Soldiers** is essentially a hackneyed war film trading on Gibson's "warrior" persona as established in **Braveheart** and **The Patriot**, and part of the uncannily timed batch of militaristic pictures released soon after September 11 2001 that included **Black Hawk Down** and **Behind Enemy Lines**.

NOTES

1.   The next Australian movie to show conflict with the Vietnamese would be **Romper Stomper** (Geoffrey Wright, 1993), a modern tale of urban neo-Nazi skinheads and their attacks on the local Vietnamese community (who they refer to as "gooks" in honour of the War), notable for its breakneck amoral violence and the film debut of Russell Crowe.

2.   Unlike America, France has always preferred to keep quiet about its overseas conflicts such as those in Algeria and Vietnam. Very few French films deal with France's occupation of Nam, and those which do – such as **Les Dimanches De Ville D'Avray** (1962, about a traumatised bomber pilot) – tend to focus on human interest rather than "war" itself.

3.   As the 1990s progressed, the Desert Storm genre began to develop in a similar – though much smaller scale – way to its Vietnam predecessor, with the release of exploitation movies like **Uncle Sam** (1997), in which a Desert Storm vet who was killed in combat rises from the grave on July Fourth to slaughter the unpatriotic citizens of his hometown, after some teens burn an American flag over his burial site.

4.   There have been numerous TV movies about combat or captivity in Vietnam, including: **When Hell Was In Session** (1979); **In Love And War** (1987); and the trilogy **Vietnam War Story** (1988), **Vietnam War Story II** (1989), and **Vietnam War Story III** (1989). Relating to combat – specifically the My Lai massacre – was Stanley Kramer's **Judgement – The Court Martial Of Lt William Calley** (1975), with Tony Musante as Calley and also featuring a young Harrison Ford. There has also been one major TV series centred around Vietnam combat – *Tour Of Duty* (1987–1990) ran for 58 episodes, commencing with the feature-length pilot **Hard Rain – The Tet**.

CHAPTER 2
THIS IS THIS:
"THE DEER HUNTER"

The Deer Hunter, a cornerstone of the Vietnam war movies cenotaph alongside **Apocalypse Now** (1979), **Full Metal Jacket** (1987), **Platoon** (1986) and (arguably) **Born On The Fourth Of July** (1989), is, like the others, a memorable, provocative, but often flawed picture. No Vietnam film has yet adequately explored all sides of the conflict, and this one both fails to address the tumultuous involvement of the US Government and, perhaps most seriously of all, cruelly stereotypes the Viet Cong as latter day Japanese-style prison camp sadists.

At the end of the late 1970's, the Vietnam War was still a deeply unpopular subject with countless millions of Americans. Producers of tentative war films including **Go Tell The Spartans** (1978) and **The Boys In Company C** (1978) found this out to their cost when their films bombed at the box office [see previous chapter]. The resultant gloom with the war and the film genre itself meant that Cimino had to turn to the British Film company EMI for his initial financing of the film at some $7.5m. EMI saw the great potential in Cimino's idea, which simplistically tells the story of a group of steelworkers in fictional Clairton, Pennsylvania whose relationships would be dramatically altered by their leaving for the Vietnam War.

Michael Cimino earned a bachelor's and then a masters degree in art from Yale University in the early 1960's. He studied acting and directing with Lee Strasburg and then worked in New York on industrial films, documentaries and TV commercials. As a screenwriter he had a shared credit on films including the low budget sci-fi classic **Silent Running** (1972) and Clint Eastwood's **Magnum Force** (1973). He would soon become one of Hollywood's hottest properties with the success of **The Deer Hunter**.

Narratively, **The Deer Hunter** is roughly divided into equal thirds or acts – (1) the development of characterisations and symbolic rituals of the second-generation Russian-Americans in their small Pennsylvania steel community before war-time. This section includes a wedding and a long reception sequence – the first act in life's cyclical passage; (2) the harrowing, sensational, and violent war-time experiences of the Americans in Vietnam – the psychologically-destructive scarring of life; and (3) the aftermath of the war and its physical and psychological effects upon the three male participants in the war and those left at home (wives, families, and friends).

The film's credits, white letters on a black background, are accompanied by Stanley Myers' music and the main title theme (by John Williams). The opening scene occurs at the end of the night shift in the small, dingy, industrial Pennsylvania town of Clairton. In the local iron foundry, fiery, bright flames, smoke and sparks emerge from the blast furnaces – the powerful, hellish fire a symbol of productiveness and destructiveness both in peace and in war-time. In the early morning, the protagonists of the film are introduced as hard-working blue-collar workers as they shower and leave the factory for the last time before three of them ship out for a tour of duty in Vietnam. One of their colleagues warns: "Don't get your ass shot off." The three close, hometown, "macho," working-class, male-bonded Russian-American buddies who will be testing their masculinity in war are Michael Vronsky (Robert De Niro), Nick (Christopher Walken), and Steven (John Savage). They join up with weasly, insecure, would-be womanizer Stan (John Cazale), and massive, heavy-set, brutish, and grunting Axel (Chuck Aspegren).

Steven is taking the extra commitment of marriage and tying the knot with already pregnant Angela (Rutanya Alda). It's a great source of despair for Steven's first-generation, immigrant mother (Shirley Stoler). The wedding is held inside the local cathedral, an enormous, glitteringly decorated testament to the unshakeable faith of these Russian-Americans. It's a lengthy affair, with Nick and Linda acting as courtiers. The unfortunate thing is that while these two are a couple, Nick's buddy Michael also covets the attention of Linda. At the reception, everyone relaxes in a whirl of vodka, stylised dancing and feasting sufficient to set the happy couple off on their matrimonial journey. As friends are inclined to do, the core group of Michael, Nick, Stan, John (George Dzundza) and Axel celebrate the coming battles. All are used to hunting deer in the mountains, so they can extrapolate the thrill of sighting an enemy.

The first act of **The Deer Hunter** then belongs to Steven, encouraged into a shotgun marriage for two reasons; Angela is with child, and Steven may never come back from Vietnam. Now is the time to make an honest woman of her, for tomorrow may be too late. In the second act (in Vietnam), the inner strength and determination of Michael comes to the fore. While Nick and Steven visibly disintegrate under the abuse and torture of their captors, Michael refuses to capitulate. In fact he grows stronger, channelling every emotion through his self-will and harnessing the power. By the final segment this inner light has dimmed, without failing completely; the tragic core is now Nick, lost both in location and mind. For all that friendship binds the three together in post-conflict trauma, they prove unable to save one another. This is a tale of missed opportunity, where all see the possibility of returning intact slip through their fingers; these losses hurt.

When Michael, Nick and Steven are thrown headlong into the horror of battle, the severe intensity of their predicament is soon made all too obvious. (With his deep-seated need for realism, Cimino relocated the cast and crew to Thailand for the war scenes using it as a substitute for Vietnam. Even so, it was still a potentially dangerous location for filming, and was at the time undergoing serious political turmoils of its own – so much so that Royal Thai policemen were assigned to protect the unit, one policeman for every three crew members).

In **The Deer Hunter** the pivotal character in the film, Michael is somewhat awkward and shy, completely moral (at least in his mind) and at times brutish. He has trouble communicating with his love interest Linda. He finds his most lasting bonds with the male characters of the film, yet he reacts quixotically when faced with slight apprehension. When one of his comrades refuses to do as he says in the beginning of the film, he reacts with an intense stare. Michael is portrayed as intensely loyal, and prone to self-sacrifice in a heart-beat

The three friends in Vietnam

throughout the film. He is the true hero of the film, and one of his favorite pastimes with his friends involves the hunting of deer. He is adept at this sport, and he makes it clear to his friends that the best way to hunt the elusive deer is to "kill in the first shot". In his quasi-articulate, quasi-mystical way, Michael expresses this "one shot" philosophy in a key scene in the mountains, holding up a single bullet with the mantric affirmation, "this is this". He practices his philosophy of mental precision coupled with fluid violence later in the film to life-saving advantage, when he frees his friends from the Russian Roulette practicing torture camp by his decisively abrupt and clinical action.

When Michael returns from Vietnam back to a hero's welcome in Clairton, he is again depicted as awkward and overly modest. His attempts to woo Linda are misguided and stilted. Only when he has a gun in hand and is actively hunting deer, does he feel at home again. When Michael hears about his beloved friend Nick being alive in Vietnam, he goes back in an attempt to save him, which tragically fails with Nick's death. It is here in the film where he experiences his first truly tragic loss. He loses someone, one of the few people he was able to truly connect with, to circumstances beyond his control. Although the film ends on an uplifting note, with a eulogy being expressed for the group's common friend, the experience undoubtedly had greater mental consequences

Combat

for Michael than was made clear by the film's end.

When the film finally opened to the public in early 1979 (it had been released in Los Angeles in December 1978 to be considered for Oscar nominations) there were predictably diverse and extreme reactions. For many, the war was still a deep wound and America was still deeply divided over both the conflict itself and the resultant aftermath. Perhaps, while ultimately **The Deer Hunter** didn't actually resolve the conflicts of its survivors, it did allow them to minutely examine their feelings under their own personal life microscopes and, by extension, allow those who watched the film come more to terms with their own personal demons.

Moreover, **The Deer Hunter** wasn't a story about big government making wrong decisions, it was about the choices of one man and his friends, a microcosm of American culture. Yet this meandering, sometimes harsh but undeniably raw film remains controversial on many accounts – both political and emotional. On the downside, the extravagantly-expensive film is often pretentious, ambiguous, overwrought and excessive. It is loosely edited, with under-developed character portrayals and unsophisticated, occasionally careless film techniques. The most talked about sequence in the film is (most critically) the contrived, overly theatrical, and fictional Russian Roulette torture, imposed on the American POW's during wartime and later played as a game in a Saigon gambling den. The Russian Roulette sequence is a metaphor operating on several

Escape

levels. Superficially it ties in with the joy that these working men feel when they go hunting, beyond which there is the similar mindset that both activities possess. Each is highly ritualised, a macho path whereby the soul can become purged and the thoughts calmed, preparation for death. Unfortunately, when the hunters become the hunted, the facade of their "sport" becomes apparent. The mindless pursuit of Russian Roulette comes to represent war as an entity, in all of its random futility and psychologically devastating consequence. Narratively this sequence, as Cimino had predicted, caused the greatest controversy. Many critics considered the roulette scenes exploitational and gratuitously violent, their weight given extra argument in the knowledge that the sequence was a fictional situation created by Cimino as "metaphor" and with no genuine grounding in historical fact. Yet, paradoxically the Russian Roulette scene remains one of the most suspenseful and cathartic in all movies depicting the horrors of war.

Stylistically speaking, **The Deer Hunter** is indicative of the time period in which it was made. The mid-seventies feeling of malaise and unwillingness to cope with the war or its after-effects themselves were the main factors contributing to the Vietnam War film's rather late coming. **The Deer Hunter**, along with **Apocalypse Now** were the first films to portray combat in Vietnam in over a decade after John Wayne's nationalistic, jingoistic, propaganda-entrenched **The Green Berets** (1968). Instead, the films of the mid-seventies, like **Coming Home** and **Taxi Driver** (1976), dealt with the issue of Vietnam rather indirectly, or more metaphorically, as opposed to head-on, like **The Deer Hunter**,

Pennsylvania mountains to a drug-hazed blood sport wherein the gun is pointed only at oneself. Just as Michael's drive for control reflects the nation's own sense of imperial authority then Nick's (not entirely unconscious) rejection of his homeland represents its collective, psychic collapse. If Michael's quasi-mythic persona reveals that to which America aspires, Nick's physical and mental disintegration demonstrate truly what it has become. Nick ends up dead after letting his fear consume him.

In **The Deer Hunter**, the performances are everything and the cast is excellent, draining and economical. De Niro, the lynchpin of the trio, is exceptionally satisfying, scaling the pinnacle of emotion. The scenes in which Mike returns home a hero, without choosing the honour, and feels compelled to avoid his welcome are tremendous. He seems blank, wiped clean by the struggle and distanced from old friends. Streep is equally impressive, allowing subtle needs to flit across her face as she tries to keep a lid on her fraught psyche. In the third corner of this triangle, Walken is chillingly effective in his transformation. Psychologically ruined, he's a haunted shell. Finally, the more peripheral actors are all uniformly excellent, with the acting of Cazale (who was suffering with terminal cancer during the film and died before its release) being particularly poignant.

Ultimately, **The Deer Hunter** excels in most departments; not least by dint of featuring one of the most memorable of all modern movie scores. The central theme rises up throughout the film, a comforting constant, accompanied by smartly placed sound effects (such as the thudding of chopper blades announcing a shift to Vietnam).

In detailing how war destroys individuals, relationships and communities, **The Deer Hunter** is moving, disturbing and profoundly sad. The waste of life is almost too much to bear, and Cimino's film leaves nowhere to hide. It was winner of the New York Critics Award before collecting the best picture Oscar, while Walken won a best supporting Actor statuette against nominations for De Niro and Streep. The precocious Cimino picked up the direction Oscar in only his second film as director (**Thunderbolt And Lightfoot** being the other, four years earlier) before setting out on the disastrous trail to the monumentally expensive, often striking but heavily overwrought box-office suicide, **Heaven's Gate** (1980). His career pinnacle to date therefore remains this hauntingly shot epic of male bonding in peace and war, from small town Pennsylvania to the hell of Vietnam and back.

CHAPTER 3
THE HORROR, THE HORROR:
"APOCALYPSE NOW REDUX"

Few cinematic masterpieces have been as closely and methodically scrutinised, discussed, analysed and, indeed, mythologized to the extent of Francis Ford Coppola's **Apocalypse Now**.

A film that perhaps comes close is Ridley Scott's 1982 science fiction classic, **Blade Runner**. Years of speculation and "academic" analysis of the film could still not determine the answer to questions such as: "Is Deckard a replicant?" Even the release of a director's cut in 1991 failed to lay ghosts to rest. The debates and near fist-fight arguments continue today, fuelled, to a large degree, by the proliferation of the internet and its dedicated fan-boy fan-base.[1]

But **Apocalypse Now** is a beast all of its own in terms of depth compared to its (not inconsiderable) breadth. It remains to be seen if the release of Coppola's directors cut, **Apocalypse Now Redux**, will entirely satisfy the army of fans that have spent 20 plus years watching and re-watching the most complex Vietnam film ever produced. (Of course **Apocalypse Now** is far more than "just" a Vietnam film.)

Indeed **Apocalypse Now** is as famous for its extended and tortuous creation process as it is as a finished film. It is the cinematic equivalent of the Sistine Chapel – we may marvel at it in terms of the its sheer power as an aesthetic or narrative masterpiece, but it is the dedication, time and the sheer madness that went into its creation that will always fascinate. The title of Carol Reed's 1965 film about the life and obsessive work of Michelangelo, **The Agony And The Ecstasy**, would serve as an excellent sub-heading for Coppola's own production.

Apocalypse Now could have been a *very* different film indeed. Consider some of these permutations: George Lucas as director; Steve McQueen as Willard; John Milius as director; James Caan as Willard; Steve McQueen as Kurtz; Jack Nicholson as Willard; Jack Nicholson as Kurtz; Al Pacino as Willard; Gene Hackman as Kilgore; Robert Redford as Willard; Harvey Keitel as Willard. All of these were, at one time or another, real possibilities. Indeed Keitel, a one-time Marine in real life, was initially cast and spent considerable time shooting before being unceremoniously and publicly fired. Coppola rather off-handedly recalls, "He found it difficult to play him as a passive onlooker."[2]

Before we begin to explore the new journey into the heart of darkness that is **Apocalypse Now Redux**, we should turn first to the stated intentions of the director himself in presenting this new (improved?) version. Coppola states, "When I started **Apocalypse Now**, my intention was to create a broad, spectacular film of epic action-adventure scale that was also rich in theme and philosophic inquiry into the mythology of war... More than 20 years later, I happened to see the picture on television. What struck me was that the original film – which had been seen as so demanding, strange and adventurous when it first came out – now seemed relatively tame, as though the audience had caught up to it. This, coupled with calls I received over the years from people who had seen the original 4 hour plus assembly, encouraged me to go back and try a new version."[3]

During a six-month period, Coppola worked to re-edit from the original "dailies" (unedited, raw footage.) The film was re-formed from scratch with Coppola able to pay more attention to what he calls "morality in war."[4] The result is a cut running a full 53 minutes longer than the version most commonly screened or, intermittently, available on either video or DVD. Key sequences were reinstated – in particular the Playboy playmates' second appearance and the French plantation scenes (glimpsed in the documentary **Hearts Of Darkness: A Filmmaker's Apocalypse**[5]). The much-discussed Brando scenes are also expanded, providing more of the incredible and almost entirely improvised performance that Coppola bought for himself for a *mere* $3million. There are two new musical themes on the soundtrack, both covering scenes in the French plantation sequence, which were taken from the archives of Coppola's late father, Carmine, who scored the original feature. Ultimately **Apocalypse Now Redux** is a film that Coppola describes not only as "a richer, fuller and more textured film experience", but also as, "Sexier, funnier, more bizarre, more romantic and more politically intriguing."[6]

Although the film is a tour-de-force for Coppola, it is also one of the most collaborative films ever produced. The key writing and endless rewriting was divided between three major players: Francis Coppola, writer/director John Milius and war correspondent Michael Herr (other contributors included Walter Murch and, arguably, George Lucas.)

Milius, like Coppola, was a "graduate" of Roger Corman's American International Pictures. Unlike Coppola his views, preoccupations and themes show a strong right-wing sensibility, and a brief look at his filmography (**Magnum Force**, **Red Dawn**, **Conan The Barbarian**, etc.) confirm this stance. He was also a failed Marine recruit, rejected because of his chronic asthma, and typically talks in pseudo-militaristic terms; describing his work on **Apocalypse Now** as, "the longest tour of duty"[7] and referring to Coppola as Führer. He worked on the first ten drafts of the script, but Coppola disliked his presence on location because he feared a mutiny from his exhausted, but predominantly loyal, crew. Milius later reprised the "Kurtz" theme of **Apocalypse Now** in his 1988 film, **Farewell To The King**.

Incredibly Coppola had originally perceived **Apocalypse Now** as a film that wouldn't require a voice-over narration (another similarity to Scott's **Blade Runner**), but during the editing Walter Murch was able to win him over and introduced Michael Herr to the project. Herr, originally a film critic for the American *New Leader* magazine, had worked extensively in Vietnam providing evocative copy for publications such as *Esquire*. By 1977 his features had been edited together and published as the incomparable *Dispatches* – a book of anecdotal reports that seemed to sum up the very essence of a filthy war. His work on **Apocalypse Now** provided the film with many of its most memorable quotes and it is hard to imagine the film existing in any meaningful form without his contribution. Herr would later write **Full Metal Jacket** for Stanley Kubrick.

Of course there is a fourth voice, perhaps more of an echo than a fully formed vocalisation, that cannot be ignored in **Apocalypse Now** – it belongs to Polish born writer Joseph Conrad, upon whose novella, *Heart Of Darkness*, the story is based. Conrad was in essence an adventurer, travelling extensively throughout Africa and the Far East. His *Congo Diaries*, his first written work in English, record his experiences along the African river and formed the basis for *Heart Of Darkness*, which, although not expressly set on the Congo, is clearly intended to be. Obviously the Nineteenth-Century Congo journey is a far temporal and geographical/geopolitical jump to a Twentieth-Century Vietnam/Cambodia river journey, but many of the core themes of exploration (inner and outer) remain. Conrad also created the character of central adversary, Kurtz, a rogue ivory trader. Additionally there are snippets of dialogue that survive intact between novel to screen, most notably Kurtz's dying words, "The horror! The horror!" A literal film adaptation of *Heart Of Darkness* had been envisioned by a young Orson Welles, but was ultimately shot for television by Nicolas Roeg in 1994, with John Malkovitch as Kurtz.

With such a gaggle of competing, and often wildly contradictory, chattering voices, it is a miracle that anything near a comprehensible story emerges from **Apocalypse Now**. This is undoubtedly Francis Ford Coppola's greatest triumph.

The film's opening sequence combines two key images familiar to – in fact inseparable from – Vietnam and Vietnam films – helicopters and napalm. The first helicopter is heard before it is seen and introduces us to the quadraphonic/quintrophonic sound (today often call 5.1) that was developed for the film by Walter Murch in his role as Sound Designer. The multifaceted sound could be expanded or contracted as the film required, creating either audio-surround effects or single-speaker dialogue, which subliminally directed the audiences' attention. The second helicopter signals the explosive destruction by napalm of the tree line and the almost too-deliberate joke of Jim Morrison singing "The End" right at the beginning of the film. Of course this is more than a simple, ironic pun. The lyrics of the mystically obsessed Doors' most enigmatic songs are a perfect precursor to the film's action:

"Of our elaborate plans, the end
Of everything that stands, the end
No safety or surprise, the end"

Slowly the image of Willard's face is faded through (he is upside-down), he closes his eyes as Morrison sings, "I'll never look into your eyes...again. Can you picture what will be?"

A subtle, but vital visual motif is imposed on the already multilayered screen – an ancient carved stone Godhead. One of the key readings of **Apocalypse Now**, as we shall see, is that the journey "up river" is an allegorical journey back through time itself, a journey from the modern to the primal (possibly even more literally the urban to the natural) that takes on mythical properties – as befits a project part written by John Milius.

The first line of voiceover dialogue has become a classic: "Saigon. Shit! I'm still only in Saigon." And it is certainly a brave opening gambit, if we are to sympathise with the central character. This is a man who not only wants to be in Vietnam as opposed to "back home", this is a man who wants to be *deeper* in Vietnam – "back in the Jungle." Willard elaborates, explaining that it was worse

The boat crew steal Kilgore's surfboard

though his voiceover to the distinguished career and subsequent enigma that the Colonel has become. The sounds of explosions alert the crew to the presence of the Air Cavalry, their escort to the mouth of the river.

As the crew of the PBR beach to meet the Air Cavalry, Coppola can be seen in a rather self-conscious cameo playing a news camera director. Willard continues past him and is directed toward the commanding officer, Colonel William Kilgore, brilliantly portrayed by Robert Duvall. Whilst the name may be a simple trope – Kill + Gore – the origin of the name is, in fact, rather more prosaic. Michael Herr wrote in *Dispatches* about meeting a charismatic helicopter gunner who hailed from Kilgore, Texas – an incident that almost certainly provided the character's name. Colonel Kilgore is an amalgam of real and imagined characters, who also projects mythic qualities; Willard speaks of him possessing a, "weird light around him." To further Milius's *Odyssey* connection, the writer compares the character to that of the Cyclops, from which Odysseus and his men must escape. But Kilgore doesn't present a threat to Willard and his crew from which they must escape; they must simply survive his company and tolerate his extreme idiosyncrasies.

As evening falls Willard begins to discuss entry points to the Nung River with Kilgore. At first the Colonel is sceptical about the possibility of passing through Vin Drin Dop village, until one of his men informs him that the beach provides an excellent surf-zone. When he is warned that the point is, "Hairy," that it's, "...Charlie's point," Kilgore responds with his famous: "Charlie don't surf!"

The following morning the helicopters are underway, heading for the deadly beachhead. A mile off shore Kilgore instructs his men to turn on the music and, to the bemusement of Willard, Wagner's "The Ride Of The Valkyries" blasts out of the helicopter-mounted speakers. Not only does the accompanying power of Wagner's music make for impressive cinema, it also has deeper implications. Wagner was a composer of famously rightwing leanings and reportedly Hitler's favorite composer – further, the movement in the opera occurs whilst dead warriors are being transported by flying horses (air cavalry?) from the battlefield to Valhalla.

The attack on the village is one of the most bravado pieces of filmmaking ever undertaken. It lasts in excess of six minutes and the final napalm blast alone saw 1200 gallons of fuel detonated in a 90 second period.

Once established on the beach, Kilgore and his men prepare to surf. Having delivered his second classic line of the film, "I love the smell of napalm in the morning," Kilgore leaves Willard with the resigned comment, "Some days this war's gonna end." Probably not for Willard. The Kilgore sequence ends slightly differently in **Apocalypse Now Redux**, than in the original, with the PBR crew stealing Kilgore's surfboard. It is a minor point but it does slightly reinforce the Kilgore/Cyclops relationship and more importantly helps to lighten our perception of the crew – they are not above silly practical jokes.

The PBR continues its journey into the mouth of the Nung River. Clean and Lance smoke dope, Willard drinks brandy. Again this sequence is slightly more protracted in the **Redux**; there is more interplay between the crew and Willard, more camaraderie. The extension of this sequence strengthens audience sympathy with the characters and ultimately, as Coppola states, "Helps underscore the tragedy of what befalls them as their journey unfolds."[10]

When the boat is moored, Chef, escorted by Willard, enters the jungle in search of mangos. What they find is a tiger, which chases them back to the boat. Chef frantically repeats the line, "Never get out of the boat," like a mantra (we have previously seen him silently praying or perhaps repeating a mantra of some kind during the helicopter attack sequence.) Willard's narration concurs with Chef. "Never get out of the boat. Absolutely Goddamn right. Unless you were going all the way." This is the first time they have been "touched" by the jungle and as we shall see they will become slowly consumed by it. This is part of the elaborate construct that sees the jungle as savage (remember the Godhead in the opening sequence?) and Willard's absorption into it.

The Playboy bunny sequence is the most hallucinogenic in the whole film. The brightly lit anachronistic stage/compound appears in a phantasmagoric blur of light and smoke. Milius has likened the bunnies to *The Odyssey*'s Sirens – tenuous in the original release, but strengthened in **Redux** by their second appearance in which they are stranded and exchange sexual favours for fuel. As Willard leaves the boat, Chief enquires, "Captain, are you giving away our fuel for a Playmate of the Month?" "No," Willard replies, "Playmate of the Year, Chief." Typically Coppola sees the bunnies' role in less mythical terms: "In their

way, the girls are the corresponding characters of those young boys on the boat, except they're being exploited in sexual ways. But it's the same thing, you know how they're being consumed—used up by a society that calls itself moral and yet isn't."[11]

When the PBR comes under "friendly fire" from another boat (they throw a smoke grenade) the boat's canopy is damaged. Lance – later the first to adopt camouflage – repairs it with palm leaves, so again we see the jungle's insidious invasion.

The PBR routinely stops to check a sampan and in the confusion that follows (a woman is reaching for a puppy *not* a weapon) the Vietnamese are mown down. The sequence is one that Milius fought hard not to have included in the original release. It seems rather heavy to recreate a mini My Lai (a real incident that saw almost 350 innocent civilians massacred) and there is a danger of jettisoning any audience sympathy with the PBR crew. This is also the first time we have seen Willard as anything but a passive observer of events. How much more powerful to have reserved his explosive violence for the film's climax. Regardless the sequence remains, for better or worse, in the **Redux**.

The Do Long Bridge scenes that follow are the film's most insane and perfectly encapsulate the futility of the Vietnam conflict: "We build it overnight. Charlie blows it back up again." The otherworldly feel is heightened by the soundtrack that combines ghostly cries and half-heard dialogue with strangled carnivalesque music – Eleanor Coppola confirms, "Parts seem like a circus."[12] The bridge represents the furthest official position of US military activity and can be read, in terms of a quest, as gates that must now be entered. There can be no turning back for Willard or the PBR crew.

Do Long Bridge ("Asshole of the world") was also one of the most gruelling and logistically complex of Coppola's shoot: "500 smoke bombs, 100 phosphorous sticks, 1200 gallons of gas, 50 water explosions of 35 sticks of dynamite each, 2000 rockets, flares, tracers and 5000 feet of detonating cord are used in the finale."[13]

In the moments before Clean's death, the mail that was collected at the Do Long Bridge provides two significant diversions. Willard receives an update on his mission informing him that a previous soldier, Captain Colby, had already been sent to "terminate" Kurtz's command and is believed to have joined the renegade Colonel. The audience begins to more fully recognize the danger that Willard is in – Kurtz, like the jungle, has the power to consume those sent to challenge him. The second, less significant, letter is for Chef. A newspaper cutting reporting the Manson murders provides the film's only true temporal pointer and also helps to establish a sense of American history outside of the Vietnam War. Manson also represents the other dark-side of American counter-culture and in terms of the media helped to spell the end of the flower-power years.

Moments later the PBR is under attack. Clean is shot and killed whilst a tape from his mother, also collected at Do Long Bridge, is heard playing in the background – "Stay out of the way of the bullets," she warns, seconds too late.

In the original release of **Apocalypse Now** Clean is denied a burial, in fact he is never really mentioned again. In the **Redux**, however he is afforded a proper burial, thanks to the reinstating of the following French plantation sequence.

The French sequence has always been one of the most eagerly discussed of the "missing" scenes, due mainly to its extensive inclusion in both **Hearts Of**

Opposite: Chef, Willard; "Never get out of the boat".

Entering Kurtz's compound

Darkness: A Filmmakers Apocalypse and Eleanor Coppola's *Notes On The Making Of Apocalypse Now*. Francis Coppola had intended it to serve two purposes beyond the burial of Clean. Firstly it would emphasise the river journey as a journey back through time, showing as it does a plantation that has barely changed from the 1950s. Secondly it acts to highlight issues of colonialism within South East Asia. The scenes are certainly a triumph of production design, with the ghostly ambience enhanced by the flickering candlelight and shimmering gauzes. The leaden dialogue and the rather stilted acting (Coppola was never happy with the chosen actors) let the sequences down and create a rather heavy-handed history lesson – making explicit what was previously implied. Coppola pretentiously argues for the inclusion of the sequence by stating that it "captures an exotic yearning, groping for long-vanished ideals and a crumbling way of life that presages and essentially predicts the folly of America's experience in Vietnam."[14]

Willard is seduced by one of the women, Roxanne, who helps to underpin the feeling that Willard and Kurtz are no more than a murky reflection of each other: "There are two of you, don't you see? One that kills... And the other that loves." Again, this is making the point a little too obvious.

The film now enters its final act as the PBR draws nearer to Kurtz's lair ("He was close. He was real close") The arrow attack on the boat that kills Chief is lifted almost directly from Conrad's source material and again emphasises the power of the "savage" over the "civilised." The attack is straight out of the stone-age and Chief's final utterance is more a bemused question than statement of fact: "A spear!(?)" Lance, now fully camouflaged, delicately paints Chief's face before lowering him into the river in an imitation of baptism or perhaps something more pagan. The river swallows another soul.

The PBR nears the compound, passing through rafts of clay-clad Montagnard soldiers – pure stone-age warriors. As they come in to land the photojournalist (manically portrayed by Dennis Hopper) appears and urges Chef to, "Zap 'em with your siren!" to scare them away. This is the last time the crew will be under any delusion that modern trappings can prevent them from being consumed by natural forces.

The photojournalist introduces himself (although only as "a photo-journalist") and when asked who all the tribesmen are, he responds, "These are all his children. Hell man, out here we are all his children!" And, as we know from the words of Jim Morrison, "All the children are insane." Amid the photojournalist's ramblings he likens Kurtz to a "warrior-poet" and begins to quote Kipling:

"If you can keep your head when all about you
Are losing theirs and blaming it on you
If you can trust yourself when all men doubt you..."

Not only is the quote deeply ironic, given the severed heads that litter the compound and the fate that awaits Chef, it also serves to establish the role of poetry that will have greater resonance when we are introduced to Kurtz himself.

Chef, who accompanies Willard ashore, is also showing signs of absorption into the jungle, wearing a palm leaf as a hat. Willard observes, "If I was still alive it was because he wanted me that way." Overtones of divine power, which are echoed when Chef is informed that the code to call in the air strike is "Almighty."

Willard is taken for his audience with Kurtz. The scenes between the two are extended in the **Redux** in part to provide the audience with more of the outstanding, and largely improvised performance, that Brando gives[15]. The warning, "Don't try to escape, or you'll be killed," is added at their first meeting. But Willard knows that escape is already pointless – their lives, their destinies, are already too intertwined.

At first the conversation between Willard and Kurtz seems to be almost pedestrian. Kurtz asks where he comes from and when Willard replies, "Toledo", Kurtz asks, "How far from the river are you?" Interestingly the question isn't, "How far from the river *were* you?" it is asked in present tense. Is Kurtz also using the river as analogy? Is he really asking Willard how closely they have become

(Ernie Fosselius, 1980), about a deranged butcher.

Another hardcore porn film set against the background of Vietnam is Charles De Santos' **China DeSade** (1977), the story of Ming Lee, a luscious ex Chinese spy in Saigon, who falls into the company of a cruel Green Beret commander, Colonel Krieg. Back in the U.S., Krieg and Ming Lee are sought by Mercenary Philip Weyland. Weyland infiltrates Krieg's lair in an attempt to kill Krieg and capture Ming Lee and becomes involved in a series of bizarre sexual encounters.

2.   *Apocalypse Now*, Karl French, p.145.

3.   *Apocalypse Now Redux* official website, www.miramax.com/apocalypse now.

4.   ibid.

5.   *Hearts Of Darkness: A Filmmakers Apocalypse* Dir. Fax Bahr & George Hickenlooper.

6.   *Apocalypse Now Redux* official website, www.miramax.com/apocalypse now.

7.   *Apocalypse Now*, Karl French, p.194.

8.   *Notes on the Making of Apocalypse Now*, Eleanor Coppola, p. 104.

9.   *Hearts of Darkness: A Filmmakers Apocalypse* Dir. Fax Bahr & George Hickenlooper.

10.   *Apocalypse Now Redux* official website, www.miramax.com/apocalypse now.
11.   Ibid.

12.   *Notes on the Making of Apocalypse Now*, Eleanor Coppola, p.106.

13.   Shooting Log – Original theatrical brochure.

14.   *Apocalypse Now Redux* official website, www.miramax.com/apocalypse now.

15.   In his autobiography, Brando describes Coppola shooting Kurtz's "death monolgue", an extempoized sequence by Brando which "...must have been 45 minutes long. It was probably the closest I've ever come to getting lost in a part, and ones of the best scenes I've ever played..." Journalist Paul Cullum, writing in *Film Threat* magazine in 1995, claims to have viewed this entire scene, and reproduced the following transcription of Brando's improvised soliloquy: "[Deep breaths] I...I...I...I had....I had immense plans. I was on the threshold of great things. And what you've hacked here to the ground like a tree is not the end of it. No, you've also shaken the seeds from that tree. And I will take root in you. I will sprout. I will be nourished by your violence. Nothing. Nothing. To look into the abyss without drawing away is everything. The highest...The highest of honours. To approach the horizon of endurable anguish and to pass it, you must have eyes without eyelids, for if you blink once, you will incinerate.

We are winning this war. We are winning it. And you will...you will help to win it. And just beneath the surface is your strength. Just below your skin are your vital forms, your vital forces running like eternal springs. Wild. Restless. They will guide you, and give you counsel.

And when they call you murderer, and when they judge you, then turn on them, hang them, all of them, by their lying jaws on meat-hooks till they soil themselves and ask forgiveness. The bloodlust. The bloodlust – you don't think of it. You don't think of the bloodlust; you experience it. You must experience it. Masses.... people – any people – they will go anywhere, do anything, as long as the ring of faith is in their noses. Yes. Put the rings in their nose. Call it God. And Country. And Mother. Then you run a slim cord through the rings of all of them – ten million, a hundred million or more – and herd them wherever you will.

The human animal has no limits. He will generate a force to overcome the gravitational pull of society and fling himself into outer space to find a new orbit around Jupiter or the sun, determined by far greater forces. And the instinct to submission, the longer to obey, to be ruled by the strong, the will to submission, is stronger than the will to power... Eichmann...Eichmann... Six million Jews jumped into their graves... Dusseldorf... Bremen.... Wounded Knee... Coventry....Nagasaki...Ten-year-old boys carrying...carrying grenades in baskets of fruit. And pregnant women, nursing women, carrying explosives in their vaginas... inside their vaginas, crossing beyond our checkpoints.

Extremism in the defence of liberty is no vice... No... No vice... No vice...

This war will never be won by the priests of misery, the Rand Corporation and not in the Situation Rooms in Washington. The people here, those yellow and white who lie in the much and who can stand the rain and no food, the stink and the rot of dying... People who get sick and wake up numb and still have the will to fight. They're the ones who will stand it. And the ones... and the ones who will win... None other... None other... They just need the will, the guns and the grace of God. The enemy, well-trained, experience no fear. VC gun... NVA... no fear in their gun....Not in their gun.

Their minds. Have fear of their minds. You hack them to pieces and they say nothing. They only inspire respect. God help you if you.... God help you. The strong...the strongest leaders don't want to lose this war to little yellow men in black pyjamas, so they lie. Presidents, all of them, all the presidents, want to retain power, so they lie. Congressmen, our... lies. Lies. Magazines... lies. This is not a war of people and freedom and rights and self-determination. Lies. Only oil, power, manganese, cobalt, geopolitics, staying in office... must have these... we must have these... lies. Remain strong. Remain free. Regret... regret... never saw a flower being pushed into the end of AK-47 muzzle. Children put their flowers where I can see them. I'd like to see their faces if they'd put the flowers in VC guns. The top of their heads would come off... [incomprehensible]... Forbidden to kill... Slay animals... Across the centuries... [incomprehensible]... Lies. Lies.

They are right. They are right. We should not intervene. No intervention here. Civil war. Their war. No intervention. They are right. Not intervene, but to invade, inundate all of Southeast Asia with fire enough to eliminate... eliminate our intentions here for two centuries. They don't want my mission to succeed because they would be wrong, and they would rather be dead.... dead than wrong.

No. Stay with the primitive here. Stay with these people. Stay with them. They're small feathers in this hurricane of change, this whirlwind. But they know, they understand, they're made of the earth. They live without fear. They do not hide in masks of guilt. Platinum. Platinum. There are some things, there are some things of which I cannot, I dare not speak.

To raise a stench, a stench so strong as to break the stride of.... of a pack of jackals. To be as familiar with death as maggots are with manure. The world needs us now, and we will stay here until mushrooms grow out of our faces. These men, these tired ticks that crawl across....across the anvil of history. A time for giants, and they send us pygmies armed with chalk, computers, tennis rackets, Santa Monica hotlines to human misery. The eager students of suffering and violence. The sick and twisted hippies, long-haired hypocrites, rotting with decay. In every powerful civilization for the past 35 centuries, violence stills those inner ancient passions, that primordial slime that lies in the bottom of our minds waiting aeons and aeons to be ...only to be stirred and – what? And the silkworms... the silkworms writing those fawning reports of victories while we die out here like blind martins. The experts, the air-conditioned priests, who only look for the break point in human misery. McNamara... Bunker... Rostow... Bunker... Bundy... Bunker... Bunker... Johnson...."

In the same article, Cullum describes many other unused sequences, some of which duly appear in **Apocalypse Now Redux**. Scenes apparently still missing include Hopper's photojournalist being blasted with a shotgun, and Willard running an infant through with a spear.

16.   *The Golden Bough*, Sir James Frazer, p.266.

17.   Coppola's single subsequent return to the Vietnam War movie genre, **Gardens Of Stone** (1988), is also about as antithetical to **Apocalypse Now** as possible. **Gardens Of Stone** is a film about the keepers of the War Cemetery at Arlington, during 1968. Starring James Caan and Anjelica Huston as the decorated sergeant and the anti-war correspondent who strike up an unlikely relationship, **Gardens Of Stone** is set entirely Stateside, whilst **Apocalypse Now** is all "in-country"; **Gardens** is quiet and reflective while **Apocalypse** is explosive; **Gardens** is insular and regulated, while **Apocalypse** is limitless, psychedelic, chaotic. It seems as if, after a decade, Coppola was seeking to redress the balance.
       Another film examining the Stateside military during Nam is Joel Schumacher's **Tigerland** (2000). Like a cross between **Full Metal Jacket** and **Southern Comfort**, **Tigerland** shows the explosive fallout when a combative group of Marines training for Nam go on exercise in a shotgun swamp. Also dealing with the Stateside military are **Heartbreak Ridge** (1986), which stars Clint Eastwood as the Nam veteran who must prepare raw recruits for the US invasion of Grenada, and **Private War** (1988), with former Warhol superstar Joe D'Allesandro as a crazed Nam vet drill instructor. **Streamers** (Robert Altman, 1983) is set in an army barracks and centres around a group of recruits awaiting the call to Vietnam. **Dogfight** (1991) concerns a bunch of recruits on R&R in San Francisco the night before shipping out to Nam. After a night of drinking and misogynistic pranks, they leave for the combat zone. A single, short combat sequence then shows all of them, except the lead (River Phoenix) get blown to pieces in a mortar attack.
       The earliest film to depict military training for Vietnam was **Tribes** (1970), a movie made for TV but later released theatrically under the terrible new title **The Soldier Who Declared Peace**. Frederick Wiseman's documentary **Basic Training** (1971) is a typically revealing *cinema-verité* glimpse at a real-life army drill camp, where boys are turned into soldiers fit to fight in the Nam and elsewhere.

CHAPTER 4
JUNGLE FEVER:
"THE LAST HUNTER"

1. TAPPING A VEIN

The most profound and thought-provoking of war films employ the battleground as a dramatic device, one which naturally encourages the purest of emotions. The fear and violence of war is perfect as a hyper intense back-drop against which the film's true driving force, the raw human experience, can be played out; Captain Willard's military objective in **Apocalypse Now** is a subsidiary plot mechanism used to carry the character's meandering and introspective exploration through the mortal condition and into the stark realisation of true madness. Noble sentiments indeed – but Italian exploitation filmmakers weren't in the business of creating soul-searching epics; they were in the business of making money fast and inexpensively. All they needed for a war film was a vaguely plausible plot that could carry as much swearing and shooting as a feature running time would allow. Welcome to war – Italian style.

"Today it is almost impossible to compete with American million-dollar budget movies"[1]

The Italian film industry experienced a period of prolific filmmaking during the 1970's and '80's, producing a barrage of quick and cheap thrill-packed movies that raised levels of on-screen sex and violence to dizzy new heights. The inspiration and format for these films, more often than not, came from box-office successes in America; once a film had proved itself to be a money-maker in the US, its format was instantly re-crafted into a salacious and blood-soaked Euro copy. The till-clanging approval of George Romero's **Dawn Of The Dead** (1978) led to a rapid flow of flesh-tearing zombie movies[2], the universal popularity of 1971's **Dirty Harry** and **The French Connection** mutated into the blistering "Poliziotteschi" genre[3] of renegade cops and tyre-screeching chases and, likewise, even the futuristic nightmares of **Mad Max 2** and **Escape From New York** were dutifully answered by a batch of hit and miss "post-apocalyptic" action epics[4]. So, it was no different when, in 1979, Michael Cimino's haunting Vietnam fable **The Deer Hunter** hit Italian cinema screens, re-titled in Italy as **Il Cacciatore** (translated as "The Hunter"), followed shortly by Coppola's monumental war essay **Apocalypse Now**.

2. GUNS FOR HIRE

Producer Gianfranco Couyoumdjian, the man behind such grindhouse fare as Aristide Massaccesi's **Emanuelle E Gli Ultimi Cannibali** (1977) and Marino

Girolami's **Zombi Holocaust** (1980), quickly came up with a story that could neatly side-step the more problematic social and emotional aspects of Cimino's film, concentrating more on the extreme content. Put in the capable hands of seasoned writer Dardano Sacchetti[5], it was fleshed out into a dynamic and visceral script peppered with heroic action, macho dialogue and blood-soaked gristle. Under the legally dubious shooting title of **Il Cacciatore 2**, the film was lensed in the Philippines (reportedly using some sets left over from **Apocalypse Now**) with interiors shot at Incir De Paolis Studios Rome, by the uniquely versatile and jungle-savvy director Antonio Margheriti[6], who had just finished the infamous Vietnam shocker **Cannibal Apocalypse (Apocalisse Domani** aka **Invasion Of The Flesh Hunters)** [see chapter 7]. Released in 1980 as **The Last Hunter (L'Ultimo Cacciatore)**, the film was a hit in its homeland before going on to find an enthusiastic audience in UK and US cinemas[7].

Even in his weakest productions, Margheriti had always managed to give a glimpse of his master craftsmanship; whether it be an elaborate camera set-up or a stand-out special effect, he refused to be constrained by the meagre budgets he was given. In fact, it was exactly this quality, mixed with his energetic "gung-ho" cinematic flair, that lent itself perfectly to the fast and frenzied world of war films. Who else could handle a mixed-bag of international actors, unreliable indigenous locals in the sweltering jungle heat on a tight schedule and even tighter funds?

3. "THE LAST HUNTER"

The Last Hunter stars New Zealand born actor, and ex-catalogue model, David Warbeck as tough Marine Captain Harry Morris; a macho character haunted by memories of a life before war with his close friends Steve and Carol. Warbeck carved a long and successful career out of the Italian film industry, appearing in numerous other exploitation titles, but is best known to horror fans for his role in Lucio Fulci's 1981 zombie masterpiece **The Beyond**[8]. Appearing alongside Warbeck in **The Last Hunter**, as reporter Jane Foster – a female incarnation of Dennis Hopper's **Apocalypse Now** photo-journalist – is another Italian horror favourite Tisa Farrow (sister of Mia, daughter of Maureen O'Sullivan and director John Farrow), who also featured in Fulci's equally unforgettable **Zombi 2** (aka **Zombie Flesh-Eaters**, 1979) and Aristide Massaccesi's (aka Joe D'Amato) sleazy **Grim Reaper** aka **Anthropophagous** (1980). Margheriti regular and industry veteran "Alan Collins" (Luciano Pigozzi), likened to an Italian Peter Lorre, dutifully turns up as a surgeon.

"It's not a bad picture; I like that one" –Antonio Margheriti[9]

"The Screen Explodes In A Blazing Spectacle Of War"[10]

The film's opening "whorehouse" scene is one of Margheriti's career triumphs (and of exploitation filmmaking in general) and stands as the film's aesthetic as well as emotional highpoint, an artsitic plateau sadly unacheived anywhere else in the picture. Using a stream of evermore obscure angles and sweeping moves, the camera, within a matter of minutes, captures a stifling atmosphere and establishes a pervading anti-war pathos.

"January 1973 – Outskirts of Saigon"... Inside a sweaty bar, packed with

The Last Hunter – victim of a VC booby-trap

GI's on recreation leave, a disco track pulses as go-go dancers perform on a small stage. Marine Captain Harry Morris sits smoking, seemingly oblivious to his surroundings, whilst, behind a curtain, his anxious friend Steve tries to relax with one of the Vietnamese working girls. A roughneck GI paces nearby, crunching beer cans as he waits his turn eagerly.

Roughneck: *"Your balls could fucking steam in here..."*
Captain Morris: *"Why don't you go and cool yours off and stop breaking mine!"*

Pleading for the girl not to touch him, Steve becomes increasingly tense and agitated as she continues to caress his chest whilst the impatient GI taunts him ("Can't get it up?"). The atmosphere builds until, unable to cope ("I can't take anymore!"), traumatised Steve takes a revolver and aims at the roughneck's head. Before Captain Morris can intervene – BANG! ...The loud-mouthed GI falls to the floor dead.

Steve: *"Where's Carol? Why isn't she here anymore?"*

Morris tries desperately to calm his disorientated friend when suddenly a bright red flare smashes in through the window. In the ensuing panic Steve puts the revolver in his mouth. The gun-blast illuminates the young soldier's cheeks as the back of his head sprays out...

Captain Morris is sent on a top secret assignment to silence a VC propaganda

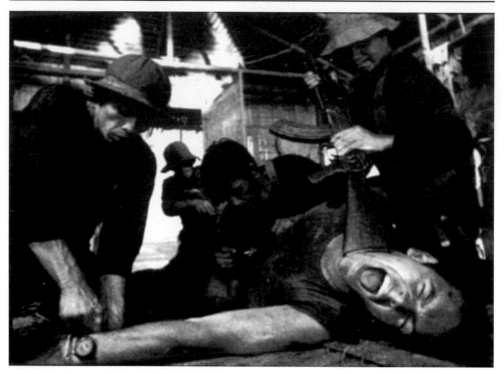

The Last Hunter – victim of VC torture

radio, broadcasting moral-destroying messages to tired US soldiers from deep down river ("Throw your rifle away... Disobey your Commander... Go home, American boy") – a literal interpretation of Willard's objective to silence the renegade Kurtz in **Apocalypse Now**. Despatched into the jungle by helicopter, Morris is met by an escort troop of soldiers, led by George "Midnite" Washington ("The only kind of chocolate I eat is white"), played by Tony King from **Shaft**, and accompanied by sassy journalist Jane Foster ("What kind of mission are you on? I mean, what can you do that helicopters, jets, tanks can't?"). Surviving the hazards of the jungle (swinging spike traps), the group make it to the relative safety of cave-dwelling Major Cash ("Their propaganda is doing more damage than all our napalm!"), played by John Steiner; whose drug-addled, sex-starved men sit around drinking beer and smoking joints in a well-equipped bar – predating the potent drug culture revealed in Oliver Stone's **Platoon** by several years. When some of Cash's marines try to rape Jane, the Major sends one of the guilty soldiers out on a "coconut run", a seemingly suicidal dash behind enemy lines to retrieve a coconut – seemingly a lacklustre attempt to re-enact the manic surf antics of Robert Duvall's napalm-smelling Major in **Apocalypse Now**..

　　　The local VC stage a daring attack on the cave, in which Jane is snatched and flame-throwing Captain Morris escapes on a boat with a severely injured Washington. Leaving Washington to fend for himself (a knowingly impossible task), Morris sets out on land to continue his mission, but before long is captured by a VC troop. He is taken to an army base down river where he discovers Jane is also being held, but (more importantly?) on arriving he spies his primary target;

Tiger Joe – David Warbeck

the radio aerial, rigged nearby. Morris is thrown into an underwater bamboo cage (as in **The Deer Hunter**), where a badly scarred soldier warns him of the ravenous rats that attack at night ("They come in here by the hundreds"). Morris is dragged out for a vicious torture interrogation by VC officers – attempting, in vain, to recreate the lethal atmosphere of the infamous "Russian roulette" scene in **The Deer Hunter**. Jane manages to overcome her guard and she rushes to rescue Morris from the vermin-infested cage. Whilst Jane hides in the bushes, Morris enters the radio control room where he calls for US assistance before discovering the shocking (and ridiculous) identity of the broadcaster's voice – Carol, dead Steve's girlfriend and long time Vietnam objector ("We all three thought the same way... I followed my ideals through"). An American air attack is on the way; Carol is shot dead, and the radio station goes up in flames whilst Morris escorts Jane to a waiting chopper. She calls out for him to join her, but Captain Morris can never return home. His mission complete, Morris rips off his dog-tags and stands alone as the music begins: "Peace and love is all we're asking for all around the world..."

4. THE TIGER & THE TORNADO

The Last Hunter team regrouped for the inevitable follow-up film: **Tiger Joe** (aka **Fuga Dall'Arcipelago Maledetto**, 1981). Most of the essential ingredients were there (Warbeck, Tony King, Alan Collins) for Margheriti to re-hash the success of the original, but the absence of screenwriter Sacchetti is all too apparent. Written with little verve by Tito Carpi, Warbeck plays the gun-running pilot "Tiger Joe" who flies firearms for villain Bronski, played by Giancarlo Badessi from **Caligula**, through South East Asia. Following a crash in the jungle, Joe is captured by government rebels, falls in love with local girl Kia (Annie Bell) and becomes a "freedom fighter", helping destroy a bridge used to carry government soldiers and equipment[11].

Margheriti returned to bona-fide war territory, and somewhat to form, with the fast paced **Tornado** in 1983; with presentiments of **Platoon** (betrayal, redemption), it is a solid action film with kinetic force, and features some memorable dialogue (Captain:"Well buddy, you got your purple heart" – Soldier: "I'd rather have my fucking leg!"), but is ultimately let down by its lifeless hero, played by "Timothy Brent" (Giancarlo Prete).[12]

NOTES

1. Antonio Margheriti, quoted in *Bizarre Sinema! Horror All' Italiana*, published by Glittering Images.

2. For example, Lucio Fulci's **Zombi 2** (1979), Marino Girolami's **Zombie Holocaust** (aka **Doctor Butcher M.D.**, 1980), and Umberto Lenzi's **Nightmare City** (aka **Incubo Sulla Citta Contaminata**, 1980).

3. For example, Enzo G. Castellari's **La Polizia Incrimina, La Legge Assolve** (aka **High Crime**, 1973) and **Il Cittadino Si Ribella** (1975), Umberto Lenzi's **Violent Naples** (1976), Fernando Di Leo's **Milano Calibro 9** (1972), and Sergio Grieco's **La Belvia Col Mitra** (aka **The Mad Dog Murderer**, 1977).

4. For example, Aristide Massaccesi's **Endgame** (1983), Sergio Martino's **2019 After The Fall Of New York** (1983), Enzo G. Castellari's **1990 – The Bronx Warriors** (1982) and **The New Barbarians** (1983), and Bruno Mattei's **Rats Night Of Terror** (1984).

5. Amongst numerous others, Sacchetti worked on: Dario Argento's **Cat O'Nine Tails** (1971) and **Inferno** (1980), Mario Bava's **Bay Of Blood** (aka **Reazione A Catena**, 1971) and **Shock** (aka **Transfert-Suspence-Hypno**s, 1977), Ruggero Deodata's **Cut And Run** aka **Inferno In Diretta** (1985) and **Camping Del Terrore** (1987), and Lucio Fulci's **Sette Note In Nero** (1977), and **City Of The Living Dead**.

6. Unknown by the film-going audience at large and often unfairly regarded amongst genre fans as nothing more than a "hack", Antonio Margheriti (aka "Anthony M. Dawson" – his earliest work was signed "Anthony Daisies", the literal translation of the Italian word "margheriti", but he then changed it to "Anthony Dawson", later adding the "M" to avoid confusion with the British actor of the same name), with more than fifty films to his name, remains one of the most underrated of all Italian directors.

Overshadowed by such influential luminaries as Riccardo Freda and Mario Bava, who have rightfully received critical reappraisal in recent years, Margheriti's career is equally as diverse and dynamic. Starting out as an assistant editor in 1950, Margheriti soon distinguished himself in special effects cinematography and assisted Bava with maquette and miniature work. By 1954 he was put in charge of all effects duties on **The Five From Adamello** (aka **I Cinque Dell'Adamello**), before finally, in 1959, Titanus Studios granted his directorial debut **Assignment: Outer Space** (aka **Spacemen**). Supposedly made for $30,000, this impressive sci-fi adventure set Margheriti out as a director able to conjure fantastic visions from truly limited resources – a skill that was to stand him in good stead for his entire career.

Dictated by the ever-changing international market, Margheriti, like most of his native peers, moved quickly through an array of genres with varying degrees of success. He excelled at Gothic chillers with the likes of **The Long Hair Of Death** (aka **I Lunghi Capelli Della Morte**) and **The Virgin Of Nuremberg** (aka **La Vergine Di Noremberga** aka **Horror Castle**), both from 1964, but seemed to flounder within the "giallo" (Italian thriller) format, resulting in uninspired efforts like 1968's **The Young, The Evil And The Savage** (aka **Nude...Si More** aka **Schoolgirl Killer**) or the interminably slow **Seven Deaths In The Cat's Eye** (aka **La Morte Negli Occhi Del Gatto**) from 1973. He was credited as co-director on the two Paul Morrissey 1974 horror spoofs **Blood For Dracula** and **Blood For Frankenstein**; his films between then and **The Last Hunter** range from the western **Take A Hard Ride** (1975), to the thriller **Death Rage** (1976), to the **Piranha** rip-off **Killer Fish** (1978).

7.	Subsequent Nam-related Italian war films have included: **Warbus** (Ferdinando Baldi, 1985), **Cop Game** (Bruno Mattei, 1988), **Leathernecks** (Ignazio Dolce, 1988), **Jungle Heat** (Jobic Wong, 1989), and **Dog Tags** (Romano Scavolini, 1991).

8.	Warbeck also appeared in, amongst others, the British horror films **Trog** (1970) and **Twins Of Evil** (1971), Sergio Leone's **A Fistful Of Dynamite** (aka **Giu La Testa**, 1972), Martin Campbell's **The Sex Thief** (1973), Russ Meyer's **Blacksnake** (1973), and Giuliano Carnimeo's **Ratman** (aka **Quella Villa In Fondo Al Parco**, 1987).

9.	From an interview conducted by Peter Blumenstock in Rome, March 1994 and published in *Video Watchdog* No.28.

10.	Text appearing on the film's promotional artwork for the original UK VHS distribution by Inter-Light Video.

11.	Sadly, on the last take of the arduous **Tiger Joe** shoot, another victim was added to the list of actors and technicians struck down in action, when cinematographer Riccardo Pallottini was killed in a plane crash. He had previously worked on Margheriti's Gothic shockers **The Virgin Of Nuremberg** and **La Danza Macabra** (1964), and his dark westerns **Vengeance** (1968) and **And God Said To Cain** (1970).

12.	Amongst various other jungle adventure films, Margheriti teamed up with the Swiss exploitation producer Edwin C. Dietrich for a series of three action films starring Lewis Collins, from *The Professionals* TV show, as an expert mercenary soldier hired to annihilate opium-growing Mafia or overthrow banana republic presidents. The first of these was **Code Name: Wildgeese** (1985) featuring Lee Van Cleef, Ernest Borgnine and Mimsy Farmer, followed by **Commando Leopard** (1987) co-starring Klaus Kinski and John Steiner. The last in the trio was **The Wildgeese Commander'** (1988) with appearances from Lee Van Cleef and Donald Pleasance. He also lensed three Indiana Jones-style action adventures: **I Cacciatori Del Cobra D'Oro** (aka **Hunters Of The Golden Cobra**), **I Sopravissuti Della Citta Morte** (aka **Ark Of The Sun God**, both starring David Warbeck), and **La Leggenda Del Rubino Malese** (aka **Captain Yankee And The Jungle Raiders**) starring Lee Van Cleef, all from 1983.
	Margheriti's last tour of duty into the jungle was for two eco-friendly "Indio" films (the first, **Indio**, in 1988 and the second, **Indio: The Revolt**, in 1990), starring Marvellous Marvin Hagler, Brian Deheny as an ex-Army Colonel, and Francesco Quinn as an ex-Marine fighting to preserve the Indio peoples' land – something akin to an Italian version of John Boorman's **The Emerald Forest**. But guiltless exhilaration and unashamed violence had finally been replaced by human rights issues and ethnic politics; the volatile spark that distinguished heyday Italian exploitation cinema had long since gone and with it, maverick heroes like Marine Captain Harry Morris of **The Last Hunter**.

dangerous, heavily scarred and blood-lusting Sgt Barnes (Tom Berenger), at permanent odds with the more paternal and almost saint-like Sgt Elias (Willem Dafoe)[1]. It is no coincidence that our first shot of Elias, gun behind his head, carries a Christ-like sense of imagery, a recurrent image that finds its fullest force in his later bullet-riddled death. The triad of the two ideologically divided sergeants with Taylor intertwined, drives the film's narrative.

Ostensibly then, this is a simple tale of life in the firing line and, apart from the terrified responses of the villagers we learn practically nothing of the feelings of the Vietnamese. The enemy itself, like the GIs, we barely ever get to see other than in silhouette and deeply camouflage. Moreover, other than the garbled and increasingly frantic communications via radio while the GIs are in the field, we learn very little of the orders or motivations of the US military commanders, thousands of miles away back in the States or safely ensconced in safe bases in Vietnam itself. Stone's film narratively, is solely concerned with the GIs' often confused patriotism, the moral strengthening and undoing of his characters and the heat of the war itself. But the commentary comes from within the plot, between those of a higher consciousness and those of lower.

By examining the various lives and attitudes of the members of the platoon, we come to learn why America was in Vietnam. Historically the film immediately pronounced itself a polar opposite to the cod patriotism espoused in Reagan-era films including **Top Gun** and **Rambo: First Blood II**. Ted Kotcheff's **First Blood** (1982) with Sylvester Stallone as the misunderstood vet John Rambo carried enough bloodletting and emotional manipulation to achieve at the box office, but its story played itself out after the war had finished and Rambo had returned home. **Platoon** thrust us screaming into the hell of the war itself, and ultimately **Platoon** fully deserves its reputation as the proper American admission of pain over Vietnam.

Further back, films like **Coming Home** eight years earlier were marked with a genuine sense of cloying sentimentality. Although actors Jon Voight and Jane Fonda picked up Oscars for their roles, **Coming Home**, released the same year as Michael Cimino's infinitely superior (though still inherently flawed) **The Deer Hunter** had a cliché'd archetypal Vietnam storyline – Fonda falls for paraplegic veteran Voight while her vet husband Bruce Dern goes mad and drowns himself. And it is telling that while **The Deer Hunter** succeeded at the box office, **Coming Home** was a financial failure.

Filming of **Platoon** began in February 1986. Stone gathered a strong cast, although the actor James Woods was eventually to turn him down (they had worked on Stone's earlier **Salvador**) and said "I couldn't face going into another jungle with Oliver". Rising "Brat pack" star Charlie Sheen was chosen for the lead role of Taylor. Tom Berenger and Willem Dafoe, two powerful character actors, were set to play opposite each other as the dark Barnes, his face grotesquely scarred like a parody of Prussian duelling scars, against the glow of light from Elias.

Arriving in the Philippines, the actors were sent on an intensive two week "training course". This training was under the command of Captain Dale Dye, who had served in Vietnam and was here Oliver Stone's right hand man and the film's Technical Adviser. Living in the jungle, the actors were prey to forced marches, digging foxholes, even night ambushes complete with special effects explosions. The reasoning was obvious for Stone's military manner as he and Capt

Dye systematically broke the actors down. He was to tell *New York* magazine; "We did it to fuck with their heads so we could get that dog-tired, don't give a damn attitude, the anger, the irritation, the causal way of brutality, the casual approach to death". During the pre-film training the young cast including Sheen, Kevin Dillon, Forest Whittaker and a young Johnny Depp were kept in character twenty-four hours a day and even between takes, were forced to unquestionably respect the command hierarchy, and to address actors like Tom Berenger and Dafoe with their characters' names in the film.

The opening scene begins with the new recruits disembarking from a carrier plane and straight into the heat and dust of Vietnam. Squinting through the dust, the young actors soon see body bags waiting to be returned to the States and a line of a seemingly shell-shocked platoon returning from an arduous tour of duty. The morality and core of the film has been set, as Taylor sees one particularly haggard, sunken-eyed soldier walking past and at that moment is aware that perhaps he is looking at a hellish vision of his own future. The new recruits immediately find themselves in the darkened, foreboding claustrophobia of the jungle and Taylor soon chances on the blackened corpse of a Vietnamese fighter, vomits and then, suffering from energy-sapping heat exhaustion, promptly collapses. And it is here that we immediately get introductions to Taylor's superiors and their own opposite psychologies. Sgt Barnes shouts at Taylor for his lack of character, but Sgt Elias helps up the young recruit with some encouraging words and a desire to lighten the back pack of the young inexperienced recruit. Good and evil in the hell of the jungle have been established in the length of a three-minute sequence of dialogue.

The GIs set up camp for the night and Taylor takes his first opportunity to write a letter home to his Grandmother (a recurring theme of the film and a chance for Taylor and the audience to be aware of the fragility of both his own existence and the distant thought that there is life elsewhere on the planet away from the jungle bloodletting and moral and idealistic turmoil which the GIs are going through). The recruits go on a night time look-out duty and after Junior (Reggie Johnson) falls asleep during his watch, the mosquito-riddled Taylor awakes suddenly to see the rapidly approaching Vietcong approaching in silhouette through the trees. In the explosive battle that follows, one soldier is killed and Taylor is wounded. Junior falsely claims that Taylor fell asleep on his watch and Taylor is consequently sternly berated by Sgt Barnes.

Scenes of late night marijuana- and alcohol-fuelled reverie back at the base camp for the young recruits – their only temporary means of emotional escape from the day to day carnage of hostilities – helps to set up the film's later civil war which will erupt between the "juicers", who drink alcohol, and who will do anything to survive – exemplified by the commander Sgt Barnes – and the "heads" who smoke pot, trying to survive with some shred of humanity left intact with Sgt Elias their natural and charismatic leader. In that sense then schematically, Sgt Barnes represents the film's death instinct with his personal vendetta towards the Vietcong, while Sgt Elias represents life.

Cast against type, Dafoe, who had spent a career playing psychos and villains to that date, was turned humanist by Stone who, by turning a classic villain into a saint, was attempting to give the sense of the anguish of sainthood – as it is entirely plausible that Elias had battled back his own dark side. Barnes and Elias then are soon to become explosive, mythic Titans in a terrible struggle for the soldiers' souls.

Barnes threatens summary execution

The film returns to the field and on New Years Day, 1968, the platoon makes it way through the jungle, and finds an abandoned bunker complex which is booby trapped. One soldier gets his arms blown off before they find another soldier, brutally executed and tied to a tree. Barnes particularly reacts to each GI death like a wounded animal and becomes more emotionally unhinged each time. Soaked with a testosterone-heavy lust for revenge, the platoon descends on a village in search of the Viet Cong. Taylor finds two civilians, shoots the ground in front of them in a style of torture before coming, horrified, back to his senses. His compatriot Bunny (Dillon) soon reveals he has joined the side of evil like Sgt Barnes and, in perhaps the film's most disturbing scene, takes gleeful pleasure in clubbing the young Vietnamese man to death with his rifle so brutally that his brains are splattered everywhere. Outside, Barnes, desperate for information on the whereabouts of the Viet Cong is at the point of executing a villager by way of gleaning information, when he is stopped by Sgt Elias and a violent fight ensues. Later on another ambush, while the GIs are pinned down by enemy fire, Elias goes out into the jungle alone in an attempt to stop the Viet Cong from ensnaring the soldiers; but after killing some of them he comes face to face with

Elias and Barnes clash

Barnes, who promptly shoots him. Believing him dead, Barnes tells Taylor that Elias has been killed, but later when Barnes and Taylor are in a helicopter, they see Elias, bleeding heavily and being chased by the Viet Cong. Repeatedly shot, Elias finally succumbs to his mortal wounds and at this moment, Taylor realises Barnes' self-evident guilt.

At the film's climax lies a ferocious, awesome nocturnal firefight. This sequence is a visceral *tour-de-force*, and probably comes nearer to conveying to the viewer the catalclysmic reality of jungle warfare in Nam than any other movie. It is a veritable firestorm of blinding explosions, noise, abject terror, confusion and sudden, brutal death. After this final battle sequence, Taylor executes an already severely wounded Barnes. At that point Taylor has become Barnes. Taylor has become Vietnam, a transformation neatly summed up by the film's tagline, "The first casualty of war is innocence".

Platoon took 54 days to shoot at a then cost of $6.5m, and some 15 percent of the script was dropped in edit. A deal was struck with the Philippines Army to use their military equipment, as had been done for **Apocalypse Now**, filmed in the same country.

have an obligation to build again, to teach to others what we know, and to try with what's left of our lives to find goodness and meaning to this life." It is as though we are listening to Oliver Stone's personal motto on life. Which we unquestionably are.

The film opened on the 19th December 1986 and on only six screens, but the instant word of mouth that grew from the screenings hammered home that it had hit a core nerve in heartland America. This was not a Vietnam film made by a group of Hollywood aesthetic visionariess, nor was it Vietnam as metaphor or even Vietnam the way it should have been. Instead it was simply and explosively Vietnam as it was, alive with authenticity and imbued with a cinema-verité realism. By the beginning of February 1987, **Platoon** had arrived at the top of the box office in the USA. The reasons were clear; the film's powerful autobiographical elements so expertly brought to film reality by Oliver Stone, linked strong arms with the film's charged circle of truth. The success of the film brought open discussion of the Vietnam war, which had long since been quietly kept in denial by the American public.

The film took $136m in the US and received eight Oscar nominations. Winner of the best Picture Academy award, it also gained an Oscar (and Bafta) for Stone's direction, the best editing and the best sound. Stone's script was also nominated, as were Dafoe and Berenger in supporting actor roles (symbolising the outstanding ensemble cast) alongside Robert Richardson's photography. **Platoon** remains as powerful a film now as on its release, and one of cinema's greatest war films.

NOTES

1.   Willem Dafoe is another actor with several roles pertaining to the Vietnam conflict. In 1987 he appeared alongside Gregory HInes as a military policeman in 1968 Saigon, in Christopher Crowe's **Off Limit**s; Oliver Stone cast him as a disabled vet in the "sequel" to **Platoon**, **Born On The Fourth Of July**, in 1989; in David Lynch's **Wild At Heart** (1990) Dafoe plays wired Viet vet cocaine dealer Bobby Peru, a true psycho who gets his head blown off – way off; and in John MIlius' super-patriotic **Flight Of The Intruder** (1991), he plays a pilot involved in "payback" bombing raids over Hanoi.

CHAPTER 6
WAR IS HELL:
"FULL METAL JACKET"

It is striking how some of the key Vietnam war movies are as much expressions of their makers' personal obsessions as they are reflections of a deeper, collective attitude to the conflict itself. It seems that the confusions and traumas of the war brought the prevailing concerns of particular filmmakers into sharp, brilliant focus. **The Deer Hunter** presented its vision of Vietnam against the mounting doubt the war casts over the title character's quasi-mythic "one shot" ethos. **Apocalypse Now** (1979) filtered the political, historical and philosophical implications of the war through the figures of Willard (Martin Sheen) and Kurtz (Marlon Brando), two morally fragmented but symbiotically fused figures. **Platoon** (1986) focused on the central conflict for the soul of Chris (Charlie Sheen) between two surrogate fathers, Barnes (Tom Berenger) and Elias (Willem Dafoe). Seen in the context of the careers of Michael Cimino, Francis Coppola and Oliver Stone respectively, each film marked a pivotal moment and a definitive artistic statement. **Full Metal Jacket** (1987) on the other hand, has been often written off as a lesser, late period work of a filmmaker who had long ago insulated himself from the world and left his best work far behind. Yet, Stanley Kubrick's vision of Vietnam remains distinct and unique and in many ways it is his most concise expression of the human condition. Like those antecedents above, the film is focally concerned with links between war, masculinity and sexuality. However, Kubrick retreats from the engagement with mythical archetypes so evident in much of the Vietnam cycle, stripping the film down to the point where it almost seems detached from its historical reference points.

Such is the sparse, minimal narrative of the **Full Metal Jacket**, Kubrick could have fashioned it regardless of the conflict under consideration. This might seem an apt feature for a film which was shot in and around London, thousands of miles from its supposed location by a filmmaker who was already firmly ensconced in the English home counties by the time the war ended. The film depicts a combat zone beyond the dense jungle landscapes of other Vietnam films, presenting its conflicts within the sterile confines of a training camp and the urban desolation of a ravaged city. It largely eschews any deliberate political analysis and instead randomly scatters all manner of terminology and events emergent from the war. For example, "search and destroy", "the thousand yard stare" and "Tet" are all namechecked at some point but receive scant exploration beyond their almost perfunctory reference. As if in response to the mythic resonance of Coppola, Cimino and Stone's interpretation, the film climaxes in a simple encapsulation of the war as a bloody showdown between a disorganized, frightened platoon and a lone, but equally terrified sniper.

Divided into two distinct sections, the structural division of the film is striking and initially jarring. Upon this structure, Kubrick constructs a clinical, distanced meditation on the jarring contrasts between the preparation of men for conflict and their responses to its terrible actuality. At first, there is a dislocated feel to the narrative, a feeling that the meticulously designed parts do not constitute an organic whole. Indeed, the first section, set on the Parris Island boot camp ("home of the phoney tough and crazy brave") is tight, contained and relentless whereas the latter segments in Vietnam seem loose, episodic and fragmented. This is crucial however to the film's play on "duality", a theme exemplified by the protagonist and narrator, Private Joker (Matthew Modine), who wears a peace symbol button on his chest in conjunction with a slogan on his helmet proclaiming "born to kill". After the intensity of the opening forty five minutes, the sudden transition from a sterile barrack room toilet to the chaotic streets of Vietnam reinforces this observation of "duality", altering the geographical and psychological profile of the film and blurring the important connections to be made between the training and combat sequences.

If war is Hell (a cliché verbally mocked at one point by a demented helicopter gunner) then the boot camp represents a military inversion of purgatory, a cleansing of all the moral detritus which might impede the killer instinct. The training sequences pre-echo the later Vietnam episodes through the examination of obsessively sexual, hyper-masculine rituals. The boot camp is singularly concerned with the shedding of moral, social and spiritual conscience in the service of creating institutionally approved killers, a reversal of the Ludovico technique in **A Clockwork Orange** where anti-social impulses were eradicated in order to create model citizens. The Vietnam section sets out to demonstrate the absurdity of such preparation in the context of a war which is fought in terms far beyond the hopelessly idealised concepts defined by American military imperialism. The film's very title alludes literally to the physical properties of weaponry but is also redolent of the mechanized human, a theme that has of course fascinated Kubrick previously, from the thinking computer Hal in **2001: A Space Odyssey** (1968) to the brainwashed Alex of **A Clockwork Orange** (1971). A full metal jacket is the copper casing around a bullet which assists its feeding through the rifle barrel. However, in changing the title of Gustav Hasford's source novel from "The Short Timers", Kubrick evokes a sense of technology and the body in fusion, a model of masculine aggression that is dismantled against its (literally) feminized enemy. This reflects the overriding sense of collective impotence which manifested itself in a variety of Vietnam narratives. In **Born On The Fourth Of July** (1989), Oliver Stone uses his protagonist's paralysis (and more specifically, his sexual impotence) as a metaphor for a deeper, national affliction. Kubrick too draws from this castration motif but links it much more systematically to the symbolic function of phallus as weapon.

For all of its concentration upon the assertion of masculine aggression, the film begins with an intimation of child-like or infantile passivity. Seated in a barber's chair, seventeen young men, their expressions alternately blank, sullen or resigned, form a montage of unidentified faces as they endure the first stage in a systematic process of physical and psychological deprogramming. The individualization of each trainee is largely avoided throughout the course of the boot camp sequences, which concentrate chiefly on the triangular interaction of Private Joker, Private Pyle (Vincent D'Onofrio) and Drill Sgt. Hartman (Lee Ermey). Somewhat wryly therefore, the film gives the recruits their close-up at the moment their defining physical features are being stripped away. The ambience is that of an operating theatre, the indifferent yet brutal sweep of the barber's clippers suggesting not so much military protocol as preparation for brain surgery, a sense underlined by the icey, desaturated colour and precise, static images. The final shot of the montage, depicting a floor buried beneath a mass of human hair, merely affirms Kubrick's indifference to the mythic individualism which is so central to American notions of heroism.

Nevertheless, the film is fully conscious of the potency of idealized myths of war and masculinity. The opening montage is undersored by a ludicrous, anti-communist country and western song ("Goodbye My Sweetheart, Hello Vietnam") laced with trite observations on America's moral obligation to respond to distant "bugle calls". The cowboy song may invoke the romantic image of the western hero but actually prefigures the film's frequent parody of western mythology, a tendency exemplified by Joker's contemptuous John Wayne impersonations. The film develops an intermittent commentary on the Reagan era action film, where the hero (exemplified by Rambo) was a muscular, instinctive, all-conquering masculine ideal, psychologically damaged yet physically potent and committed to a recuperative mission of personal and national redemption. Kubrick concentrates the first section of his film on the very process necessary to harness and manufacture such figures yet places emphasis on Joker, who emerges as the irreverent antithesis of Hartman's ideals, and the "disgusting fatbody" Pyle, who defies all notions of the body conscious action hero but becomes Hartman's most potent recruit.

As Hartman addresses his recruits for the first time in the Parris Island barracks, the camera tracks in reverse, completing a 360 degree movement almost in terrified apprehension of his approach. The wide angle lens, utilised in so many of Kubrick's iconic images, imbues the unnaturally clean barrack room with an oppressive geometry and the sheer functionality of the training grounds later finds stark contrast in the ruins of Hue City. Hartman describes his charges as "pukes", "maggots", "ladies" and "the lowest form of life on earth... not even human fucking beings" but "unorganized, grab-asstic pieces of amphibian shit". Introductions are bawled, nicknames ("Snowball", "Joker" "Cowboy" "Pyle") instantly assigned, racial and ethnic identities insulted, local affiliations mocked ("Texas! Only steers and queers come from Texas!") and conventional modes of verbal interaction ruthlessly negated. Daily routine is marked by the maintenance of cleanliness, the tackling of physical obstacles and the absolute imperative of mass obedience. The film's nominal star (Modine) provides brief voiceover but such is the clinical gaze of the camera eye that any empathy is instantly neutralized. His presence in the first section of the film is often secondary to the Oedipal trajectory of Hartman/Pyle relationship, yet he provides an essential link between the stark ambience of the training sequences and the broader, satirical intent of the latter sections. Joker functions primarily, as his name suggests, to mockingly observe the rituals of training and combat yet remains powerless to provide any radical disruption to the familiar Kubrick obsessions with the formal and thematic implications of order, symmetry and control.

The relentless tirade of scatalogical and sexualized verbal abuse consolidates the links the film draws between the sex and death drives. In the (both physical and symbolic) absence of the feminine at the boot camp, sexual humiliation becomes one more means to masculine subjugation. The strict hierachy of the military is shown to draw sustenance from pre-ordained codes of homosocial intimacy. Hartman's order that each soldier provide his rifle with a

female name underlines this sexualized harmony of men and weaponry, bypassing the common phallic connotations of firearms in order to construct a relationship as much reciprocal ("without me, my rifle is useless, without my rifle, I am useless") as masturbatory. Identifying the gun ironically as man's best friend, Kubrick pursues the sexual connotations with a singular precison. Hartman assures his soldiers that the weapon is going to be the "only pussy they're going to get" before leading them in a ritualized march whereby, with his rifle in one hand and his cock in the other, he intones "this is my rifle, this is my gun, this is for fighting, this for fun". While Hartman imbues the gun with feminine characteristics, his chanted couplet also conjoins the phallus and the gun barrel. This dual form of sexual power conflates masculine control and aggression with the sensual properties of a weapon's internal mechanics, man and weapon as conjoined, polymorphous entity. Man is seen as both the master and accomplice of the gun, a relationship which is dramatically inverted by the film's concluding section.

Through his obscene verbal tirades, Hartman affirms his position as the tyrannical military patriarch, presiding over an institutionalized culture of control that informs all social and spiritual impulses. A low angle shot of an incensed, finger pointing Hartman (as he berates Joker's first jocular indiscretion) serves as a grotesque parody of the Uncle Sam recruitment posters used in previous, perhaps more just conflicts. In his pride at the sterile cleanliness of the "head" (communal toilets), he orders Joker and Cowboy to attend to it until "the Virgin Mary herself would be proud to take a dump in there". A Christmas day celebration becomes one more opportunity to inform the recruits of their obligations to serve both God and country in the eradication of communism and Hartman informs his men that God Himself has a "hard on for marines, because we kill everything we see". The harnessing of the killer instinct is posited as an expression of almost sexual and spiritual purity, a characteristic reflected environmentally in the antiseptic, reflective surfaces of the barrack interiors. The eradication of morality begets the model marine and Hartman's celebration of Charles Whitman and Lee Harvey Oswald's (both ex-marines) murderous marksmanship highlights with grim irony the devastating potential of the "motivated marine". The place of Whitman and Oswald in the pantheon of American psychos and miscreants points briefly to the role Hartman's trained killers might play "back in the world", when their talents serve no further purpose in the distant struggle to combat a presumed ideological foe. Unbeknownst to him, Hartman is also celebrating the process which leads to his own demise, to a recruit raised in his own charge.

Through the figure of Pyle, the film frequently returns to the childhood motif introduced from the outset, his fumblings and incompetence in all manner of military life (save for one terrible, latent talent) offsetting the relentless interrogation of a peculiarly institutionalized form of masculinity. Initially, the prime incompetent in the corps' orderly universe, he becomes its ultimate creation through the absolute divorce from previous moral and psychological characteristics. Transcending an extended programme of humiliation, Pyle becomes the most ruthlessly efficient embodiment of Hartman's creed of a "hard heart that kills". However, this is a hard heart born of innocence, transformed via forced rituals which require him to enact infantile remorse at his incompetence. This includes sucking his thumb while marching with his trousers around his ankles, eating jelly donuts while his comrades endure push ups administered because of his indiscretions and, most crucially, a nocturnal beating from his fellow recruits. Carried out in a cold, blue light, Pyle's beating (using bars of soap wrapped in towels) marks the moment when the litter finally turns on the runt, his sobs in the darkeness further reducing him to an infantile state. The sequence is accompanied by a rhythmic, electronic drone which, before building to crescendo, suggests an aural fusion of the mechanical and the organic, a machine gasping for air. Its use here underscores the reduction of the recruits to mechanised beings, their accelerated rejection of empathy for their comrade hastening Pyle's own deadly transformation. From this moment, his fumblings are supplanted by an eerie calm, evoked by the slow, sensuous zoom into his brooding stare. Effectively, he becomes Hartman's blankest canvas, his alienation and isolation enabling totally the killer instinct sought by the surrogate father.

From malfunctioning component to perfect mechanism, Pyle crystallizes the marriage of man and weapon, informing his rifle of its beauty in a tender whisper as he cleans and assembles its constituent parts. His execution of the military patriarch concludes the Oedipal trajectory of the film's opening segment. The setting for his final mortal act amplifies the film's scatological obsessions through its enactment in the "head", a literal "world of shit". As a privileged male space, the visualisation of the "head" reflects the contrasts of order and filth, symmetry and chaos from which the film draws. The morally desolate, pre-programmed "world of shit" which Pyle inhabits finds physical expression in the eerily symmetrical, reflective surfaces of the pristine toilet room. Once representative of Hartman's quest for a purity of purpose, the cleanliness of the "head" provides the site upon which the drill sergeant falls prey to the instrument of his own making. Bathed in the same cold blue glow which marked his nocturnal beating, and methodically recounting the technical specifications of his rifle, Pyle's ritulized actions instantly eliminate the oncoming Hartman with a decisive, devastating squeeze of the trigger. In an instant, the incessant verbal onslaught of Hartman that has provided the film with its aural rhythms, is silenced, his body hurled backwards by the impact of the bullet. In turning the rifle on himself, Pyle enacts his final indiscretion, the splattering of blood and brain matter on the walls of Hartman's beloved, anti-septically clean "head", fusing him terminally with the physical space of his final transformation.

From Pyle's death in the clinically sparse interiors of the head, the film fades to black and suddenly transports the viewer to the urban space of Vietnam. A slow, deliberate forward tracking shot, underscored by Nancy Sinatra's "These Boots Are Made For Walking", follows a prostitute in a leather mini-skirt as she struts into view. Self-consciously, she makes outwardly sexual gestures as she approaches the seated pair of American soldiers across the street, the camera discreetly continuing its forward movement behind her. The previous absence of the feminine is answered directly here, instantly defining Vietnam as an object of sexual as well as political and ideological exchange. This is a key transitional point which has crucial ramifications for the presentation of the conflict as an emasculatory process. The empowered, sexually aggressive connotations of the Sinatra song provide an ironic counterpoint to the objectified female figure on screen but assumes a greater significance later when a lone female sniper methodically eliminates members of Joker's platoon. Obliquely referencing the sexualization of weaponry in the early sequences, the marines encounter Vietnamese women only as prostitutes and assassins, both objects of total objectification and the living embodiment of castration anxiety. This is made

doubly ironic later after a teenage prostitute refuses to go with Eight Ball (Dorian Harewood) on account of the sexual stereotype of the "soul brother" black man. Her protestation that he will be "too beaucoup" is met with amused jeers and mockery. However, Eight Ball's obvious pride in his "magnificent specimen of Alabama blacksnake" is mortally dented in his later confrontation with the sniper – in all deliberation it seems, she shoots off his genitals.

If Hartman's creed stressed that all of his recruits are "equally worthless" under his command, there is a sense that all social, cultural, racial and gender hierachies have been restored in Vietnam. This ranges from a colonel's proclamation that "inside every gook there is an American trying to get out" to Animal Mother's threat that "all fucking niggers must fucking hang". All of the early Vietnam sequences contrast vividly with the brutal order of Hartman's boot camp. Joker's first scenes in Vietnam depict him debating over a price with a prostitute, insolently addressing his superior officer and lying around bored in a bunk. His brief encounter with a street thief, who warns off Joker with a fluent, elegant display of martial arts calisthenics, prompts him to respond in a clumsy, awkward imitation which mockingly recalls Hartman's earlier demand to see his "war face". The film also contrasts Joker's conscious attempt to avoid actual conflict (through his job as a military journalist) with his new companion, Rafterman (Kevyn Major Howard)'s desire to prove himself in the field because, as a photographer, all he ever does is "take handshake shots at award ceremonies". Joker's status as "military journalist" was earlier mocked by

Hartman ("Who do you think you are, Mickey Spillane?") and he becomes one tiny cog not only in the military machine but also in the workings of the propaganda effort. The sequences in which Joker meets with his colleagues on the "Stars And Stripes" newspaper extend the film's satirical aspirations and introduce the now familiar notion of a war partly defined by the manipulations of the news media. As he did in the boot camp, Joker mocks the processes and attitudes of the newspaper but is powerless to alter the manipulation of facts and terminology that become central to the ideological underpinnings of the war. The editor of the paper demands that the phrase "search and destroy" is altered to "sweep and clear" and the whole attempt to alter public perceptions of the war is given extra irony by the editor's insistence that he remains in Da Nang away from combat, "in the rear, with the gear".

Kubrick utilises the notion of a "media war" and more specifically, a conflict which is partly shaped and defined through a prying camera lens. At one point Joker retorts to *Variety* speak ("scuttlebut") in his enquiries about strategic developments and meets Animal Mother's contemptuous questioning on how much combat he has actually experienced by replying sarcastically that he has "seen a little on TV". The sense of the war as a giant media event is exemplified by the extraordinary sequence in which a laterally tracking camera depicts the systematic bombing of Hue City by tanks as, in the foreground, the covered marines address a television crew through a range of dark wisecracks. Counterpointed by the song "Surfin' Bird", the pulverization of the city is narrated by the marines who greet the cameras by welcoming them to "Vietnam: The Movie". Referencing John Wayne, General Custer, horses and Indians ("we'll let the gooks play the Indians"), the conflict is presented in terms of an elaborately choreographed spectacle in which fictional and mythic archetypes are assigned to conform with "traditional" notions of how war should be fought. This is coupled with a later interview montage which demonstrates a jumble of individual beliefs and motivations as the marines address the camera directly. Again the sequence throws up a series of fractured, incoherent attitudes and responses which conflate historical, political, and cultural attitudes. Animal Mother's suggestion that they just "blow the place to Hell" and Cowboy's gripe that there isn't a single horse to be found in the whole of Vietnam are juxtaposed with the direct quotation of Lyndon Johnson and the observation that the war simply doesn't correspond to preconceptions of how armed conflict should be conducted ("there's the enemy, kill them"). These are capped by Joker's wry remark that he wanted to visit Vietnam, "the jewel of south-east Asia" to "meet interesting and stimulating people of an exotic culture and kill them". Extending the attempt to alter the language of war through ambiguous terminology, the procession of soundbites emphasises the contradictory motivations that drive the grunts on. These sequences make apparent the impossibility of the media attempt to impose meaning and moral order upon the war while its ground level participants can't quite identify just what the war is actually been fought over and why. Where the boot camp suppressed and eliminated individual opinion, the attempts of the "Stars And Stripes" newspaper to sweeten the bitter truth are countered by the grimly honest reactions of the marines to their direct experience in the line of fire.

The complacency of presumed masculine power is underscored by echoes of the film's earlier sexualization of military ritual. Where in the boot camp the recruits stood rapt, stiff and attentive to Hartman's instructional tirades, the film develops a recurring pattern in Vietnam whereby the marines stand blank and disillusioned over the corpses of the war's casualties. This inversion of military procession initially defines the marines' direct confrontation with death. Joker's observation that "the dead know only one thing; it is better to be alive" serves as a concise summarization of the fatalism so evident in Kubrick's other work. In one sequence, the short laments of the grunts as they stand over their dead comrades are coupled with a rhythmic, circular camera movement which depicts them from an extreme low angle. Empty tributes are paid to the stiff, bloodied corpses and the film again draws explicit parallels between the sex and death drives. Animal Mother, the film's embodiment of the redneck, trigger happy action hero, rejects the suggestion that the marines were killed in the name of freedom. Instead he states that the only word he'd be willing to get his "balls blown off for" is "poontang". The democratic or patriotic impulse is displaced by that of self-preservation and the phallus, with its connotations of both sexual and combative power, is defined as the focal embodiment of masculine concern. Such is the proliferation of frustrated sexual impulses that the imminent catastrophe of Tet is ignored in favour of the excitement induced by the impending arrival of a Hollywood glamour figure. The "Stars and Stripes" editor's dismissal of the rumours of a possible Tet offensive are coupled with his instructions to Rafterman that he wants to see plenty of revealing photographs of Ann-Margaret's imminent morale boosting visit ("I wanna see fur. And early morning dew"). The soon to be non-existent arrival of Ann-Margaret stresses the elimination of all traces of Western femininity from Kubrick's film. Hartman's earlier invocation of "Mary Jane Rotten Crotch" and Joker's final voiceover, which describes his "homecoming queen fuck fantasy", present two stereotypes of American femininity which further enhance the sense of divorce from "traditional" values back "in the world". In achieving this, the film also enhances the castrating function of the Hue City sniper through a mortal confrontation with a model of femininity that is the antithesis of the ideals fantasised by Joker.

In brutal contrast to Hartman's preparatory rituals, disorganization and chaos is central to the climactic confrontation between the marines and the unseen sniper in the ruins of Hue. Calculating and proificient, the sniper enacts the very qualities which Hartman espoused to his recruits, assuming the very same methods as Oswald and Whitman, those figures namechecked as the ultimate embodiments of the "motivated marine". However, the sniper killings are marked not by an lethal single shot but by a process seemingly designed to prolong the death agonies of the victims. The sniper shootings are photographed with a graphic but cold detachment. The clinical dismantling of men's bodies is accentuated by slow motion images and heightened sound designed to maximize the velocity and impact of rifle fire. Furthermore, as if to emphasise the methodical poise of the sniper in contrast to the shambolic platoon, the film allows the audience to share her point of view as she takes careful aim at a series of figures isolated in the distant rubble of the city. Feet, arms, thighs and genitals are ripped apart in graphic explosions of blood and tissue, emphasizing the sheer vulnerability of bodies refined for combat. The precision of sniper fire is met with the aimless discharges of Animal Mother's M-60 and the platoon's automatic rifles. Hartman's creed is turned against his own progeny with the marines' desperate return fire is directed blindly into a mass of ruined concrete. The ruins of the city stand as a visible monument to futile, destructive masculine impulses enacted in the guise of the democratic principle.

The revelation of a young female as the deadly assassin in the midst of a destroyed city answers comprehensively the film's relentless associations of masculinity with violence. Contemptuous references to womanhood have echoed across the film, articulating both the suspicion of "feminine" traits in men and the emasculatory potential of the female. The previous encounters with Vietnamese whores were marked by the arrogant assumption of superiority by the American marines. However, oblivious to their lone enemy's gender and removed from the power structures and rituals of sexual exchange, the marines respond with panic and hysteria. Having tracked down the sniper, Joker's rifle (without which, Hartman informed him, he is "useless") malfunctions and he is forced to cower from his foe as she sprays bullets in his direction with a frightened but steely resolve. Only the intervention of Rafterman, elated at his first taste of active combat, saves Joker. The film repeats the imagery of men stood over a dying body, this time as it prays in anticipation of imminent death. The killing of the sniper is met with an empty relief, a partial recognition that the former bravado has been severely undercut by the supine, terrified young female form beneath them. Having failed to achieve symbiosis with his rifle, it is left to Joker to finish the sniper off with a single shot to the head by handgun, a personalised act which contrasts the sniper fire that killed his comrades. This final killing at close quarters is defined through his reluctance and hesitance, a response which offsets the moronic whooping and hollering of Rafterman at having cut down the enemy. The camera holds on Joker's face as he administers

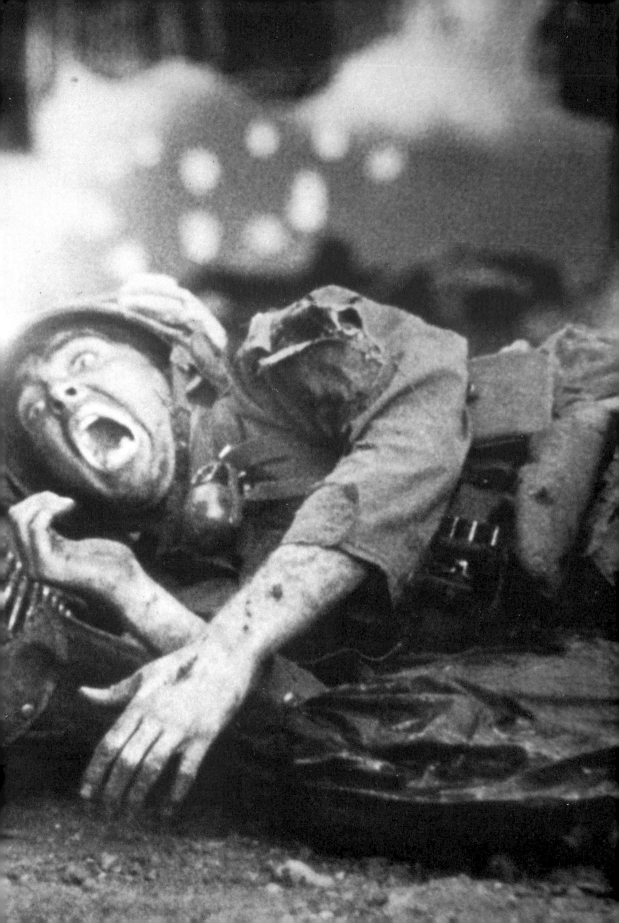

the final, mortal shot, his mournful gaze signalling that his own transformation reaches deeper than that of his fellow grunts. If the killing legitimizes Joker in the mind of Animal Mother ("fucking hardcore man" intones the trigger happy redneck), it is Rafterman's suggestion that he should be awarded the "Congessional Medal of Ugly" that expresses the final terrible break from the heroic ideal.

In his extermination of the sniper, Joker is partly estranged from the philosophy of Hartman but ironically fulfills his former drill instructor's ideal of a "hard heart that kills". As the marines march in the decimated ruins of the infernal city, Joker's voiceover expresses a naive level of personal awareness while yearning for adolescent gratifications. His "erect nipple wet dreams" are contrasted to the recognition that he inhabits a "world of shit". Moreover, his suggestion that the marines have "nailed their names in the pages of history enough for one day" is undercut by the film's obliteration of "history" and military "tradition" in the face of a conflict that pays no heed to vague notions of the "rules" of combat. The final declaration by Joker that he is "alive and not afraid" suggests that he does indeed boast a "hard heart", a new killer instinct born paradoxically of a strangely humanitarian act. He has harnessed the ability to kill out of a terrible compassion which has somehow survived his moral blankness. Just as it began, the film concludes on an expression of mass infantilism as the grunts, silhouetted against the distant flames, chant a rendition of the theme from the Mickey Mouse Club. If Joker has indeed recognised his essential humanity it seems to be at the cost of mass regression. Unlike his comrades, Joker is allowed a brief moment of realisation, an understanding that the "hard heart" may yet yield to a purer influence. But he remains the child of Hartman, the "minister of death praying for war". A dark sky enshrouds the ruins of Hue at the film's conclusion – as if in empathy, and as articulated in the Rolling Stones song that concludes the film, Joker has looked inside himself and seen his heart is black.

PART TWO

AFTERMATH

CHAPTER 7
GUN CRAZY:
VIETNAM VETERAN FILMS

1. MOTORCYCLE PSYCHOS

"Three motorcycle-riding hoodlums led by an ex-Viet Nam medically discharged veteran BRAHMIN brutally beat an unsuspecting fisherman before the eyes of his voluptuous wife and proceeds to physically assault her.

Their voracious appetites for criminal violence still unsatisfied, they proceed to terrorize GAIL MADDOX wife of CORY MADDOX a young veterinarian. MADDOX forcefully interrupts the harassment of his wife. Revenge is in order and BRAHMIN, DANTE and SLICK criminally assault GAIL. MADDOX is absent administering to a mare belonging to the wealthy / stunningly / frustrated sex-machine, JESSICA FANNIN. She comes very close to swaying MADDOX' affections.

CORY discovers his wife GAIL brutally beaten and criminally assaulted when he returns home. With the indifferent attitude of the local sheriff, CORY takes the law into his own hands. This results in a dangerous desert chase involving a lusty Cajun girl named RUBY BONNER and her murdered husband HARRY BONNER, incidentally, by the same three hoodlums.

Together, CORY and RUBY stalk the killers. Excitement runs rampant with BRAHMIN murdering SLICK, his buddy, in cold blood; CORY experiencing a deadly snake bite with RUBY withdrawing the venom from his leg with her mouth, saving his life. She further defends CORY'S helplessness by permitting DANTE to crudely make love to her, and at the same time placing a hunting knife between his shoulder blades! Thus DANTE meets his end.

CORY foolishly follows BRAHMIN. RUBY is critically wounded by BRAHMIN's rifle. The desert-crazed BRAHMIN believes that he is back in Viet Nam fighting Commies. RUBY and CORY with only the meager protection of a shallow mine trench, manage to kill the insane BRAHMIN at the critical moment with the aid of a crudely fashioned hand grenade. (Materials, of course, conveniently attainable from the mine immediate.)"

–Description of Russ Meyer's **Motorpsycho!** on Meyer's own RM Films website

Russ Meyer's **Motorpsycho!** (1965) is notable for featuring the earliest screen appearance of that latterday icon of exploitation cinema: the deranged, maladjusted Vietnam war veteran[1]. Brahmin, the gun-toting combat-scarred killer, remains the very prototype of this new breed of sociopath. The film also anticipates the mid-'60s revival of a motorcycle hood genre instigated in 1954 by **The Wild One**, but allowed to lapse in the intervening decade. It was exploitation king Roger Corman who breathed new life into the biker movie with

Motorpsycho!

Wild Angels, starring Peter Fonda, in 1966. For the next few years the genre flourished, and several biker movies featured as characters Vietnam vets who either rode with, or were terrorized by, Hell's Angels motorcycle gangs.

Born Losers (1967) instigated the character of Billy Jack, an angry half-breed Viet vet played by Tom Laughlin. Billy Jack clashes with violent redneck bikers who are terrorizing girls in a small California town, and becomes an anti-hero. Laughlin went on to reprise this role in the highly successful **Billy Jack** (1971). This was followed by the progressively less well received sequels **The Trial Of Billy Jack** (1974) and **Billy Jack Goes To Washington** (1977).

In **Angels From Hell** (1968), a "cycle psycho" played by Tom Stern reverts to his pre-war biker days when, as a returning Viet vet, he is unable to readjust to society. His military combat skills earn him new respect and he is soon elected leader of the local biker fraternity. In a suitably downbeat ending, he is shot and killed by police. **The Angry Breed** (1968) features a Viet vet called Johnny who comes into conflict with a biker gang when rivalry erupts between him and the gang leader over a Hollywood part. After various attempts by the bikers to kill Johnny (including driving him mad with LSD), the soldier hero elopes with the film producer's daughter in a rare happy ending.

Satan's Sadists (1969) is one of the roughest of the biker flicks, featuring much violence, murder and rape perpetrated by a vicious bike gang led by Russ Tamblyn. Another Viet vet named Johnny finally brings them to rough justice. Billed as a tale of "human garbage in the sickest love parties", **Satan's Sadists** is another outrageous offering from Al Adamson, director of sleaze

classics such as **Brain Of Blood** and **Lash Of Lust**.

The Losers was directed by ace trash film director Jack Starrett in 1970. Its premise – Viet vets team up with Hell's Angels in order to go back into Cambodia and cause mayhem – anticipates the **Rambo** films of the 1980s. A gang of Angels (including biker film stalwart William Smith) with armoured hogs finally ship out to the east, but most of them die before the end of the movie. **The Losers** was remade in 1986 under the title **Nam Angels**, a film produced by Roger Corman and directed by Cirio H Santiago in the Philippines[2].

1971 saw two late entries in the Viet vet/biker stakes[3]. **Chrome And Hot Leather** (directed by Lee Frost) features a Viet vet Green Beret who wreaks revenge on the bikers who killed his fiancée. One of his vet friends is played by Marvin Gaye, and William Smith also stars. Here the violence escalates into full-out war between the two factions, with the vets bringing all their military training and hardware to bear. **The Hard Ride** (directed by Burt Topper) tells the tale of a Viet vet who returns with the body of his best friend, a black soldier killed in action. More flashbacks to the war are included than is customary in these films, and the relationship between the two men is fully stated. In the end, the hero is killed in a brutal gang rumble and buried alongside his dead buddy. With its emphasis on the ethnicity of the dead soldier, **The Hard Ride** is also notable for including elements of another rising genre of the early '70s, the blaxploitation movie. Bikers, blaxploitation and the war finally fused in Matt Cimber's **The Black Six** (1974), in which a gang of black, Viet vet bikers avenge a soul brother's death, finally defeating a rival gang of white bikers.

2. IN THE GHETTO: BLAXPLOITATION

The blaxploitation genre is generally accepted as having started with Melvin Van Peebles' **Sweet Sweetback's Baadasssss Song** in 1971, and it wasn't long after that before the Vietnam vet factor would begin to be added to the mix. That same year, in an urban drama called **The Bus Is Coming** directed by Wendell Franklin, a black vet returns home to LA only to find that his brother has been murdered by the police. Naturally, he teams up with a group of black militants and goes up against the racist pigs.

1972 saw three additions to the blax/Viet vet sub-genre. Barry Pollack's **Cool Breeze** features a black vet who leads a team of robbers in a $3 million bank heist. Blaxploitation queen Pam Grier has a small role in this action thriller. **Black Gunn**, directed by Robert Hartford-Davies, was the first of two 1972 vehicles for Jim Brown, perhaps the first blaxploitation superstar. Here, Brown plays a nightclub owner in LA, who goes up against the mob after they kill his Viet vet brother, Seth, who used mob money to fund a revolutionary faction called the Black Action Group. Brown next played the eponymous Viet vet in Jack Starrett's **Slaughter**, his most famous role and one of the all-time great blaxploitation movies. Once again, Brown goes up against the mob – this time after they kill his parents – and uses all his army-taught killing skills to wipe them out.

A sequel, **Slaughter's Big Rip-Off**, appeared in 1973 and featured such bizarre scenes as Slaughter bedding a white dwarf. That same year saw several other entries of varying quality. **The Bad Bunch**, directed by Greydon Clark, features a vet who must go to Watts, the black LA ghetto, to deliver a letter from a black comrade who was killed in Nam. Also known as **Nigger Lover**, the film

Slaughter

has been reviled as racist in tone. **Gordon's War** was a violent 1973 entry from Ossie Davis, in which a group of black Viet vets are called upon to use their military expertise in Harlem, where they must combat street crime in vigilante fashion. **Mean Mother**, another Z-movie directed by Al Adamson (this time assisted by Leon Klimovsky), is about two Viet vets, one white one black, who somehow end up in Europe and get involved in stupid adventures.

The final film for 1973 was William A Levy's **Blackenstein**, an entry into the "blaxploitation horror" sub-genre that began with **Blacula** (1972) and also included the likes of **Sugar Hill** (1974) and the **Exorcist** rip-off **Abby** (also 1974). In **Blackenstein**, a black GI is blown apart in Nam but reconstructed as a monster by a mad scientist and his jealous assistant. The monster rampages around for a while before being killed by a pack of dogs. Unfortunately, it's as bad as it sounds.

Films after 1973 were sporadic: **The Black Six** came in 1974 [see above]; 1976 produced the Fred Williamson vehicle **Mean Johnny Barrows**, in which a black vet (dishonourably discharged for assaulting his superior officer) comes up against a powerful crime boss; 1978 saw the release of **Youngblood**, in which a black vet returns to The Los Angeles ghetto and joins the fight against drug pushers; **Ashes And Embers** (1982) tells of a black vet's struggle against poverty and racism; and **Messenger** (1987) is another typical Fred Williamson film, in which he plays a Viet vet who turns to crime, comes out of prison and goes up against the drug barons. It would be another eight years before the best movie of them all appeared.

Gordon's War

Dead Presidents (1995) was the second film by the Hughes Brothers, whose debut feature **Menace II Society** was perhaps the bleakest and most violent entry in the "new wave" of blaxploitation movies which erupted in the late '80s/early '90s. **Dead Presidents**, a story of the black experience immediately before, during, and immediately after service in the Vietnam war, is equally brutal. After a deceptively low-key opening segment concerning the coming-of-age of the film's key young protagonists, the action abruptly moves to Vietnam for a middle section which is probably the most shocking, bloody and ultra-violent "in-country" sequence yet filmed. Here we see not only point-blank shootings and bodies blown apart, but atrocities committed on both sides. The film's focal character, Curtis, finds himself in a Recon unit along with some of his associates from Harlem who include Skippy, a junkie, and Cleon, a preacher's son. The unit is all black except for its psychopathic leader. After one bloody firefight Cleon hacks off a dead Vietcong's head with a machete, keeping it in his pack as a good luck charm until the stench of rotting flesh becomes unbearable and he is forced to bury it. But the most unpleasant scene here is an atrocity committed by the VC on an ambushed GI, who is eviscerated and castrated then left, still alive, with his severed genitals stuffed in his mouth.

Once discharged and back in New York, Curtis struggles to find work and ends up in a butcher's shop. Soon, scenes of meat, corpses and maggot-riddled flesh fill his traumatised nightmares. When he is laid off, he decides to raise cash by means of a heist, roping in Cleon, Skippy and others (including his girlfriend's sister, who has now become a Black Panther militant). Of course the heist goes

A HUGHES BROTHERS FILM
DEAD PRESIDENTS

wrong and ends in an extremely bloody shoot-out, with fatal casualties on both sides. Curtis escapes, but is soon apprehended and sentenced to the penitentiary. Underpinned by an amazing soundtrack of classic black American doo-wop, soul and funk – no white rock Nam clichés here – **Dead Presidents** is a downbeat but viscerally explosive film, and surely the last word on the black experience in and after Nam.

3. HELL TRIP: HORROR/SF

Bob Clark's **Deathdream** (aka **Dead Of Night**, 1972) was the first horror movie to incorporate a Viet nam vet – in this case, a dead one. This under-rated film opens with a brief Vietnam combat sequence in which we see a GI shot and killed, then the action switches to a suburban household back in the States where the Brooks family anxiously await news of their son, Andy, who is in Nam on tour of duty. One evening, a knock comes at the door – it is the news they have been dreading, Andy has been killed in action. Andy's mother goes into shock, refusing to accept the news as truth, and spends the midnight hour in prayer for her son to still be alive and to come home. Later, in the dead of night, they are disturbed by a noise downstairs. When they investigate they find Andy, standing in the shadows, still wearing his army uniform. Although they are overjoyed at this apparent miracle, Andy seems different – cold, withdrawn, distanced. He also has zero appetite. Andy had hitched a ride home with a truck driver; the next morning, the trucker is found murdered, his throat viciously slashed open and a strange puncture mark in his arm.

Over the next few days Andy's strange behaviour continues, taking a turn for the worse when he strangles the family dog to death. By night he heads to the local graveyard. When the town doctor becomes suspicious about Andy's connection to the murder, Andy follows him to his surgery. Here, he reveals to the doctor that he is dead – no pulse, no heartbeat – before savagely killing him in a frenzied attack. Andy then draws blood from the doctor's arm and injects it into his own veins. It seems that Andy has become a zombie vampire of the most modern kind, one who must feed on the blood of others to stay alive, and who considers this blood "donation" nothing more than what he is owed for having given his life in service of his country.

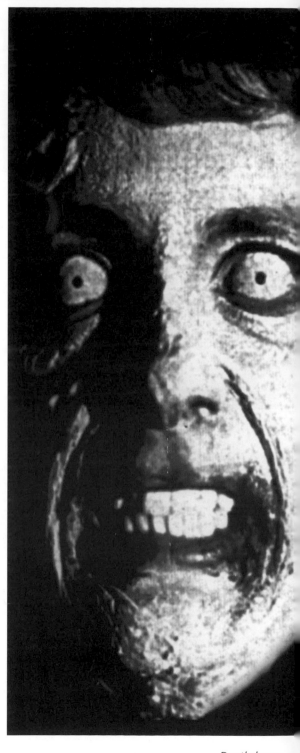

Deathdream

Andy's father faces the truth about his killer son, but his mother remains loyal. Meanwhile, Andy starts to age and decompose, donning a disguise of dark glasses and gloves when he goes out with his former girlfriend, his sister and sister's boyfriend. At a drive-in the girlfriend notices his advancing state of decay, and he kills and partially eats her. He then kills his sister's boyfriend before driving home, where his father commits suicide at the sight of him. Pursued by the police, he and his mother drive to the local graveyard where Andy, now wretchedly putrefied, flees to the last refuge left to him – his own grave, which he has dug out by night, a shallow trench surmounted by a stone crudely etched with his epitaph.

Like **Clay Pigeon** (1971), **Deathdream** was based on a classic story of the supernatural – in this case, WW Jacobs' *The Monkey's Paw*, whose "moral' is: be careful what you wish for – you just might get it. Well-shot and grimly effective, it was one of the first films to feature the horrific make-up work of Tom Savini. Savini was about to start work on a film directed by his friend George Romero – **Night Of The Living Dead** – when he was called in for photography training by the Army. He was then sent straight to Vietnam as a combat photographer, thus missing out on Romero's landmark 1968 film altogether. Vietnam changed Savini's life forever; he would later describe the horrific bloodshed, maiming and mutilation which he encountered there, and its effect on his life and career. "Like everyone else who went to Vietnam, I was real screwed up when I got back. My marriage went instantly into the toilet," he would recall in 1982. "Vietnam changed my life; it made me want to escape from reality forever... much of my work for **Dawn Of The Dead** [1980] was like a series of portraits of what I had seen for real in Vietnam. Perhaps that was one way of working out that experience." In this sense **Dawn Of The Dead**, with its graphic depictions of the human body being violently destroyed by hardware (including helicopters), can be seen as a Vietnam veteran movie with a difference.

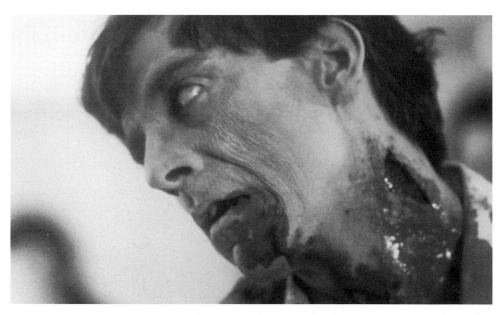

Echoes of war; *Dawn Of The Dead*

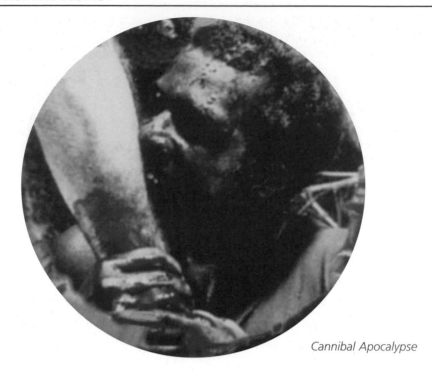

Cannibal Apocalypse

Blood Sabbath (aka **Yyalah**, 1972) is an extremely weird tale of sex and witchcraft. This low-budget film, directed by Brianne Murphy, stars Tony Geary as an itinerant Vietnam vet who is accosted by five naked girls, who turn out to be witches and the servants of one Queen Alotta (Dyanne Thorne, showing off her breasts in yet another topless role). Yyalah is the name of a water nymph who fatally attracts the disturbed young man. The Nam vet suffers intense combat flashbacks (including shooting Vietnamese children), and there is plenty of nudity and occasional violence in this highly unusual psychedelic movie.

Typically, it was an Italian exploitation film maker who next seized the potential for horror involving Vietnam vets. Antonio Margheriti's **Cannibal Apocalypse** (1980) comes towards the end of the cycle of Italian cannibal movies which flourished in the 1970s with the likes of **Cannibal Ferox**, and stars John Saxon. Saxon plays Hopper (a tribute to Dennis?), a Viet vet plagued by nightmares about his war buddies Bukowski and King. When Hopper freed them from a bamboo VC trap, he saw them gnawing on human bones, and one of them bit his arm. It turns out that they are vectors of a cannibal virus acquired in Nam, and soon are all rampaging through the streets of Atlanta in search of human flesh[4]. **Cannibal Apocalypse** is a gory horror movie, with only half-hearted attempts at laying the blame for its horrible events at the feet of US foreign policy-makers.

The same year, Margheriti stayed with the Vietnam theme to produce the blood-splattered combat movie **The Last Hunter** [see chapter 4], while his contemporary Ruggero Deodato peaked with **Cannibal Holocaust**. Deodato's

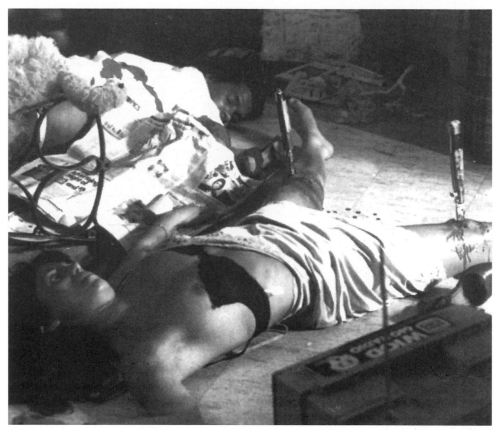

Cut And Run

routine SF actioner **Raiders Of Atlantis** (1983) featured a pair of rugged Vietnam vets sent to rescue a female explorer who has raised the lost city. Far better was the same director's **Cut And Run** (1985). In this very violent and bloody movie, Richard Lynch plays Horne, a Nam vet colonel now involved in the South American drugs trade. In one clever flashback sequence, Horne is seen at the site of the Jim Jones/Guyanatown mass suicide, perhaps perpetuating the myth that the US government was directly responsible for those multiple deaths. Horne now controls a sadistic, ultra-violent hit-squad of Indio natives (led by Michael Berryman) in his quest to "purify" the world by destroying the weak with overdoses of cocaine. In this sense Horne is portrayed as a Kurtz-like figure, lording it over jungle tribesmen and spouting quasi-Nietzschean cant, though the more profound sentiments of **Apocalypse Now** are very absent from **Cut And Run**.

Another cult exploitation film director, Jess Franco, offered a bloody mixture of cannibalism and Nam fallout in his 1980 production **Man Hunter**. This visual compendium of atrocities involves a stalking, man-eating zombie, a kidnapped actress and cannibal Vietnam vets amid scenes of human sacrifice and dismemberment deep in the jungle. Like many Franco films, a catalogue of depravity with little to offer beyond its surface horrors.

Twilight Zone – The Movie (1983) was a compendium film version of the classic SF TV series, with segments directed by George Miller, Joe Dante, Steven Spielberg, and John Landis. Only Miller's segment – a remake of

"Nightmare At 20,000 Feet", an episode which had originally starred William Shatner – was worth watching, but the film will always be remembered for John Landis' contribution, a story of racism set partially in Vietnam during the war. Remembered for the horrific deaths of actor Vic Morrow and two young Vietnamese children, hacked to bits and decapitated by a crashing helicopter during filming. As a result of this hideous accident, Landis was prosecuted for involuntary manslaughter. Snuff footage of the event later turned up in the neo-mondo video compilation **Death Scenes 2**. Mikita Brottman, in her fascinating study of "cursed" movies *Hollywood Hex* (Creation Books 1999), describes the accident as follows:

1.30AM, July 23rd, 1982, Indian Dunes Park, nr. Saugus, north of L.A: *Director John Landis is busily preparing to shoot the scene described in the screenplay above, in which the character of Bill, played by veteran screen actor Vic Morrow, is fleeing hostile soldiers in Vietnam. In the screenplay, Bill comes across two Vietnamese orphans and rescues them from an air attack. The scene allows Landis to blow up the entire village, and thus end his segment of the movie on a remarkably apocalyptic note. Few of the cast or crew present, however, have any idea just how memorable or apocalyptic the scene will turn out to be.*

Landis goes to confer with Paul Stewart, the special effects supervisor, and the two of them stand to one side and begin an animated conversation. After a few minutes, Stewart seeks out special effects technician Jerry Williams and asks him to prepare an eighteen-inch mortar filled with sawdust and gasoline and plant it under a four-legged wooden structure next to one of the village huts.

This is the last scene to be shot for the Landis segment, and it has to be perfect, because the explosions are set to destroy the entire village in a series of enormous fireballs. After three straight weeks of night-shooting in a tight location with little manoeuvrability, the entire company is feeling tense and worn down.

1.45AM: *The two Oriental children who've been hired to play the Vietnamese orphans, Renee Chen and Myca Le, are being made up for their brief part in the scene. Production assistant Hilary Leach rubs mud in their faces then leads them over to the village set.*

Renee is nervous. "What if we get sick?" the child asks her.

"You won't get sick. You'll be fine," Leach reassures her.

Nearby, John Landis is giving similar assurances to Myca Le. Elsewhere, cameraman Michael Scott is positioned on the cliff behind the mock village. Concerned about the possible impact of the explosions, he asks one of the special effects men whether the fireball in the next scene will reach as far as the top of the cliff.

"Where will you be standing?" asks the powder man.

"Right here," says Scott, indicating his spot at the edge of the cliff.

"I hope your life insurance's paid up," the other man replies.

2.00AM: *Vic Morrow is pacing up and down on the banks of the Santa Clara river, preparing himself for the gruelling shoot ahead. Landis brings up the two Asian-born children and chats to them for a while, trying to calm their nerves. A* few moments later, the signal is given that the cameras are ready to roll.

2.10AM: Landis wades into the shallow waters of the river to signal the start of filming. The helicopter hovers above the set, its forty-four-foot blades whirring viciously.

"Scene thirty-one! Take one!" yells a crew member. The cameras begin to roll.

"Action!" yells Landis.

Morrow begins his slow progress across the river, picking up the two children and pressing them tightly against his body as he wades through the water.

The first three bombs at the rear of the village are detonated at one or two second intervals. The force of the blasts is terrifying; the camera operators on top of the cliff are suddenly engulfed in an unanticipated cloud of smoke and ash. Their cameras still running, they dash up the slopes of the cliff to escape the heat of the explosions.

2.12AM: The second series of mortars begins to go off directly beneath the helicopter. Fragments of wood and debris begin to rain down on the cameramen and crew members; the camera lenses are splattered with mud. Above the set, the helicopter wobbles dangerously, surrounded by clouds of flames and debris, and begins to career out of control. It tries to lift and then starts to spin, turning over on its left side.

Special effects man Jerry Williams, in the middle of detonating a round of explosions, hears a sudden change in the noise of the helicopter's rotor. Looking up, he sees the massive craft falling out of the sky. He turns and runs for his life.

2.14AM: Stumbling through the shallow water, Vic Morrow is hit full on by the force of the explosions. He loses his grip on Renee and drops her in the water. He stumbles and tries to retrieve her, but it's too late. The gigantic helicopter, turned on its left side, crashes into the water, landing on top of the body of Renee and crushing her to death immediately. The still-spinning main rotor blades, filled with an immense power, cut through the river with an enormous splash, sending up a massive spray of water. One of the blades, functioning as an enormous scythe, slices through the necks of Vic Morrow and Myca Le, decapitating them at virtually the same moment.

John Landis, in a moment of terrible shock and confusion, is unable to understand what's happened. "What the fuck is this helicopter doing in my shot?" he asks himself in bewilderment. Then a sudden chill runs through him.

"Oh my God!" he shouts. "Where are Vic and the kids?"

He drops his megaphone and runs towards the helicopter. Also running towards the helicopter is the second *assistant director, Anderson House. House arrives at the crash scene and sees something large and rubbery lying in the river. There's no blood anywhere, and his first thought is that a dummy must have fallen out of the helicopter. Then he spots Vic Morrow's head lying near the shore, and suddenly realizes the magnitude of the disaster.*

"Oh my God!" he screams.

Only when the crew members on the bank hear his screams do they understand what's happened. Renee's mother, Shyan Huei-Chen, runs down to the river bank only to discover the crushed remains of her dead child. She begins pleading with the girl to wake up, and her pleas turn into horrified wails. Myca's father, Dr. Daniel Le, spots the body of his son "with his neck sticking out and headless", as he later puts it. Myca's arm and shoulder have also been chopped off. Dr. Le runs screaming towards the river, and has to be restrained by two crew members.

As the people aboard the crashed helicopter are pulled out of the debris, Jack Rimmer, one of the fire safety officers on the set, along with special effects supervisor Paul Stewart, drag Morrow's headless body back to the peninsula. They set it on the bank, and cover it with a blanket. Wading across the river, Rimmer discovers Myca's head in the water. A crew member brings over a plastic garbage bag and the child's severed head is placed inside. Special effects technician Kevin Quibell locates the head of Vic Morrow, which is placed in another black garbage bag.

The helicopter pilot, Dorcey Wingo, is led in a daze from the scene of the crash. He spots people in the water picking up papers and manuals that have fallen out of the helicopter. Suddenly, he gets worried.

"Where's Vic?", he asks.

The fuel truck driver pus a hand on his shoulder. "Dorcey," he says quietly, "the main rotor got Vic and the kids".

Dorcey becomes suddenly faint, and slumps back into a nearby chair.

"Leave your equipment where it is!" shouts a voice over the loudspeaker into the darkness. "Go home. Please, everyone go home. That's a wrap!"

In a bizarre case of life imitating art imitating life, these orphaned children had escaped Vietnam to a "better life" in America, only to be slaughtered while acting in a Hollywood movie about the conflict from which they had managed to flee just a few years earlier. In that sense, Vic Morrow and the two orphans had just become the latest casualties of the Vietnam War.

House (1986) was the first in a bunch of horror movies made over the next five years which contained some Viet vet connection. Directed by Steve Miner, **House** is a haunted house story concerning a Vietnam combat vet who is now a novelist. To complete his latest book, the writer holes up in an old house where he duly suffers visions of ghosts and monsters, including the rotting zombie figure of his old army buddy, over whose capture and torture in Nam he has unshakeable guilt.

Tobe Hooper's **Texas Chainsaw Massacre 2** (1986) featured a new addition to the cannibal family from the first movie – Choptop, another deranged brother returned from Vietnam with a metal plate in his head and terminal shellshock. Choptop likes to scratch his surgical plate through unhealed skin with a coathanger while screaming one-liners like "incoming!" or "Nam flashback!".

House

Jim Muro's outrageous **Street Trash** (1986) is a low-budget gore spectacular, concerning the in-fighting between a bunch of winos who live in a wrecked car yard. Their leader is a homicidal Viet vet who suffers wild flashbacks. When a case of contaminated Tenafly is unearthed from the cellar of the local booze store, everyone who drinks it seems to explode or liquefy. Other delights in the film include a guy having his penis severed and trying vainly to catch it as his assailants throw it to one another, necrophilia, and gang rape.

Gary Graver's **Moon In Scorpio** (1987) has an interesting cast of former stars on the way out (Britt Eckland, John Phillip Law, Robert Quarry), but is a pretty dull movie. A trio of Viet vets – still haunted by Nam flashbacks and the

Street Trash

memories of a My Lai-type massacre in which they participated – set out on a cruise, but their boat is stalked by a psycho killer (one of the men's girlfriends).

Blood Massacre (Don Dohler, 1988) is a low-budget entry concerning a bunch of psycho Viet vets who end up holding a family hostage; the movie takes a twist into horror when their prisoners turn out to be cannibalistic zombie ghouls who turn on the vets and butcher them.

In David A Prior's **Night Wars** (1988), two Viet vets are still having recurring nightmares about the war, reliving their torture by sadistic captors. Eventually, they start to wake up from these nightmares with real wounds, just like in **Nightmare On Elm Street**. Seeing a chance to rewrite history and rescue a friend who died in a POW camp, they get guns and take them with them into this parallel dreamscape. The movie ends with a massive explosion.

Terrorgram (Stephen Kienzle, 1988) is a horror movie in three segments. The last story concerns a vicious drunk who had apparently been responsible for the drafting of a student to Vietnam in the late '60s. The drunk ends up with horrible visions of Nam; after being caught up in a firefight he is captured and tortured, and haunted by the rotting corpse of the young man he condemned to death.

Faceless (1988) was Jess Franco's blood-soaked return to the surgical mutilation themes of his earlier **The Awful Dr. Orloff**. Always keen to incorporate popular trash tropes into his movies, Franco makes the private eye in this film a Vietnam vet.

Universal Soldier

Universal Soldier (1992) combines SF with elements of horror and martial arts mayhem to forge an enjoyable if ridiculous pulp thriller. The film stars Dolph Lundgren as Scott, a psycho army sergeant, and Claude Van Damme as Deveraux, his adversary, and opens in Vietnam where Scott has gone on a killing spree, butchering unarmed Vietnamese and wearing a necklace of their hacked-off ears. Deveraux intervenes and in a fierce struggle, both men die. We next see their bodies being appropriated by a special medical team. The men are designated "Missing In Action".

Cut to the USA some 20 years later, where we see a team of highly-powered soldiers in action. Two of them appear to be Scott and Deveraux – the latter plagued by flashbacks to his dying moments. It turns out that the men are Universal Soldiers – Unisols for short. A rogue unit within the government has created these super-troopers from the cryogenically preserved corpses of Nam combat troops. The Unisols are kept alive by serum injection, and must not overheat. Reanimated by "cell acceleration", they are in effect high-powered zombies. The experiment soon goes wrong; Scott suffers from "aggressive traumatic recall" and believes he is still in Nam. He and Deveraux are soon in conflict again, and the rest of the movie details Scott's pursuit of Deveraux until the two finally meet in a rain-soaked, climactic martial arts fight to the death.

Two dire TV movies, **Universal Soldier II: Brothers In Arm**s and **Universal Soldier III: Unfinished Business** were made in 1998, before Van Damme returned in the big-screen **Universal Soldier: The Return** in 1999.

4. PSYCHO KILLERS

All Viet vets in cinema are, it seems, mentally disturbed to varying degrees. Tormented by flashbacks, unable to readjust to "normal" society, unemployable except maybe as hired muscle. Some become mercenaries and return to the jungle for revenge; others become vigilantes and clear the criminals and scum out of their home towns; but in movieland there is a third group, an "alpha group" of sick Viet vets who go beyond the pale, who become vicious rapists, brutal murderers, and walking timebombs primed to erupt with cataclysmic violence [see also chapters 8, 9, and 10]. The cinematic descendents of Brahmin from Russ Meyer's **Motorpsycho!**, these are the psychotic loners and losers who gave Vietnam vets a bad name.

Targets (1968), the first film from Peter Bogdanovich, was vaguely based on the true case of Charles Whitman, a Marine marksman who went crazy in July 1966, knifing first his mother and then a young woman before hiding in a campus lookout tower. From this elevated position Whitman fired at random into the crowds below, killing another 14 people and injuring 30 more before police shot him dead. Whitman, it should be noted, was not a combat veteran – but Bobby, the sniper in **Targets**, is.

Starring Boris Karloff in his last film as an ageing horror movie icon who finally confronts Bobby, **Targets** relocated the murderous action to a freeway, and then a drive-in cinema, where the young shooter fires from behind the movie screen. Fittingly, as Karloff bowed out from the "horror" film arena with **Targets**, the film – released the same year as **Night Of The Living Dead** – helped usher in a new era of more realistic, Vietnam-conscious terror.

Targets

Hi Mom!

In 1969, Brian De Palma (and Robert De Niro) revisited the character of Jon Rubin from **Greetings** (1968) [see chapter 12] in **Hi Mom!**, a harder-edged movie in which Rubin has returned from Vietnam as a troubled combat vet. Looking (and acting) just like a younger incarnation of Travis Bickle from **Taxi Driver**, he becomes a full-time photographer and drifts into porno, indulging his penchant for voyeurism to the full. Complete with intimations of impotence, and a fondness for blowing things up, this is a portrait of the assassin as a young man – a disturbed young man just started out on the path which will lead inexorably to terrible violence. **I Feel It Coming** (Sidney Knight, 1969) features a Viet vet similarly numbed by combat, and impotent as a result. In this sleazy movie, we see him unable to perform with either his wife or a prostitute. Attempts to arouse him by watching striptease and live sex also fail. As a last resort they try cannabis; unfortunately, the drug delivery girl refuses to join the man and his wife in bed and the film descends into sexual violence with the man raping her. Impotence, voyeurism, violence and rape: the tone was well and truly set for a decade of films in which Viet vets were presented as the ultimate losers of society.

The Ravager (Charles Nizet, 1970) presents a character even further down the line to carnage. This Viet vet was stranded in the jungle, and witnessed the horrifying rape of two Vietnamese women. Traumatized, he is treated with therapy upon his return to society, but soon erupts with violence whenever confronted by the sight of young lovers. Very much like the real-life Son of Sam, who would come to prominence in 1977, the title crazy of **The Ravager** is

Delirio Caldo

compelled to kill anybody having sex in parked cars. That same year saw two more psycho Viet vet movies: in **To Kill A Clown**, Alan Alda plays a crazed, half-crippled Nam vet who terrorizes a young couple with his trained-to-kill mastiffs; and in **Ten Seconds To Murder** (aka **Booby Trap**) a peace-hating psycho vet tries to blow up a rock festival, killing plenty of innocent folks along the way.

    Glory Boy (1971) featured a psycho Viet vet sergeant who twice attempts to rape a young peacenik; when his second attack is successful, he is shot dead by the father of another vet.

    Rape also figured in **The Visitors** (Elia Kazan, 1972), which featured a young James Woods in his first leading role as a Viet vet who has returned to the US as a confirmed pacifist. He lives quietly with his wife, but is tormented by her father, who lives nearby and disapproves of his beliefs. One day they are visited by two ex-combat comrades, a white sergeant (Steven Railsback) and his black buddy. It turns out that these two have just been released from prison, where they were serving time for the brutal rape and murder of a Vietnamese woman – and it was Woods's testimony which put them behind bars. Though friendly at first, the pair's behaviour gradually darkens, and they win the father-in-law's approval with their boasts of rape and other atrocities. Finally they attempt to rape Woods's wife; he tries to save her and is beaten unconscious. In an unexpectedly low-key ending (no **Straw Dogs**-style worm-turning and slaughter by Woods), the two psycho soldiers simply wander off to find their next victims.

    1972 would prove a bumper year for Viet vet psycho movies, and not just from the USA. From Italy came Renato Polselli's **Delirio Caldo** (aka **Delirium**).

This ultra-violent *giallo* featured a gratuitously rampant and sadistic woman-killer. In the US release of the film, Nam flashbacks were edited into the movie in order to provide the killer with motivation: now, he was a tormented Viet vet. Juan Logar's unusual Spanish production **Autopsia** tells of a different kind of combat vet: this one is not an ex-soldier but a war photographer, equally traumatised by what he has witnessed. In this gory mondo-type movie, we see the confused man watching a lengthy autopsy on a corpse; apparently, this is his means of dealing with the reality of the Vietnam experience, and the footage is interspersed with philosophical ruminations on death, and other bizarre imagery.

Back in the USA, **Stanley** (William Grefe, 1972) was a low-budget horror about a crazy Viet vet who keeps deadly pet snakes. Stanley is the king killer snake. The psycho is an American Indian with the unlikely name of Tim, and **Stanley** may well be a serpentine variation on **Willard**, the hit killer rat movie from the previous year. **Caged Terror** (1972) tells how a hippie couple are preyed on by a gang of psycho Nam vets, but the film fails to deliver a satisfactory pay-off. In **Skyjacked** (1972), one of the early '70s cycle of disaster movies, a plane is hijacked by a demented, bomb-toting Viet vet, played by James Brolin, while **Girls On The Road** (1972) features a Nam vet sheriff who suffers from flashbacks and ends up killing young female hitchhikers who stray into his territory.

The best entry of 1972, **Welcome Home, Soldier Boys** tells the story of four returning Viet vets who take off on a road trip across America. After many sexual encounters they arrive in the New Mexican town of Hope. Here, provoked by a potshot from a gas station owner, they go on a terminal rampage. Dressed in their army uniforms and armed with a huge arsenal of weapons, they proceed to wipe out the whole town in a **Wild Bunch**-like stand which ends as the massed National Guard advance, ready to exterminate the four men who are out of time, out of place.

Poor White Trash 2 (aka **Scum Of The Earth**, 1974), directed by SF Brownrigg, is a tale of violent, in-bred hillbilly trash that set the tone for the Viet vet psycho films of 1974. An insane Nam vet killer is involved at the film's climax. **The Recon Game** (aka **Open Season**, 1974), directed by Peter Collinson and starring Peter Fonda and John Phillip Law, is one of many variations on **The Most Dangerous Game** (1932), the seminal horror film about humans hunting other humans[5]. Here, the hunters are deranged Viet vets who need to continue the thrill of slaughter they first experienced in the Nam. **Two** (Charles Treischmann, 1974) was another edgy production in which a hospitalized, mentally unstable vet escapes from a psycho ward and kidnaps a young woman. He is eventually shot dead while robbing a bank. **Johnny Firecloud** (also 1974) is one of the goriest and most violent of the psycho vet cycle. Johnny, the title character, is a tough American Indian Viet vet who flips when members of his tribe are tortured, raped and murdered by local racists. As if these atrocities aren't gruesome enough, Johnny's revenge is portrayed in the graphic extreme and includes blinding, skull-slicing, and even castration by dynamite – probably a movie first. David F Friedman produced this "anti-racist" counterpart to his equally violent "fascist" film of the same year, **Ilsa – She Wolf Of The SS**.

But even more alarming than **Johnny Firecloud** was **Forced Entry** (1974), a hardcore porn movie written and directed by Shaun Costello (under the cinenym Helmuth Richler), and also the most powerful and disturbing Viet vet psycho movie to date, taking the premise of 1970's **The Ravager** to new

extremes of sexual mayhem and violence. Porn star Harry Reems takes the lead role as Joe, a very, very sick ex-combat soldier now running his own gasoline shack in downtown New York. **Forced Entry** opens with a newspaper report and quotes about the psychosis suffered by returning Vietnam veterans, overlaid by sounds of gunfire, then cuts to a flashing police siren and then a shot of a bloody male corpse being photographed by detectives. The camera homes in on a section of the gunshot victim's exposed brain, over which the title "Forced Entry" is flashed. Cut to a grimy gas station, where we first glimpse Joe, the greasy, sleazy-looking pump attendant. Serving a pretty female customer, he contrives to get her name and address before she drives away. Later that day, we see him approaching the building where she lives. This sequence – and most of the ensuing action – is intercut with genuine footage from Vietnam, uniformly grainy and monochrome, showing various images from Saigon street scenes to aerial bombing raids. The soundtrack moves swiftly from pulsing, swirling Oriental music with high-pitched vocal inflections to jazz elegies to classical and back again in seemingly random order. Peering through the woman's apartment window, Joe sees her making love to her boyfriend. During a prolonged voyeuristic sequence, he plays suggestively with his army bayonet and pistol as he watches the couple indulge first in oral sex and then full penetrative sex. At one point Joe goes up the fire escape to a higher level, where he spies a girl alone in her apartment. He then returns to watch the couple's climax, as the boyfriend cums over the woman's ample buttocks. Joe then enters the building lobby and climbs the stairs to the higher apartment. Breaking in silently, he grabs the lone girl from behind and brandishes his knife, threatening to disembowel her unless she "sucks his cock". This sequence of intense sexual violence is intercut with scenes of distressed Vietnamese womenfolk, implying that Joe may well have honed his deadly craft on the indigenous female population whilst on his tour of duty.

As the terrified woman sucks his large, thick-veined penis, Joe continually taunts and threatens her, finally sneering the telling insult: "What do you think you are – some kind of gook from Nam?". As this gruelling scene builds to a crescendo, so do the images from Vietnam – burning villages, whirring choppers and, just before we see Joe cum all over the woman's face, a nightmarish napalm strike. Sated, Joe flatly announces that he didn't enjoy her act of fellatio "one little bit", seizes a dagger from the apartment wall, and coldly, slowly slits her throat. As she slides to the floor he kisses her dying mouth, a terminal ironic gesture intercut with real footage of dead, female Vietnamese children laid out after a US raid.

Cut to the gas station; new day, new customer. Joe gives a young woman directions to where she is staying, and soon heads off after her. As he takes short-cuts through the New York streets, his progress is intercut with Vietnam footage, culminating with explosive battle scenes as he reaches her house. He breaks in and heads upstairs, knife in hand. She is in the shower when he grabs her, pulls her out and throws her naked on the bed, setting the scene for the film's central – and most disturbing – session of prolonged sexual assault.

First, Joe strips and forces the woman to fellate him at gunpoint, a lengthy sequence devoid of flashbacks. Then, his oil-stained hands digging into her white flesh, he flips her over and roughly drives his glistening erection into her anus, as images of female VC prisoners being hooded flash up on screen. The lengthy and harrowing sequence of savage anal rape that follows is constructed as a powerful montage of anamorphic penetration shots, explosive Vietnam scenes and a soundtrack of battle noise over which Joe's taunts and curses are fired off like sniper's bullets. "Starting to bleed a little in there? – You don't know what bleeding is," he threatens, delivering his customary "gook in Nam" insult as he nears climax. Napalm strikes and shellfire fill the screen as he finally cums over her buttocks, the "little death" of his orgasm refected in the culminatory shot of dead Vietnamese girl-children. Once again, Joe follows rape with a homicidal attack; informing the traumatised woman that he failed to enjoy the sex, he berates her ("you got my prick all full of shit") over and over, provoking his anger to the point where he is compelled to plunge his knife into her. This murder scene, simultaneously brutal and matter-of-fact, is unpleasant in the extreme.

First Joe slashes the woman down the side of the neck, then sticks his blade into her stomach, and finally drives it into her left breast. He is cold, methodical, silent as he butchers her. As she expires, he kisses her dying mouth in valediction.

Cut to a road where a young woman driving a camper van stops to pick up a stoned, teenage hippie girl hiker. Their conversation soon turns to sex and drugs, and they head home – unfortunately, stopping at Joe's for gas on the way. As they talk to Joe he seems to fade into a reverie. The phrase "five dollars worth of gas" is looped and repeated like a mantra over images of napalmed Vietnamese children. Joe sees himself in battle gear, aiming an army revolver at their heads. Snapping out of it, he fills up the van. We now hear his interior voice, a hateful sneer repeating the phrase "scummy hippies!" over and over again (cut to images of long-haired anti-war protesters) as he plans revenge on these girls who have dared to violate the space of his gas station.

Later that day, Joe is positioned where he can spy on the couple back at home, who are high on LSD and indulging in lesbian sex play, kissing and fondling each other's breasts. He watches with growing revulsion and fury ("scummy hippies!") as they progress to cunnilingus, before finally entering the apartment and pulling his knife with the customary "suck my cock". Which is where the film turns on its head.

In a climax which somehow manages to invert the savage misogyny of the preceding sixty minutes, the naked hippie chicks are so stoned that they respond to Joe's outburst with laughter. He pulls out his gun, but the more aggressive and phallic he becomes, the more they collapse with amusement, seemingly completely unphased by his macho posturing and threats. As shots of Vietnamese women flash on screen, Joe starts to fall apart. The girls begin to dominate the situation, turning the tables on Joe as they fondle their tits and cunts suggestively, at one point standing over him as he flinches back to the floor. "Stay away from me!". Vietnamese chanting fills the soundtrack as Joe's madness implodes; he raises the gun to his own head as images of both Nam and his recent victims flash up in quick succession. Finally, he pulls the trigger. The final images of the film are those from the beginning – the police siren, and Joe's bloody corpse.

Even leaner and meaner than De Niro in **Taxi Driver**, the wild-looking Harry Reems – seemingly living proof that "big nose = big dick" – is all too convincing as a rape-killer who revels in the pain and humiliation of his victims. Further realism is afforded through the film's downbeat, washed-out look and feel, and by the "natural" look of the performers, whose untrimmed body hair and floppy breasts present the antithesis of modern, streamlined, body-enhanced porno stars. Fucking is portrayed flatly as an ungainly and noisy act, and the close-ups of penetration are anything but glamorous – which only serves to augment the film's sordid aura of degradation and sexual disgust. Killing is likewise shown in all its prosaic, numbing futility, with a complete absence of passion or meaning.

Unjustly neglected owing to its "forbidden" status as hardcore pornography, **Forced Entry** is a sleaze classic, an inventive and relentlessly grim debut by Costello who, abetted by Reems' psycho-star turn, has produced what now stands as the first in a notable tradition of low-budget, horror-tinged Viet vet urban shockers. With its central analogy of the US invasion of Vietnam to homicidal rape, **Forced Entry** is also one of the most damning (if crudely articulated) cinematic indictments of the War.

William Devane, *Rolling Thunder*

The '70s continued to spew out Viet vet psycho movies. **Naked Massacre** (aka **Born For Hell**, 1975) seems to have been based loosely on the true case of the Chicago nurse killer Richard Speck. Here, the killer is a returning Viet vet, and he commits his atrocity in Belfast, slaughtering eight nurses (the same number as Speck). 1976 saw the release of two amazing films in which psychotic Viet vets were portrayed by two of the all-time greatest screen actors: Robert De Niro in

Taxi Driver [see next chapter], and Dennis Hopper in **Tracks** [see chapter 9]. Neither would do much to alleviate the presiding image of the stereotypical Nam vet as a fucked-up, dangerous loner – and neither did that same year's **My Friends Need Killing**, in which a returning vet suffers hideous flashbacks, turns psychotic and starts killing all his other Viet vet comrades, or driving them to suicide by reminding them of all the horrific atrocities they committed over there. This trend was continued in **Rolling Thunder** (John Flynn, 1977), in which William Devane plays the Viet vet who falls prey to local hoodlums, who rob him and mangle his arm in a garbage disposal. Now equipped with a vicious-looking hook hand, Devane turns psycho and tracks his attackers down, setting things up for a climactic firefight in a Mexican whorehouse. Co-scripted by Paul Schrader, **Rolling Thunder** developed the theme begun by Schrader in **Taxi Driver** of a vet who is tipped over the edge into an outburst of vigilante violence taken to psychotic extremes – a theme which would find its ultimate, most sleazy expression in James Glickenhaus's **The Exterminator** (1980).

But before that came several other examples of the psycho Viet vet. In **Delirium** (Peter Maris, 1979), a returning vet is hired by local right-wingers to eliminate crime in vigilante fashion; tortured by flashbacks, he goes over the top and starts to kill everybody in sight. In Luis San Andres' **Night Flowers** (aka **Night Angels**, 1979), two Viet vet buddies take an apartment in New York and lure young girls there for sex by pretending the apartment is for rent. It ends in rape and murder when a girl rejects the advances of one of them, and he turns psycho. In **When You Comin' Back, Red Ryder?** (Milton Katselas, 1979), the returning vet flips out in a diner and terrorizes the customers at gunpoint, using extreme mental and physical sadism on his victims. And in **Don't Answer The Phone** (Robert Hammer, 1980), a Viet vet photographer in LA turns psycho killer, leaving a trail of strangled, naked girls in his wake.

Don't Answer The Phone

Opening combat sequence from *The Exterminator*

The Exterminator represents the pinnacle (or nadir, depending on your viewpoint) of the Nam-vet-as-vigilante-psycho genre. A low-budget entry, it was extremely successful, perhaps for following in the tradition of the likes of **Death Wish**, and treating the theme with graphic violence. Like all good Viet vet films, **The Exterminator** begins with a Vietnam war sequence. Although brief, this is still one of the best ever, mainly due to its startling decapitation scene which occurs as three US soldiers are being interrogated by the Viet Cong. When they refuse to talk, the VC interrogator draws his machete across the throat of one soldier. Slowly, the soldier's head is unhinged and falls back from his neck. It's a realistic, and quite shocking moment. Of course the remaining two soldiers – John Eastland (played by Robert Ginty) and his black buddy – finally manage to escape in a brutal firefight which involves more violent death.

Cut to New York. Eastland and his buddy are out of the army, working as porters in a food plant which is beset by mob protection problems and petty theft. When three gang-bangers try to rob a storehouse, the two ex-soldiers use their combat training to smash them unconscious. Soon after, the black vet is stalked by the gang (known as the Ghetto Ghouls), who ambush him on some wasteland and bloodily maim him with a set of vicious metal spikes. Eastland sets out to avenge his buddy, who is left on life support.

He captures one gang member and, by threatening him with a blow-torch, gets the gang's clubhouse address. As he heads off, Eastland gets to deliver the famous **Exterminator** valediction: "If you're lying, I'll be back". At the clubhouse he shoots dead one youth and drags another back to be chained up with his fellow Ghoul. Some days later they are discovered; dead, tortured, rat-eaten.

Now, Eastland has acquired a taste for vigilantism; the rest of the film is basically comprised of his set-piece acts of violent retribution, although the story is fleshed out with a sub-plot concerning the cop obsessed with catching him (and a sub-sub-plot about this cop's unlikely romance with a female doctor). Eastland's next target is the mob boss responsible for skimming money from his place of work; he abducts the crimelord and chains him up in a warehouse, dangling in the air over an industrial meat-grinder. Under duress, the mobster gives Eastland his address and safe details, assuring him there is no other security to worry about. Eastland heads off to retrieve the extorted money. "If you're lying, I'll be back".

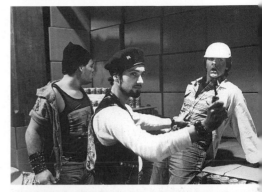

At the house he is attacked by a savage guard dog, which he manages to kill with an electric carving-knife (off-screen). Back at the warehouse, he exacts revenge on the crime boss, lowering him into the mincer. We see the screaming boss disappearing into the machine, then the camera homes in on the grille from where he is being expelled as bloody hamburger.

Cut to a brothel which caters for paedophiles, or "chickenhawks". A hooker has been tied naked on a bed and, because she refused to join in with a paedophiliac assault, she is tortured by the fat, ageing pervert who burns her breasts with a red-hot soldering iron. Some days later, the hooker is picked up by Eastland. When he sees the scars on her body he is horrified; he finds out what happened to her, and makes a note to visit the chickenshack.

The next sequence – probably the most controversial at the time of the film's release – shows Eastland making dum-dum bullets, drilling out the tips and filling them with explosive mercury. We also see the extent of his personal armoury of guns and knives. Then he pays a visit to the chicken-shack, where he beats up the proprietor before tying him up, dousing him with petrol and torching him alive. He locates the old pervert – who is in the act of torturing a trussed, naked youth – and blows him away, freeing the terrified victim.

The next major action sequence takes place in night-time Central Park, where a trio of Ghetto Ghouls are mugging an old lady. Unbeknown to them, Eastland is stalking them. As they drive away he commandeers a motorcycle and follows in pursuit. Thinking to mug this mysterious biker, the gang-bangers pull up and get out of the car. Eastland reveals himself before blasting one of them to death. The remaining two drive off again. Eastland follows, crashes the bike, and is left on foot. But as they Ghetto Ghouls drive at him he pulls his gun and shoots out the windshield. The car plunges off the road and explodes in a fireball. Eastland's acts of vigilante violence are getter bigger, more audacious, and more psychotic.

Finally, his identity is discovered by the cop, who traces him by his Vietnam service badge – it turns out the cop is also a Viet vet. Police storm Eastland's apartment, but he is not there – he is breaking the news of his black buddy's death to the man's wife. Returning home, Eastland spies cops on his roof and flees, but later telephones the cop and agrees to meet him, to surrender. At the meet, he is about to hand over his weapon when a sniper's bullet rings out, hitting the cop. The next shot hits Eastland, who cries out and plunges into the night river. We infer, from overheard dialogue, that the assassins are government agents.

The film's brief coda occurs at dawn the next day. Way downriver, Eastland – who was wearing a bullet-proof vest – staggers ashore. The end.

Exterminator is basically **Death Wish** smeared with an extra gloss of sleaze, nudity, perversion, sadistic violence and gore, and spiced with the added attraction of Viet vet psychosis. It is a violent, refreshingly amoral film which when seen today in the uncensored director's cut still has a powerful, visceral impact.

A sequel, **Exterminator 2**, followed in 1984, repeating the formula with diminishing success; and it was around then that the psycho Viet vet cycle began to wind down. **Fleshburn** (1983) featured a crazed vet who escapes from a mental asylum kidnapping his psychiatrists on the way, but it was not until the release three years later of Buddy Giovinazzo's **Combat Shock** (1986) that the genre produced its grim, terminal horrorshow.[6]

Combat Shock – originally known as **American Nightmares** – is generally considered to be by far the most serious and disturbing offering from Troma, the company better known for rubbish like **Toxic Avenger**, et al. The film opens with a protracted "in-country" combat sequence with a voice-over from Frankie, the protagonist of Giovinazzo's story (played by Giovinazzo's brother). Wandering through a landscape littered with dead VC and US soldiers and wracked by continuous explosions, Frankie is being stalked by a gang of female VC assassins. When he gets the leader in his sights, Frankie struggles with his feelings before finally squeezing the trigger and blowing her away. It's one trauma too many for the shell-shocked GI – he hurls down his weapon and flees. After traversing a killing field where dead American soldiers are depicted in terrible states of mutilation and dismemberment (heads blown off, bodies lying in two halves with guts spooling out), Frankie is finally captured. As he succumbs to a rain of blows, the sequence ends abruptly. Cut to modern-day New York, where Frankie wakes up in a cold sweat – like all the best Nam flashbacks, it's been an evil recall dream.

Frankie lives in squalour with his wife, who continually nags him to get

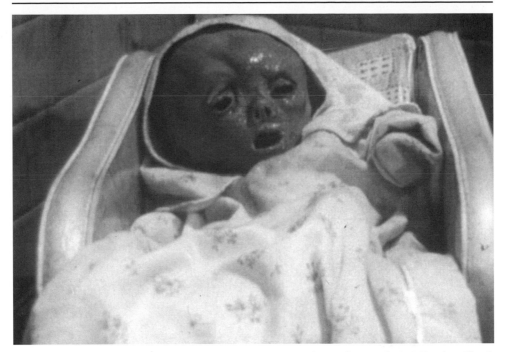

Agent Orange baby; *Combat Shock*

a job. Worse than that, they have a baby that cries non-stop, and is soon revealed to be hideously deformed – looking more like the baby in **Eraserhead** than anything human, this monstrosity is the product of Frankie's mutating genes, fatally irradiated in Nam by his own country's use of the toxic defoliant Agent Orange[7]. To cap things off, Frankie has just received an eviction notice.

Frankie – prone to sudden flashbacks which show how he was held in captivity and tortured for two years – is already a very disturbed individual. **Combat Shock** shows us the last day in Frankie's life – the day when this particular Vietnam veteran could not take it any more.

Frankie hits the street, wandering through an urban landscape of misery and squalour, rape and murder. He is beaten up by the three thugs he owes money to, meets up with Mike, a heroin-addled fellow vet, and queues for menial work only to be flatly rejected. He argues with a pimp and spins into vivid Nam flashbacks at the sight of maggots crawling in rotten meat. He even phones his estranged father – who believes Frankie killed in action – for help, but a reconciliation proves impossible. At desperation point, he decides that crime is the only solution.

Meanwhile, Mike has scored some smack, taken it – by rubbing it into the open sores on his arms – and passed out (or possibly died). A passing women robs him, taking his service revolver. This woman soon becomes Frankie's first mugging victim, as he steals her purse. The three thugs spot him and chase him to a deserted building. They beat him savagely, but the gun spills from the purse and suddenly, Frankie is armed. He guns all three down without mercy and heads back home, accompanied by a voice-over detailing Vietnam atrocities and

Combat Shock

concluding ominously that "the battlefield may have changed, but the war is not over".

Back home, Frankie's wife is still nagging, the deformed baby still puling. In the throes of terminal psychosis, Frankie stares at his blank TV and hears voices, gunfire. Images of the film's opening Nam sequence flash across his face, showing his inner delirium. He loads his gun and raises it to his head, but a vision of his wife's face superimposed on his VC victim halts and re-directs him. He tells his wife he loves her then guns her down. As she lies on the floor spewing blood, he shoots her again. Then he shoots his hideous baby, takes it to the kitchen, switches on the oven and puts the dead baby inside. Boiling blood starts to spill from the oven door.

Frankie sits down, drinks a glass of lumpy, rancid milk, then raise the gun to his head once more – this time, pulling the trigger. His head explodes in a fountain of blood and he slumps to the floor, dead. The end.

Combat Shock is more bleak, despairing and nihilistic than **The Exterminator**, and harks back to **Forced Entry** with its depiction of a Viet vet in absolute mental ruins, adrift in an inhospitable urban desolation from which suicide is the only release. Both Frankie and Joe are killers, trained to kill by the US government and compelled to kill again and again as their only mode of self-expression when that same government abandons them and leaves them to rot on the scum-ridden streets of New York.

5. VIGILANTE STORM

While a film like **The Exterminator** took its theme of vigilante revenge to barbaric extremes, a whole stream of other movies treated the theme of Viet-vet-as-vigilante with a more moderate – often mainstream – tone. Rainer Werner Fassbinder's tribute to American *film noir*, **American Soldier** (Germany, 1970), was the story of a professional hitman who had learned his trade while serving in Vietnam. In **Clay Pigeon** (aka **Trip To Kill**, 1971), a Viet vet returns home to LA and goes undercover as a hippie to battle local drug pushers, who include other, "bad" vets. This is after an opening in-country combat sequence which ends with the hero (played by Tom Stern) smothering a grenade in order to save his comrades. The film's climax is totally unexpected; after polishing off the drug dealers, Stern is transported back to Nam, where the grenade goes off and kills him. In a plot device borrowed from Ambrose Bierce's short story *Occurrence At Owl Creek*, we are left to conclude that the LA story was just a dying man's terminal vision, a final fantasy realised in the instant of his demise. This, of course, is exactly the same – equally disappointing – ending used 20 years later in the more up-market, horror-oriented **Jacob's Ladder**.

Films like **American Soldier** and **Clay Pigeon** started the trend for Viet vets to be portrayed as trained killers loose in society who, rather than succumbing to "combat shock" and putting their fatal skills to random rape and murder, could be put to more constructive use by both sides of the law. **Magnum Force** (1973), the second Dirty Harry movie, featured three vigilante killer cops who were Viet vets, while Charles Bronson starred in two such movies; in the first, Michael Winner's **The Stone Killer** (1973), he plays a vicious cop investigating a series of Mafia assassinations. It turns out that one crime family has been recruiting trigger-happy Viet vets as hired killers, assembling an army in the Mojave desert. **The Stone Killer** is something of a period classic, featuring scenes of nudity, car chases, shoot-outs, gay, straight and lesbian sex, hippy communes, Black Panthers and soul brothers, a funked-up soundtrack, and a cop whose procedures make Dirty Harry look like a bleeding heart liberal. Bronson also starred as **Mr Majestyck** (Richard Fleischer, 1974), a Vietnam vet melon farmer who comes into brutal conflict with a local hitman and aids the police capture him. Also released in 1974 was **The No Mercy Man** (aka **Trained To Kill**). This low-budget entry anticipates the Viet vet vigilantism which became rife in films of the later '70s and '80s, with an ex-soldier pitting all his combat training against a gang of sadistic hoodlums, and taking this conflict to its ultimate, deadly conclusion.

The Diamond Mercenaries (1975) was an oddity, showing how Viet vets might use their talents in pursuit of crime; however, as directed by staid British director Val Guest, these desert-bound vets (including Telly Savalas and Peter Fonda) were not particularly galvanized in their endeavours – despite the film being retitled **Killer Force** for US release.

But it was George Armitage's **Vigilante Force** (1975) which really set the macho Viet vet ball rolling. Kris Kristofferson stars as a Viet vet hired by a town to assist with keeping law and order in the face of an invasion of rowdy oil riggers. He assembles a crack team of vet mercenaries to do the job, but once they have driven out the riggers they begin to relish their position of power, taking over the town themselves. **Vigilante Force** is a powerful movie, full of gunfire and explosions but driven by Kristofferson's rugged, introspective

Vigilante Force

persona as the war veteran out to claim what he sees as his due reward.

Vigilante Force became the blueprint for a vast homogenous slurry of movies, peaking at the height of the Reagan era, peopled by edgy, wired vets (either ex-soldiers or, in some cases, ex-CIA operatives) displaying varying degrees of psychosis, unleashed on society and becoming wild pilots, war-crazed militiamen, loose-cannon cops, sleazy private eyes, vigilantes combatting street punks or organized crime, high-powered mercenaries, drug-runners, outlaws, survivalists, or just plain oddball characters fringing on "normal" society. Peaking in the 1980s and fading into the '90s, these films include: **Brotherhood Of Death** (1976); **Special Delivery** (1976); **Black Sunday** (1977); **The Domino Principle** (1977); **Green Eyes** (1977); **High Velocity** (1977); **Zebra Force** (1977); **Dog Soldiers** (1978); **I, The Jury** (1981); **Nighthawks** (1981); **An Eye For An Eye** (1981); **Kill Squad** (1982); **Firefox** (1982); **Blue Thunder** (1982); **A Breed Apart** (1984); **GI Executioner** (1984); **Riptide** (1984); **The Annihilators** (1985);

American Commandos (1985); **Alamo Bay** (1985); **White Ghost** (1985); **Year Of The Dragon** (1985); **Savage Dawn** (1985); **Latino** (1985); **Cease Fire** (1985); **Mission Kill** (1985); **Killzone** (1985); **The Enforcer** (1986); **Codename: Zebra** (1986); **Armed Response** (1986); **Band Of The Hand** (1986); **Opposing Force** (1986); **Masterblaster** (1986); **Let's Get Harry** (1986); **No Safe Haven** (1987); **Hammerhead** (1987); **Bell Diamond** (1987); **Hostage** (1987); **Outlaw Force** (1987); **Nightforce** (1987); **Lethal Weapon** (1987); **Backfire** (1987); **Act Of Piracy** (1987); **The Omega Syndrome** (1987); **Steele Justice** (1987); **Extreme Prejudice** (1987); **Tough Guys Don't Dance** (1987); **Malone** (1987); **Distant Thunder** (1988); **Mercenary Fighters** (1988); **Hardcase And Fist** (1988); **Run For Your Life** (1988); **War** (aka **Troma's War**, 1988); **Fear** (1988); **Covert Action** (1988); **Above The Law** (1989); **Operation War Zone** (1989); **Jungle Assault** (1989); **The Package** (1989); **Ghetto Blaster** (1989); **President's Target** (1987); **Far From Home** (1989); **Presidio** (1989); **Lethal Weapon II** (1989); **Snake Eater** (1989); **Ministry Of Vengeance** (1989); **The Revenger** (1990); **Cartel** (1989); **Cage** (1989); **Circle Of Fear** (1989); **Mirror, Mirror** (1989); **The Bounty Hunter** (1989); **The Fourth War** (1990); **Fatal Mission** (1990); **Street Hunter** (1990); **Project Eliminator** (1990); **In Gold We Trust** (1990); **Lock And Load** (1990); **Red Surf** (1990); **Killer's Edge** (1990); **Men At Work** (1990); **Vietnam, Texas** (1990); **Snake Eater II: The Drug Buster** (1990); **Showdown** (1991); **Street Justice** (1991); **Hangfire** (1991); **McBain** (1991); **Snake Eater III: His Law** (1992); **Death Ring** (1992); **Under Siege** (1992); **Lethal Weapon III** (1992); **So Cool** (1992); **American Eagle** (1992); **Accidental Hero** (1992); **Human Target** (1992); **Dead Boyz Can't Fly** (1992); **Gold Of The Samurai** (1992); **Cage II: Arena Of Death** (1994); and **Coyote Run** (1996).

And out of this miasma of reactionary, redneck gun-worship emerged another even more popular sub-genre: the MIA/POW movie. The movie which kick-started the MIA craze was the appropriately titled Chuck Norris vehicle **Missing In Action** (Joseph Zito, 1994) – although the theme had been addressed previously in the likes of Norris' previous **Good Guys Wear Black** (1977), **My Husband Is Missing** (1980), and in **Uncommon Valour** (1983), in which Gene Hackman starred as the Korean War veteran whose son is missing in Vietnam and who persuades a motley crew of Viet vets to go back into Nam and look for the young soldier.

Missing In Action begins, like all good Viet vet films, with a Nam flashback (actually a dream) sequence. Here we first encounter Norris' character, Braddock, engaged in a massive firefight involving groundtroops and helicopters (one of the helicopters is decorated with human skulls). The sequence ends with Braddock's two surviving buddies being brutally bayoneted by a VC assassin. Braddock unpins two grenades and leaps from above... the dream ends in a holocaustal fireball. Braddock next goes to Saigon to attend a conference on MIA POWs. Here, he meets two of his old Nam captors and is deported after killing one of them. In a seedy Bangkok brothel he hooks up with an old army buddy and they head by boat to Cambodia, pursued by the surviving Nam torturer. The film's events are punctuated by regular outbursts of predictable action, usually involving an explosion, and Braddock's grim flashbacks to scenes of torture in captivity.

The film's second half sees Braddock infiltrate Vietnam and, after dispatching dozens of "gooks" who attempt to ambush him, he finally intercepts a convoy of American POWs in transit. After many gun battles and further

Missing In Action

killings, the POWs are airlifted out of the jungle. Braddock and his newly-freed buddies burst into a televised summit on MIAs, just in time to debunk the Vietnamese government's claim that they do not exist. End.

This cheaply-made actioner struck a tremendous chord with the American public, grossing some $26m. Simply put, the MIA storyline gave the US a second chance to "win the war", to go back into Nam, kick ass and finish the job properly. Norris and co were, understandably, quick to produce a follow-up. **Missing In Action 2: The Beginning** (Lance Hool, 1985) was a prequel to the first film, showing Braddock's years in captivity and his final escape. The main body of the film is really just a catalogue of the atrocities committed by the American POWs' evil eastern captors, including physical and psychological torture and summary executions. Chuck's big moment comes in the climax, when he is pitted against his chief tormentor in a one-on-one martial arts duel. Reprising and inverting the climactic fight of **Way Of The Dragon**, when Norris was the American bad guy slaughtered by Bruce Lee, this time Chuck is the hero, and after battering his sub-human opponent into submission he gets to deliver the same bare-fisted death-blow which Lee had dealt him a decade earlier.

Of course, Norris went on to star in **Braddock: Missing In Action 3** (1988), as well as in other patriotic, all-action vehicles like **Delta Force** (1986). In **MIA 3**, Braddock returns to Nam in search of his Vietnamese wife and son and perpetrates the usual mayhem against more stereotypical sadistic "gooks".

The release the same year as **MIA 2** of the phenomenally successful **Rambo: First Blood II** [see Chapter 10], starring Sylvester Stallone, cemented the MIA/POW genre's popularity and ensured a steady run of imitators, including:

Missing In Action 2

Heated Vengeance (1985); **Crossfire** (1986); **Intimate Strangers** (1986); **POW: The Escape** (1986); **Ultimax Force** (1986); **The Expendables** (1987); **Forgotten Warrior** (1987); **No Dead Heroes** (1987); **Phantom Soldiers** (1987); **Forgotten** (1989); **No Retreat, No Surrender II** (1989); and **Welcome Home** (1989). **Eastern Condors** (1986, directed by and starring Sammo Hung) was an interesting Hong Kong variation on the theme, in which a ragged bunch of Chinese-American convicts are sent into post-war Vietnam ostensibly to destroy an ammunition depot deep in the jungle. **Behind Enemy Lines** (Mark Griffiths, 1996) was a late entry, but the genre had eventually run out of steam as America entered and won the Gulf War, finally obviating the psychic need for these cinematic revisions of military history.

6. THE HOLLOW MEN

Not every movie Nam veteran returns home as a rampaging psycho killer, rapist, cannibal, or invincible vigilante/mercenary; some of them are just plain fucked up, either physically – maimed, crippled, confined to wheelchairs and hospitals – or mentally – consigned to insane asylums or secure military observation units. These film portrayals run the gamut from big, serious Hollywood treatments – **Coming Home, Born On The 4th Of July** – to lurid independent productions such as **Enemy Territory** (1987), in which Jan-Michael Vincent plays a wheelchair-bound vet called in to help combat a black New York street gang called The Vampires.

Bruce Dern, Jon Voight; *Coming Home*

Robert Downey Sr's **Sticks And Bones** (1972) was an early example. Based on one of the award-winning "Vietnam Plays" of David Rabe – the others were *The Basic Training Of Pavlo Hummel*, *Streamers* (filmed by Robert Altman in 1983), and *The Orphan* – **Sticks And Bones** tells of a Viet vet who returns from the war blinded, and "sees" the reality of his family more clearly than ever before. **The POW** (Phillip Dossick, 1973) was a low-key, *cinema verité*-style study of a crippled vet dealing with the return home, a spell in a veteran's hospital, and trying to readjust to civilian life. The same year saw a crippled Viet vet figure in a totally opposite kind of film: **Fugitive Girls**, directed by AC Stevens and written by the legendary Ed Wood Jr, is a trash sex classic about a bunch of female convicts who escape and rampage around rural America. One of their victims is a paralyzed Vietnam war vet, whose house they invade.

A few years would pass before two big Hollywood productions appeared, both trying to deal with the plight of returning vets in a caring, adult way: **Heroes** and **Coming Home**. **Heroes** (1977) is the more boring of the two, one of the starring vehicles given to Henry Winkler in the ludicrous deal which saw this fairly talentless actor, famous for playing a moronic character 20 years younger than he actually was in a kids' TV series, given a string of big movie roles (they all flopped and he thankfully disappeared without trace). Winkler plays a Viet vet with "post-traumatic stress disorder", the same condition which drove the beautiful psychos in **The Ravager**, **Forced Entry**, **Taxi Driver** et al. Here, it's treated in a boring, semi-comic way, with a pathetic lead character, which makes for very dull cinema indeed. **Heroes** was essentially a retread of a lower-budget movie, **The Crazy World Of Julius Vrooder**, which had appeared in 1974. Both films demonstrate that mentally unstable Viet vets and comedy do not mix – a fact once again underscored 20 years later by **Forrest Gump** (1994). 1977 also saw the release of a TV movie, **Just A Little Inconvenience**, which dealt with a physically crippled vet, played by James Stacy. A sleazy authenticity was granted to this film by the fact that Stacy had lost an arm and a leg in real life some years earlier; when he reveals his stumps to a shocked friend, it's for real.

Coming Home (Hal Ashby, 1978) was the first really big mainstream production to focus on the plight of crippled Viet vets. Conceived by its star Jane Fonda (already a vociferous anti-war protester), the film also starred Jon Voight as the wheelchair-bound vet who becomes her lover, and Bruce Dern as her officer husband who returns home with a superficial leg wound but profound mental scarring. Featuring an extensive soundtrack of white '60s rock, the film focuses on this love triangle and the differing effects on the war on both men. Dern mentally unravels as the film progresses, and finally kills himself by drowning, while Voight grows stronger and continues to campaign against the conflict. **Coming Home**, released in the same year as **The Deer Hunter**, remains part of the first wave of big-budget, star-driven films that dealt with the Vietnam War and its consequences, and started to address America's sorrow and guilt in its aftermath.

William Peter Blatty's **The Ninth Configuration** (1979), based on his own novel *Twinkle Twinkle Killer Kane*, is the most bizarre of all movies set in and around a military hospital – in this case, specifically a mental asylum for traumatized officers. Stacy Keach is excellent in the lead role as Colonel Hudson Kane, chief psychiatrist assigned to Center 18 – a gothic retreat in Washington State, where Vietnam combat veterans and other military personnel who have seemingly succumbed to psychosis are being studied for signs of "faking it". The inmates of Center 18, led by Cutshaw – an astronaut who aborted a space mission for no apparent reason – are lunatics to a man, involved in continual charades such as adapting Shakespeare for canine actors. Into this anarchic *mise-en-scène* comes Kane, a figure of intense calm in the eye of the hurricane, who soon confides in the resident doctor that he is plagued by a recurring nightmare. The nightmare, it seems, is one that was first described to him by his brother, who he reveals is the notorious Special Forces agent Vincent "Killer" Kane, a man who would regularly drop behind enemy lines in Nam and kill "30 or 40" VC at close quarters. Killer Kane finally lost it after decapitating a young VC with wire and seeing the boy's severed head talking to him (an episode seen in flashback). As the first part of the film draws to a close, Colonel Kane encounters a new inmate to Center 18, a combat vet who recognizes the psychiatrist's true identity – "Hudson" Kane is actually Vincent Kane, the psychopathic killer.

It further transpires that the resident doctor is actually Hudson Kane, Vincent's brother. Vincent failed to recognize him because he has tried to bury the guilt of his killing ways and assume Hudson's identity. In this role as psychiatrist, he may be able to atone for his sins by helping others. After this revelation the film darkens in tone, and the action shifts when Cutshaw absconds to a local bar frequented by vicious Hell's Angels.

When the bikers recognize Cutshaw from news reports, they grab him and subject him to ritual abuse and beatings. A waitress calls Center 18 to alert them, and after a while Colonel Kane himself turns up to liberate the astronaut.

The Ninth Configuration; prelude to ultra-violence

The bikers refuse to let them leave, continuing to torment Cutshaw and heaping both humiliation and violence upon Kane, who stoically endures every indignity – even licking beer from the floor. But when one of the gang starts to piss in Cutshaw's mouth, Killer Kane finally snaps, erupting with terrible violence and brutally killing several of the bikers bare-handed before the rest flee.

Back at Center 18, Cutshaw confesses to Kane that existential terror was his reason for aborting the space mission. Trying to reassure him that God does exist, and that it is possible for one man to lay down his life to help others, Kane fatally stabs himself. The film ends with a rehabilitated Cutshaw revisiting the now-empty asylum, searching for answers and some sign from the deceased Kane that there is, after all, an afterlife.

As strange as **The Ninth Configuration** is, in the realm of hopitalized Viet vets the character of Hollis in **The Woman Inside** (Joseph Van Winkle, 1979) may just be the all-time weirdest: for Hollis comes out of hospital as Holly, a bona fide she-male, in this exploitative tale of transsexuality and trauma.

Ivan Passer's **Cutter And Bone** (aka **Cutter's Way**, 1981) is a downbeat drama featuring John Heard as Cutter, a Viet vet who lost an arm and an eye in combat, and is also confined to a wheelchair. Bone (Jeff Bridges) is his best friend, who gets dragged along by Bone's obsession to nail a corrupt local businessman. Cutter is certainly a troubled, embittered individual, but at least turns his anger into positive action to expose and eliminate the same kind of social injustice which turned him into cannon fodder.

Alan Parker's **Birdy** (1984) stars Nicolas Cage and Matthew Modine as two Viet vets – the former suffering from head and face injuries, the latter comatose from mental trauma. The film is largely set in a veterans' hospital filled with mental and physical cripples, where Cage tries to bring his friend back to sanity, but also features some brief in-country combat sequences. The title refers to Modine's bird-like posture and behaviour. **Ordinary Heroes** (1985) is a TV movie about a Viet veteran who was blinded in an ambush just before his departure from Nam, and his struggle upon returning to society.

Born On The 4th Of July (1989) was the second part of Oliver Stone's Vietnam-related trilogy, which began with in 1986, and would conclude with **Heaven And Earth** [see chapter 14] in 1993. The film starred Tom Cruise and was based on Viet vet Ron Kovic's 1976 autobiography of the same name. Originally signed up as a film project (provisionally starring Al Pacino) in 1978 but then shelved, Kovic's book told of how he was turned from an idealistic young man who volunteered for service in Nam, to a bitter wheelchair-bound cripple thrust back into a society which hardly seemed to care. (Kovic consequently acted as an advisor on **Coming Home**.)

Oliver Stone turned out to be the ideal director for Kovic's story, which he saw as an antidote to the spate of right-wing films – such as **Rambo** and **Top Gun** (which also starred Cruise, ironically) that had been so successful in the '80s. After dealing with Kovic's early life, the film shifts to Nam where we see him receive the bullet wound which would condemn him to life in a wheelchair. But the real horrors start from that point on – first in a field hospital, where Stone shows some of the terrible injuries, amputations and maimings of war, and then in a veterans' hospital back in America. This hospital is the most filthy, rat-infested hole imaginable, the treatment of the inmates carried out spuriously and in total squalour. Stone then shows the various stages of Kovic's painful, reintegration to society, including his rage at being impotent. One of the

John Heard, *Cutter And Bone*

strongest sequences is Kovic's trip to Mexico, where he hooks up with another group of paralyzed vets (including Willem Dafoe) in a haze of hookers and

Willem Dafoe, Tom Cruise; *Born On The 4th Of July*

hooch. After this low point, Kovic begins a slow rehabilitation through the protest movement, finally reaching some kind of peace with the end of the war, the publication of his book and his elevation to public speaker. **Born On The 4th Of July** is certainly the most powerful portrait of a crippled Viet vet, and as a result one of the most effective anti-war films yet made.[8]

The Desperate Hours (1990) is worth a mention here for the appearance of Anthony Hopkins – just before he first played Hannibal Lecter – as an ageing Vietnam vet who finds himself impotent against the killer (Mickey Rourke) who has invaded his home and terrorized his family. Only at the film's climax, with Rourke wounded, is the decorated vet able to reassert his masculinity. The film was directed by Michael Cimino, maker of **The Deer Hunter**, and Rourke had previously played a Nam vet cop in Cimino's **Year Of The Dragon**.

1990 also saw the release of **Blind Fury**, directed by Phillip Noyce and starring Rutger Hauer as a Viet vet who was blinded in combat but, back in the States, has somehow developed astonishing ninja-like powers of heightened perception and lightning reflexes. Completely ridiculous, but Hauer at least is good value as the most potent and positive yet of the screen vet cripples.

Article 99 (1992) is set in a veterans' hospital, and features a whole range of vets who are crippled either mentally, physically, or both. Ray Liotta stars as a doctor in this rather worthy and dull effort which refers back to the milieu of **Heroes** and its ilk.

Last and certainly least, Gary Sinise's turn as a legless, fucked-up Viet vet is by far the best thing in the otherwise terrible **Forrest Gump**, but so bad is the film that it's hard to appreciate it. This film also includes an "in-country" Nam combat sequence that must be the worst ever filmed; totally unrealistic action sequences soundtracked by a hopelessly cliché'd succession of Doors, Creedence, Hendrix, etc. One would like the think that it was meant as parody, but with a movie this bad it's impossible to give that much credit.

And even more uninteresting than the mental or physical cripples are those vets who just seem to wander around aimlessly, have domestic rows, take up dead-end jobs, talk rubbish or just quietly stew in their own juices in largely boring films such as **The Confessions Of Tom Harris** (1966), **The Big Bounce** (1968), **Norwood** (1970), **The Forgotten Man** (1971), **Jud** (1971), **Americana** (1972), **Welcome Home Johnny Bristol** (1972), **Soul Hustler** (1973), **There Is No 13** (1973), **The Stuntman** (1978), **Eyewitness** (1981), **Some Kind Of Hero** (1982), **Soldier's Revenge** (1989), **To Heal A Nation** (1989), **In Country** (1989), **Jason's Lyric** (1994), **The War** (1994), and **Ulee's Gold** (1997).

While appreciating the real-life plight of Viet vets, the viewer of these films cannot avoid a certain irritation at the mental weakness and self-pity of most of the characters depicted therein. Perhaps they should all take a leaf from the book of double amputee Ron Slinker, protagonist of the eponymous **The Amazing Mr. No-Legs** (1975), in which Slinker plays a legless enforcer in an armour-plated, gun-blazing wheelchair. Mr. No-Legs takes no shit, if necessary propelling himself from his chair to batter his enemies into submission with flailing fists and twitching leg-stumps. It's never actually specified whether or not Mr. No-Legs (or indeed Ron Slinker) is a battle-maimed Viet vet – but if he isn't, he certainly should be.

NOTES

1.   Russ Meyer also included the character of a black draft-dodger in his 1968 film **Vixen!**. Meyer's subsequent films – including **Supervixens** (1975), **Up!** (1976) and **Beneath The Valley Of The Ultravixens** (1979) – grew progressively anarchic, violent, and sexually depraved.

2.   Santiago's other Nam-related movies include **Fighting Mad** (1976), **Final Mission** (1984), **The Devastator** (1985), **Eye Of The Eagle** (1987), **Killer Instinct** (1987), **Last Stand At Lang Mei** (1990), **Field Of Fire** (1991), **Beyond The Call Of Duty** (1991), and **Kill Zone** (1993). A protegé of Roger Corman, he made dozens of Philippines-based exploitation pictures, specialising in sordid "women-in-prison" flicks. The two genres merged in **Caged Fury** (1984), in which American female POWs of the Viet Cong are brainwashed into becoming assassins. Santiago also produced **Black Belt** (Charles Phillip Moore, 1992), in which a martial arts expert must protect a singer from her stalker, a Nam-vet psychopathic killer. The pair remade this film two years later, under the title **Angel Of Destruction**.

3.   Also from 1971, a lone biker vet is the protagonist of Brad Grinter's trash epic **Blood Freak**. This strange "anti-drug" movie shows the Nam vet, Herschell, mutating into a giant vampire turkey after ingesting too much marijuana.

Lone Viet vet bikers continued to figure in films ranging from **Electra Glide In Blue** (1973, as a motorcycle cop) to **My Brother Has Bad Dreams** (1972, aka **Scream Bloody Murder**, as a catalyst to some extremely weird events). The bikers vs vets theme resurfaced some years later in the climax to **The NInth Configuration**, and in **Eye Of The Tiger** (Richard Sarafian, 1986), in which Gary Busey and his vet pals wage ultra-violent war on a cycle gang led by William Smith. Scenes include decapitations, grave-robbing, and body-blasting grenade attacks. Busey also appeared in the similar throwback **Chrome Soldiers** (1992), and was a Nam vet cop in Kathryn Bigelow's **Point Break** (1991).

4.   Interestingly, notorious real-life American "cannibal killer" Arthur Shawcross –
who boasts of having eaten the genitals of his evaginated hooker victims – dates his
cannibalism to his army service in Vietnam, where he claims to have captured and partially
cooked and eaten a young Vietcong woman.

5.   Other variations on **The Most Dangerous Game** have included: **Bloodlust!**
(1961); **Woman Hunt** (1972); Jess Franco's **La Comtesse Perverse** (1973) and **Tender
Flesh** (1997); **Deadly Prey** (1987); and **Lethal Woman** (1989).

6.   The 1980s saw just one further example of the psycho Viet vet. Josh Becker's
Stryker's War (aka **Thou Shalt Not Kill...Except**, 1987) is an unholy amalgam of
Vietnam, Charles Manson and splatter. 1969: Stryker returns home from combat in Vietnam
after sustaining a field wound. It seems that his home town is being terrorized by a local
Manson-style cult, who end up kidnapping a bunch of the locals. When Stryker is visited by
three old army buddies, they decide to check out exactly what's going down in the woods.
All-out war between the vets and the killer hippies breaks out, which is where the film
descends into ultra-gore with its depictions of the massacre carried out by the clearly
psychotic, flashback-tormented ex-soldiers. The film climaxes with a violent showdown
between Stryker and the Mansonesque cult leader, who ends up impaled on the forks of
his own chopper.
          The psycho Viet vet would surface again but briefly; in Sean Penn's **The Indian
Runner** (1991), Viggo Mortensen plays the returning vet whose behaviour grows
increasingly violent and erratic, culminating in the beating to death of a local barman
(genre stalwart Dennis Hopper). And in **Skin Art** (1994), the vet is a former tortured POW,
now working as a tattoo artist in New York and obsessed with engraving the flesh of
young Asian hookers. A study of slow-burning psychosis.

7.   The effects of Agent Orange on new generations of Vietnamese children have
been horrifyingly evident, with a huge number of deformed births. Concerns about Agent
Orange in America came up in the 1980s, but only two films, the TV productions
Unnatural Causes (1986) and **My Father, My Son** (1988), really deal with the issue. The
US government has never officially acknowledged any links between Agent Orange and
the premature cancer deaths of Vietnam combat veterans, but in 1984 veterans groups
were paid an out-of-court settlement in their compensation suit against seven chemical
companies.

8.   A documentary about Kovic, **A Good American: The Ron Kovic Story**, was
directed by Loretta Smith in 1990.

CHAPTER 8
URBAN PSYCHOSIS: "TAXI DRIVER"

"ALL THE ANIMALS COME OUT AT NIGHT..."

Taxi Driver, like other neo-noir films by Scorsese and his fellow *nouvelle vague*-influenced Hollywood renaissance filmmakers, juxtaposes generic hybridization with allusions to high art and literature. It combines elements of film noir, the Western, the horror film and the urban melodrama in its gritty, disturbing tale of social alienation. Screenwriter Paul Schrader has explicitly described the film as "an attempt to take the European existential hero – that is, the man from *The Stranger, Notes From The Underground, Nausea, Pickpocket, Le Fou Follet* and *A Man Escaped* – and set him in an American context"[1]. Other clear influences are John Cassavetes's documentary realism, the metacinematic fantasies of Federico Fellini, Powell and Pressburger's Technicolor expressionism, and the fifties B-movies of "psychotic action and suicidal impulse"[2].

The setting of **Taxi Driver** is the apocalyptic "city of dreadful night" informed by the political paranoia, economic deprivation, inner-city decay, racism and violence of the seventies. This is a New York bristling with alienation, claustro-phobia, disillusionment, and the threat of urban violence: an allegorical underworld vision of hell. The streets are either slick and rainy or oppressively hot, filled with open sewers and manhole covers from which steam vapours rise in cloudy gusts. Red neon lights illuminate the faces of lost souls, the drifters and prostitutes whom De Niro transports from place to place, wandering hypnotically through seedy streets and theatre marquees advertising horror and porno movies[3]. Bickle is disgusted by this world of sleaziness and urban decay:

"All the animals come out at night – whores, skunk pussies, buggers, queers, fairies, dopers, junkies, sick, venal. Some day a real rain will come and wash all this scum off the streets... This city here is like an open sewer, you know. It's full of filth and scum. And sometimes I can hardly take it... Sometimes I go out and smell it, I get headaches, it's so bad, you know..."

This hellish vision of bars and porn theatres is a vivid kaleidoscope of colour and movement, "vibrantly alive with the iridescence of corruption"[4]. Its inhabitants are johns and hookers, clients and cabbies, an anonymous black glanced walking down the street muttering "I'll kill 'em", a shopkeeper smiling amiably one moment, and the next savagely mutilating a corpse with an iron bar. This is a landscape whose apocalyptic decadence impels Bickle's gradual descent into a very specific kind of insanity: urban psychosis, the madness of the city. Add the shell-shocked persona of a traumatised war vet, and violence seems ineluctable.

"DAYS GO ON AND ON. THEY DON'T END..."

The hallmark of this fascinating film is the tremendous ability of Robert De Niro to totally immerse himself in the character of Travis Bickle, an enigmatic loner twitching with psychotic energy and violent tensions. Bickle has been described as a man "with a vague resemblance to nearly every misanthrope, mass-murderer, plane hi-jacker, or political assassin of the past two decades, and with a vague resemblance, also, to every man's next door neighbour"[5]. Douglas Brode describes him as "a remarkably unique human being, yet also an effectively universal symbol for the walking wounded who have, since the culture shocks of the late sixties, inhabited the mean streets of our major metropolises (along with our movie screens) in ever-increasing numbers"[6]. Some twenty-five years later, Travis Bickle still remains the single character with whom De Niro is most often associated, a character of whom he has spoken off-screen with uncharacteristic eloquence. Claims De Niro:

"I got this image of Travis as a crab. I just had that image of him... You know how a crab sort of walks sideways and has a gawky, awkward movement? Crabs are very straightforward, but straightforward to them is going to the left and to the right. They turn sideways, that's the way they're built."[7]

Previously considered for the role of Travis Bickle were Robert Blake, Jeff Bridges, and farcically, Neil Diamond, none of whom could have brought to the part the kind of precision, texture, depth and edginess of De Niro's portrayal. The critics all agreed. *Variety* insisted that De Niro gives the role the precise blend of awkwardness, naivete, and latent violence which makes Travis a character who is "compelling even when he is at his most revolting".

The shuffling De Niro is plagued by a litany of attributes and characteristics which, along with his nervous demeanour and dishevelled appearance, lead to identify him as what David Weaver has described as "a recognizable 'modern' (rather than mythic) type: the urban neurotic"[8].

The first of these attributes is strong evidence of post-traumatic stress disorder. Bickle offers only a few biographical facts about his background, but we do learn that he's a twenty-six year old ex-marine, almost certainly a battle-scarred Vietnam vet. His marine battle jacket has "King Kong Brigade" patches on it, and his psychological profile approximates those of war-zone combatants. He tells his boss at the cab company that he was discharged in May 1973, and his exact whereabouts and activities in the intervening three years are left unexplained. This dateline, however, seems to confirm that Bickle's period of service was in Vietnam. Although this is never openly stated in the film, in the years following the film's release audiences have come to identify the character of Travis Bickle with the classic alienated Viet vet; and this has never been refuted by Schrader or Scorsese. **Taxi Driver**, then, stand as the most powerful depiction ever of this abject figure, the psychologically damaged war veteran, which in the years to follow would quickly descend to the level of cliché in films ranging from **First Blood** to **Street Trash**, with De Niro's performance remaining the definitive blueprint. (Given Bickle's frequenting of porno theatres, we are also reminded of De Niro's earlier portrayal of the maladjusted Nam veteran in Brian DePalma's **Hi Mom!** [1970], who on his return to society becomes a porn film director.)

Bickle seems to be a compulsive wanderer, perpetually anxious and unable to rest, and takes the job as a taxi driver because of his chronic insomnia, having previously spent his nights wandering the streets. "I can't sleep nights," he complains, in a nervous voice, and can find nothing meaningful to do during the days. His boss suggests he try hanging out in porno theatres:

Bickle: I know. I tried that.
Boss: So whaddya do now?

Bickle: I ride around nights mostly. Subways, buses. Figure, you know, I'm gonna do that, I might as well get paid for it.

He also manifests signs of acute hypochondria, complaining about headaches brought on by the smells of the city and of the dead flowers in his apartment, rejected offerings of love. Later on, in the flat interior monologue that accompanies him through the city, he speculates that he might have stomach cancer. "I shouldn't complain, though," he adds. "You're only as healthy, you're only as healthy as you feel. You're only... as... healthy... as... you... feel".

  The twitching De Niro's urban neurosis seems to revolve around a crisis of repressed sexuality. Back inside the cab company's garage in his stall at the end of his shift (six to six), he narrates with self-loathing how he has to clean the interior of his cab after each shift. "Each night, when I return the cab to the garage," he intones, sardonically, "I have to clean the come off the back seat. Some nights, I clean off the blood". His status as a silent player in the perverse games of sexual commerce that nightly surround him serves only to stockpile more ammunition in his own arsenal of repressed sexuality. Alone during the early morning hours, he walks through the red light district and spends his free time in a Triple-X porno theatre, deliberately participating in the same scenes of degradation that he seems to find so repellent by night. Tormented by a turbulent sexual anxiety that he seems unable to acknowledge, even to himself, these violent impulses eventually begin to rupture the neurotic Bickle's own sense of identity. He starts popping pills to keep calm.

"I THINK YOU'RE A LONELY PERSON..."

What makes things worse is Bickle's complete isolation and growing sense of alienation from others. De Niro plays Travis as a complete loner, endlessly striving to bring to an end his crisis of identity, to give meaning to an otherwise insignificant life[9]. Isolated not just from other people but from the society in which he lives, Bickle's inability to connect seems to be expressive of a more general state of the psychological or even epistemological alienation of the modern subject. His predicament seems to suggest that "the fundamental human condition is one of estrangement, both from other people and from all systems of order, with the result that the onus is placed on the individual to produce meaning in a world which is insensible to his or her existence in it"[10].

  Incapable of accepting his estrangement from others as the essential human condition, Bickle begins to regard the people outside his taxicab as specifically threatening to him. De Niro's memorably droning voiceover records Travis's cynical thoughts from the tattered journal he keeps in a school composition book purchased at a dime store. His main predicament is the fact that his life seems empty and meaningless, which leads him to spend longer and longer hours with the "scum" he's grown to hate:

"May 10th. Thank god for the rain which has helped wash away the garbage and trash off the sidewalks. I'm working long hours now, six in the afternoon to six in the morning. Sometimes even eight in the morning, six days a week. Sometimes seven days a week. It's a long hustle but it keeps me real busy. I can take in three, three fifty a week. Sometimes even more when I do it off the meter..."

"A WALKING CONTRADICTION"

De Niro's virtuoso performance fills Travis Bickle with little tics and nervous twitches, the helpless death spasms of a contradictory creature trapped between the world of the day and the world of the night. He reminds Betsy of the lyrics of a song by Kris Kristofferson – "he's a prophet and a pusher, partly truth and partly fiction, a walking contradiction". It seems symptomatic of Bickle's ambiguous position in his society – embodied by De Niro's edgy, restless physical demeanour – that he's suspected by pimps and prostitutes of being a cop or a narc, and by secret service agents of being a political assassin. Similarly, he violently insists on his contempt for the night people, the pimps and pushers, yet converses more easily with them than with day-people like Betsy, just as he chooses to work at night, escaping the daylight into the artificial night of porno theatres.[11]

This sense of contradiction is carried over into the way De Niro conveys Bickle's sense of unease about his own body, and his sense of anxiety about the tensions it contains. Feelings of bodily fragmentation – another symptom of urban neurosis – are also evoked by the film's image-track, which is full of shots of Travis's eyes in the taxi rear-view mirror, shots of the back of the head, headless torsos, torsoless heads, close-ups of arms and heads, and various overhead shots of tables, counters and desks with hands extending over them. The voiceover extracts from Bickle's diary, read in De Niro's deadpan voice, also bespeak psychic fragmentation in the form of a disembodied voice laying bare his soul to an

unseen listener. Richard Martin explains how we always see the New York environment from Bickle's psychologically unstable perspective:

"[A]ll that is contained in the frame becomes on extension of Travis's troubled psyche, hence the visual stylization (the use of slow-motion and jump-cut editing, the expressionism of the colours), and the one-dimensionality of many of the characters who are little more than ciphers for aspects of Travis's own personality... In fact, Scorsese's modernization of noir expressionism, his stylistic experimentation, and his occasional employment of state-of-the-art technology frequently encourage the reader to identify with the neuroses, obsessions, and paranoia of his troubled protagonists as they negotiate the characters' complex psychic geographies."[12]

These images of fragmentation serve to foreground the film's most notorious sequence, in which an increasingly unbalanced De Niro glares at himself angrily in the mirror and recites conversations in which he threatens and insistently challenges his own image in the guise of an imaginary enemy:

"Huh? Huh? I'm faster than you, you fucking son of a bitch. I saw you coming. Fuck. Shit-heel. I'm standing here. You make the move. You make the move. It's your move. Don't try it, you fucker. You talking to me? You talking to me? You talking to me? Well, who the hell else are you talking to? You talking to me? Well, I'm the only one here. Who the fuck do you think you're talking to? Oh yeah?"

Bickle's psychic fragmentation leads him to pose compulsively in front of the mirror, but always in order to reinforce his neurotic fantasies, never to question

them, never to "look at his own eyeballs". ("What makes you so high and mighty?" the aptly-named Iris asks him at one point. "Didn't you ever try looking at your own eyeballs in the mirror?".) Yet Bickle seems almost as incapable of recognizing his literal reflection in the mirror as he is of recognizing his moral and psychological reflection in the character of Iris's pimp, Sport (Harvey Keitel)[13]. It seems ironic that this collapse of identity should be the result of

Bickle's tormented, agonized obsession with his own sense of self – what he describes as "morbid self-attention".

Although his communications with others are halting and inarticulate, Bickle's journal records a tortured, skewered, eloquent record of the utter monotony of his existence:

"Loneliness has followed me my whole life. Everywhere. In bars, in cars, sidewalks, stores, everywhere. There's no escape. I'm god's lonely man. June 8th... The days can go on with regularity over and over, one day indistinguishable from the next. A long continuous chain."

Just as Bickle's failure in human interaction sees him reduced to communicating with himself through his diary and his mirror, so his sexual and vocational failures lead him to lie to his parents about the kind of life he leads in New York. He sends them a card in which he claims that he is unable to give out his address because "the sensitive nature of my work for the government demands utmost secrecy. I know you will understand. I am healthy and well and making lots of money". He also tells them that he's been "going with a girl for several months and I know you would be proud if you could see her. Her name is Betsy but I can tell you no more than that".

Eventually, inevitably, the psychic fragmentation becomes apocalyptic. Unable to interact with the people who surround him, and disconnected from the place he inhabits, De Niro's journey through the violent streets of New York City becomes a journey into the depths of his own troubled psyche, an impossible quest for spiritual purity and integrated identity[14]. At first, he goes to fellow

driver Wizard (Peter Boyle) and tries inarticulately to explain his deteriorating mental condition, claiming that he's starting to get "bad ideas" in his head. Wizard tells him to "go out and get laid, get drunk, you know, do anything", because "we're all fucked, more or less, you know". De Niro is not comforted, and as his urban neurosis begins to build, there is almost an entropic trajectory toward solitude, alienation and silence[15]. His sense of isolation is neatly encapsulated in the café scene with his taxi driving colleagues, in which he is completely isolated in his own frame, or physically fragmented in the framing of others[16]. In the same scene, the anxiety-ridden De Niro dumps an Alka Seltzer tablet into a glass of water and the camera zooms in and lingers on the fizzing, exploding action. This is clearly symbolic of a precipitous descent into the effervescent disturbances of Travis's inner world, symbolic of a man whose psyche is gradually fragmenting to such an extent that before long, he is able to communicate his response to the urban environment only through violence[17].

"CLOSE TO THE END..."

Bickle's tenuously maintained psychosexual balance is abruptly and violently disturbed – and the action of the film set in motion – by a crisis which constitutes an enactment of his own repressed sexual desires. Betsy's angry refusal to see him again after he takes her to a pornographic movie leaves De Niro soured and bitter. "You're in hell, and you're gonna die in hell like the rest of them," he shouts at Betsy, whom he once thought of as an "angel". The failure of this abortive relationship is the crisis that impels the increasingly nervous Bickle into

isolation, psychosis and armed mayhem. From this point on, for De Niro, desire is inescapably linked to violence. This leads to his obsessive, military-style preparation for the forthcoming apocalypse – though he still seems unsure, at this stage, precisely what this apocalypse will entail:

"June 29th: I gotta get in shape now. Too much sitting is ruining my body. Too much abuse has gone on for too long. From now on, it will be fifty push-ups each

morning, fifty pull-ups. There'll be no more pills, there'll be no more bad food, no more destroyers of my body. From now on, it will be total organization. Every muscle must be tight."

Some critics found this aspect of the film to be inauthentic. Richard Schickel, for example, writing in *Time*, argued that:

"Travis's failure [with Betsy] as presented is more farcical than tragic, and it never adequately explains his becoming a killer... **[Taxi Driver]** is all too heavy with easy sociologizing to be truly moving... It is a conflict [Scorsese] can resolve only in a violence that seems forced and – coming after so much dreariness – ridiculously pyrotechnical."[18]

In fact, the precise form this act of violence takes is essentially irrelevant. What matters is its ritual significance, its purgative function, its power to release the now wild-eyed Bickle from the violent pressures of his urban neurosis. His murderous rampage is essentially an attempt to affront his own state of alienation and affirm that there is a certainty, an order that exists outside it. It is an attempt to exorcise his empty, tormented life, to enact his own, cathartic salvation, to stand up "against the scum, the cunts, the dogs, the filth, the shit". His shooting spree in the brothel is a primitive act of sacrificial mayhem, of spiritual cleansing through bloodshed, of regeneration through violence[19]. It is also an attempt to do something for which he will finally be recognized, to teach the "fuckers" and "screwheads" that "here's a man who would not take it any more... a man who stood up against the scum...".

Incidentally, many critics also rejected the violence towards the end of the film as excessive, overdone, even angering. Judith Crist in the *Saturday Review*, for example, described it (somewhat ignorantly) as "one of the most revolting outbursts of blood ever to splatter a non-'martial arts' movie"[20].

After his slaughterous rampage is over, Travis makes a futile attempt to shoot himself in the neck, but the guns click empty. Instead, his face contorted into a sober grimace, he helplessly raises a blood-soaked, dripping finger to his head and makes explosive sounds with his mouth, as he mimics pulling the trigger three times in a mock-suicide, then slowly loses consciousness as his head falls backwards. More than anything else, this final gesture seems to indicate the essentially symbolic, cleansing, purifying nature of the entire blood ritual.

"WE ARE THE PEOPLE"

The irony of De Niro's situation is that when he does manage to communicate his neurotic feelings through violence, society and the newspapers absolve him of his sins and praise him for his bloody sacrifice and vigilante bravery, according him celebrity status. Partaking of Bickle's own psychosis, society applauds the psychopathic assassin for his attempts to clean up the filth of the city through an act of monumental slaughter. Consequently, it seems, however severely alienated from his society, De Niro is also, paradoxically, representative of the society, and his private urban neurosis is therefore symptomatic of a more general social malaise[21]. It is therefore perfectly if ironically appropriate that Bickle is ultimately, although temporarily, acclaimed as a hero by this sick society in which he lives:

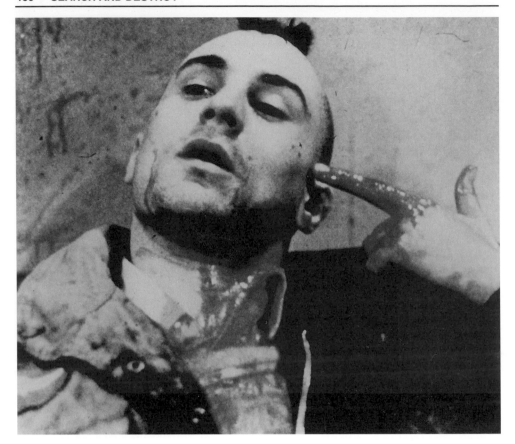

"'I don't know which of us is crazier', Iris says to Travis at one point, 'me or you'. Once we in the audience are willing to make the same admission, we appreciate just how ominously ironic Pallantine's blandly optimistic election slogan really is. 'We Are the People', it says, and so we are – all of us, including the Travis Bickles around us and within us."[22]

The purgative act of violence, however, clearly offers no lasting solution. Nothing has changed. American society remains a wasteland, characterized by "dysfunctionality, moral degradation, corruption, violence, alienation and impotence"[23]. Travis Bickle must return to the streets, unpurged of his alienation, moral outrage, and urban neurosis.[24]

NOTES

1   See David Boyd, "Prisoner Of The Night", *Film Heritage* 1976–7, 12:2, 24–30.

2.   See Richard Martin, *Mean Street And Raging Bulls – The Legacy Of Film Noir In Contemporary American Cinema*, Scarecrow Press, Lanham, Md., & London, 1997:81.

3.   In fact, screenwriter Paul Schrader claims that it was when he was wandering

around New York alone at night that the metaphor for **Taxi Driver** hit him. Schrader's own deep despair at the time – leading to obsessive behaviour, regular visits to porno theatres and recurrent fantasies of violence and suicide – brought him to the metaphor of "the man who will take anybody any place for money; the man who moves through the city like a rat through the river; the man who is constantly surrounded by people, yet has no friends; that was my symbol, my metaphor. This film is about a car as the symbol of urban loneliness, a metal coffin". Cit in Keith McKay, *Robert De Niro: The Hero Behind The Masks*, St. Martin's Press, New York: 1986, 44.

4.   Boyd, 25.

5.   Cit in McKay, 45.

6.   Cit in Douglas Brode, *The Films Of Robert De Niro*, Citadel Press, New York: 1993, 1.

7.   Ibid.

8.   David Weaver, "The Narrative Of Alienation: Martin Scorsese's **Taxi Driver**", *CineAction!* Summer/Fall 1986: 14.

9.   Richard Martin points out that **Taxi Driver** is the first instalment in a trilogy of neo-noir films scripted and directed by Paul Schrader, all featuring the existential loner hero. The trilogy is completed by **American Gigolo** (1980) and **Light Sleeper** (1991).

10.   Weaver, 13.

11.   See Boyd, 27.

12.   Martin, 87.

13   Boyd, 29.

14.   Martin, 84.

15.   Ibid., 89.

16.   Martin points out that Scorsese briefly discusses the framing in this scene in his audio commentary on the **Taxi Driver** laser disc, side 1, chapter 11.

17.   See Larry Gross, "Film Après Noir", *Film Comment* 12:4, 1976, 44–49.

18.   Cit in Brode, 98.

19.   See Julian Rice, "Transcendental Pornography And **Taxi Driver**", *Journal Of Popular Film* 5:2 (1976), 113.
20.   Cit in Brode, 99. It is debateable whether the intense realsim of this carnage is meant to reflec t the horrors of Vietnam – either in Travis' mind or in the audience's.

21.   See Boyd, 29.

22.   Ibid, 30.

23.   Martin, 89.

24.   But the reverberations of **Taxi Driver**'s eruptive gun violence did not end there. 5 years later in March, 1981,John Hinckley Jr, arrested for the attempted assassination of President Ronald Reagan, cited the film as the motivating factor behind his crime; he was apparently obsessed by the characters of Travis Bickle and the teen hooker Iris, and claimed he was acting to impress Jodie Foster.

CHAPTER 9
I'LL TAKE YOU TO NAM!: "TRACKS"

Vietnam was the first TV war. Images of the conflict were fed nightly to the folks at home, with inevitably devastating results. While every previous war had been witnessed from a safe distance, Nam was pumped directly to America, uncensored. Every atrocity, every failure, every mistake and every casualty was brought home with a reality and immediacy that cut through all the flag waving and made people wonder about just what was happening. It's unsurprising that in every war since, the authorities have sought to restrict television images of bloody, broken bodies, instead encouraging computer game-style thermal imaging of bombs striking distant targets, and reinvesting the slaughter of civilians as "collateral damage". Vietnam also spawned a unique movie genre. Previously, war films tended to show the conflicts as glorious crusades, with clean cut All-American heroes fighting for what was right. The trauma of Nam, for both veterans and the nation as a whole, changed all that for years; it was only when Reagan became President, and encouraged America to once again see war as a macho game, that Nam could become a playground for action men like Sly Stallone.

During the Seventies, movies about Vietnam tended to fall into two distinct groups. Films which dealt with the conflict itself were relatively few – **The Deer Hunter**, **Apocalypse Now**, and the little known but devastating **Physical Assault** are among the prime examples. The larger group of films dealt with consequences – mentally fucked-up kids who returned home from the war, unable to readjust to normal life. Vietnam Vets became synonymous with mental instability. When a gunman went berserk in a movie, you could be sure that he was a Vet. When a serial killer started to kill off women, it was almost certain that he would be plagued by Nam flashbacks. Bizarre films like **Cannibal Apocalypse** even suggested that the trauma of Vietnam would result in an insatiable craving for human flesh.

Falling in between these two groups is Henry Jaglom's **Tracks** – a trance-like, hallucinatory movie with psychotic interludes which plays like the missing link between **How Sleep The Brave** and **Coming Home**, and which fills in the plot holes which prevented **The Deer Hunter** from working. **Tracks** also stars Dennis Hopper, giving arguably the finest performance of his career – a career which has been consistently coloured by the Vietnam war, either directly or indirectly. While **Tracks** and **Apocalypse Now**, in which Hopper played the spaced-out photojournalist, are clearly *about* the war and its consequences, Nam has infiltrated many of Hopper's other films. In **Texas Chainsaw Massacre 2**, he not only squares up against the ultimate Nam casualty psycho ("Choptop"), but also seems like a crazed vet himself as the movie progresses; in **Easy Rider** and

The Trip, Hopper was the face of the anti-war movement, and when he's gunned down at the end of **Easy Rider**, the parallels with the Vietnam wars (both the conflict in Asia and the conflict between generations of American people) are only too obvious. Hopper's other cinematic Nam connections include: **Riders Of The Storm** (1986), in which Hopper and Michael J Pollard play bitter Nam vets broadcasting anti-right wing propaganda; **O.C. And Stiggs** (1987), in which Hopper gleefully parodies his role in **Apocalypse Now**; **Flashback** (1990), in which Hopper plays Huey, an old '60s radical activist stuck in a time-warp who still babbles on about the war; and **The Indian Runner** (1991), in which Hopper plays the bar-tender beaten to death by a psycho Nam vet. Even Hopper's psycho in **Speed** (1994) talks about a war injury and a medal, implying he is a revenge-seeking war veteran of – judging by his age – the Vietnam conflict.

　　Tracks was unusual in 1976 because it is so clearly about Vietnam, yet takes place entirely within the American heartland, on one of those endless cross-country rail journeys that seem so alien to British viewers, who can complete even the longest trip in a single day. It also seems alien to see counter-culture rebel Hopper in full military uniform, looking almost cartoonly smart. As the radio announcement at the film's opening tells us, the war is finally over – Hopper is coming home. But the radio is wrong – Hopper's war, like the internal wars of so many Vietnam vets, is far from over. It still rages inside him – a fact we almost take for granted after years of maladjusted Viet vets in countless movies from **Taxi Driver** to **Combat Shock**; more significantly though, Hopper is still on duty.

His war doesn't end until he's delivered a coffin carrying the body of one of his buddies to his home town for burial where, Hopper constantly tells his fellow passengers, "he's gonna have a band, he's gonna have a parade". We never believe such optimism – again, there is too much history, too many scenes of Vietnam vets skulking home, the losing army in a war which no-one wanted, for us to expect a hero's welcome for Hopper and his charge.

Tracks opens with a shot of Hopper addressing an unseen passenger. "Do you think about your childhood often?" he asks. "I think about mine when the going gets rough." By the end of his question, Hopper is looking directly at the camera, directly at us. He's laying out the whole central theme of the film right there. Traumatised by the present, Hopper is constantly reverting to the past. Throughout the film, he clings to ideas of a childhood which was somehow safer and easier (as all childhoods are); he listens to Forties dance tunes, morale-boosting recording from an earlier war which was only seen from the safety of Hollywood movies, in black and white. When we think of the Second World War, we see it in monochrome – a bloodless, distant event. When we think of Nam, we see grainy, hand-held newsreel footage in lurid colours, napalmed children and dangerous, drug-addled US troops out of control.

Vietnam was the only war where the public saw reality. Earlier conflicts were distanced by time and technology, while later conflicts like the Gulf war were carefully stage-managed by Governments who knew only too well the impact of burning bodies on television viewers. Nam was there in all its glory, beamed uncensored into living rooms across America and the world every night. So we can all relate to Hopper's retreat into a "safe" world (no matter that World War Two was even bloodier than Vietnam in reality).

Hopper's three day journey home is, in reality, his journey back to reality from the madness of war, and it's not an easy one. He wanders the length of the train (and again – for the sake of rail travellers in the UK – this train has spacious restaurant cars, bars, cabins etc) in search of human contact. He flits from passenger to passenger, trying to start or join conversations, but he doesn't know how to. He can't fit in. In his stiff, straight uniform, Hopper looks like an anomaly; even when he changes into street clothes, he still seems woefully out of place. Much of this is thanks to Hopper's wonderful performance – a twitchy, sweaty performance that initially makes us feel sorry for him, embarrassed for him as he nervously attempts to rejoin society.

Much of the dialogue in **Tracks** feels improvised, and the film has a documentary feel to it, using hand-held cameras and observational techniques. We catch snippets of empty conversation – talk about sex, chess, business, etc. The talk of normality. The film has an almost documentary feel during these early scenes, its deliberate banality making it more real than any stage-managed fly-on-the-wall docu-soap. The film presents a false sense of boredom – false because the viewer is never bored, yet feels as though nothing is happening. And in many ways, for the first thirty minutes of the film, nothing *is* – yet in many ways, *everything* important takes place in this opening section. We meet Hopper and his fellow passengers, we learn about his final mission with the coffin, and we experience his sense of alienation. But unlike many films which hammer such points home to the viewer, **Tracks** presents them so subtly that we are barely aware of them. Only as the film progresses do they become important.

Tracks moves forward when Hopper and fellow passenger Dean Stockwell put the make on a couple of girls who have joined the train. Hopper

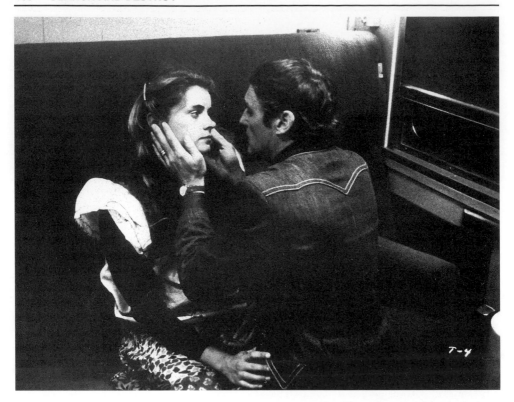

and Stockwell are an interesting mix – Hopper the shy man in uniform, Stockwell the hairy, brightly dressed easy rider. While Stockwell schmoozes his way to romantic success, Hopper is way out of his depth. He tells pretty hippie girl Stephanie (Taryn Power) "I haven't seen anything like you since I was sixteen. I'm not even sure that I saw it then." She's sufficiently interested in him to go back to his room, despite his painfully clumsy chat-up techniques, but when he comes on too strong ("let me show you how I like to kiss," she tells him after an over-enthusiastic petting session), she leaves. Hopper's desperation (for love? For connection?) has driven her away, and he starts to lose it. Slowly. The next morning, Hopper has a brief fling with an older female passenger after asking for shampoo (she washes his hair before surrendering to some intense, passionate and very real foreplay), but he still wants to connect with Power. Meanwhile, his lack of connection to everyone else is becoming more obvious. Things reach a head when Hopper is again talking about his mission. "Why do you feel you have a monopoly on feeling sorry for yourself?" asks a black Korean war veteran as Hopper explains to him that he's escorting a coffin "with a black man in it". The Korean vet is unimpressed. "You only have one, I had twenty-one," he comments. But Hopper is no longer listening. Hopper is instead watching as Power is harassed by another passenger, who then starts to assault her. Other passengers join in what soon becomes a gang-rape, and Hopper pulls his gun. Of course, none of this has actually happened. It's a hallucination, the first sign that Hopper's trip is rapidly becoming a bad one. Two days into the journey, fifty minutes into the film, and Hopper's sense of alienation gives way to mental instability.

This hallucination represents a turning point in the film, much as Max Renn's visions do in David Cronenberg's **Videodrome**. From this point onwards, we cannot trust what we see. We wonder how much is reality, and how much is false... and we begin to question what has already gone.

There is also an air of unreality about Hopper's quaintly touching relationship with Power. It's an oddly affecting, though clearly doomed affair that is old fashioned in its romance. Power seems somehow out of time; even more so as we watch the film today, her hippie look seeming almost as dated as the Glen Miller that Hopper listens to as they dance, in the final moment of lucid normality. After this touching interlude, it all comes crumbling down for Hopper.

When MP's board the train, Hopper flips – he stashes his uniform in the toilet and runs naked through the train (a nude scene which still seems startling today, given the lack of male nudity in mainstream cinema) as he seeks to escape those who are hunting him. Only it's not Hopper they want. Stockwell bursts into his cabin and reveals himself as a political radical war protester. This revelation does little for Hopper, who rejects his pleas for help. Stockwell, whose free speech is too much for the powers that be in the land of the free, is captured and taken away. The pushy real estate salesman who has been pushing land deals throughout the film is revealed as a part-time government agent. Does this feel real?

Genuine or not, Hopper's obvious hallucinations get worse. "They *know* what you've done," sneers a waiter at one point. Fellow passengers warn him of impending danger. They deny knowledge of each other. Nothing feels right. Nothing feels real.

Hopper and Power take a day out of their journey to make love in a field – Power giving Hopper the "one nice thing" that his life is missing. It's an idyllic scene – there's no sound but the wind blowing. But mid-sex, Hopper loses control. He confesses to rejecting Stockwell's pleas for help, claiming that it was impossible for him to do otherwise – "I'm on a very important mission. Guys like that have to be sacrificed". Peacenik Power is repulsed, and flees. Hopper is finally alone. No lovers. No passengers. Just him and the coffin.

When Hopper reaches the end of the line (and doesn't that suddenly sound symbolic?), there is – surprise surprise – no welcoming committee. No parade, no band. Just a couple of embarrassed looking officials to handle the funeral. Biding his time until the burial, Hopper wanders around town, even more out of place. Anonymous. Forgotten. He reverts to childhood again – visiting school rooms, an empty home. And there's the realisation. Hopper is supposedly returning his dead comrade home, but it's *him* who has returned to his home town. This is Hopper's old school, Hopper's old home, to a town that doesn't care what has happened to him, where people will come out with glib comments like "I wish I could've been there", not knowing that everyone who was in Vietnam wanted to be anywhere but there. Hopper is back in his spiritual home, and he's brought Vietnam – his mental home – with him.

Tracks ends in the cemetery. Hopper stands over the coffin, alongside the dutiful, embarrassed looking officials. "He's the biggest hero that's ever been here. No-one showed up," muses Hopper *(Hopper's the biggest hero that's ever been there. No-one showed up)*. As the flag-draped coffin is lowered into the ground, Hopper demands a moment alone. The embarrassed-looking officials leave and Hopper gazes into the grave. And finally cracks completely.

It's one of cinema's most powerful moments – a tour-de-force of acting[1], writing and controlled direction which, even seen out of context, packs a hell of a punch; within the context of **Tracks**, Hopper's final, incoherent yet revelatory monologue is what finally confirms this film as one of the finest movies to emerge in the post-**Easy Rider** era of American independent cinema[2]. It stands alongside Martin Scorsese's **Taxi Driver**, released the same year, as one of the two occasions when the "psycho vet" strand of cinema achieved a true artistic pinnacle, driven by inspired directors and by performances from two of the greatest screen actors of all time.

In the cemetery, Hopper moans: "I love... I love... I really love... I really do love... I love, I love and I hate, and I hate, and I hate, because I love... because I love I hate, because I love I hate, because I love I hate, because I love, because I love... YOU MOTHERFUCKERS!"

Hopper jumps into the grave, opens up the coffin and reveals the secret which we suddenly realise we knew all along. There is no dead buddy, no hero, no great black man. The dead man is Hopper, a small town boy who went to war and lost his mind. And now he's home. "You wanna go to Nam?" he screams; "I'll take you to Nam. I'll take you there!"

Hopper unwraps the tarpaulin, puts on the combat helmet and tools up with the guns'n'ammo that the coffin contains. Then he leaps out of the grave, ready to take the whole town to Nam...

NOTES

1. Hopper's amazing portrayal of mental disintegration and eventual psychosis here achieves the raw truth he would evince in later roles such as Donny in **Out Of The Blue**, Frank in **Blue Velvet**, and the eponymous **Paris Trout**. These are remorseless characterizations which seem to emanate from a place beyond "acting", the place that Hopper himself has alluded to as an automatic zone of "total recall".

2. And indeed the film was only made possible by **Easy Rider**'s success, which led to a string of further productions from its producers Raybert, who re-organized as BBS under the direction of Bob Rafelson, Steve Blaunter and Bert Schneider. BBS folded in 1973 after making such movies as **Five Easy Pieces** (1970), the Jack Nicholson-directed **Drive, He Said** (1971) and Henry Jaglom's **A Safe Place** (1971); but the Hollywood mould was broken, and Jaglom and Schneider were reunited for **Tracks**.

CHAPTER 10
NOTHING IS OVER!: RAMBO'S RAMPAGE

There seems to be little doubt regarding the process of conservative re-assertion undergone in Hollywood by the 1980s. The radical overhaul of generic themes and structures in a variety of post-Vietnam narratives (by filmmakers such as Michael Cimino, Sam Peckinpah, George Romero and Martin Scorsese) gave way to a general tendency which refuted many of the disillusionments engendered by the loss of the war. Labelling a variety of post-Vietnam films as "Reaganite entertainment", Andrew Britton stresses that this movement was already well under way by the mid-70s and that the phrase does not literally imply a cinema which consciously expressed the personality of President Ronald Reagan himself. Rather, he argues that many films displayed a "general movement of reaction and conservative reassurance [in which] the characteristic features... both formal and thematic, [were] substantially developed in films made before [Reagan's] election".[1]

Britton contests that titles such as as **The Towering Inferno** (1974), **Rocky** (1976), **Star Wars** (1977), **Raiders Of The Lost Ark** (1981), **An Officer And A Gentleman** *(1982)* and **E.T. The Extra-Terrestrial** (1982) express a "ritualised repetitiveness" and "interminable solopsism"[2]. This effectively insulated the films against the social context in which they were produced while satisfying a general drive toward ideological reassurance, a tacit confirmation that America was "OK". Britton's argument is supported by the fact that several of the above films spawned a series of sequels (or, to use that hideous industry term which has seeped into the pages of most popular movie magazines, 'franchises') and a rash of imitations, each seeking to work according to a prescribed formula of repetition.

Crucial to this present discussion is the inclusion above of **Rocky**, identifying Sylvester Stallone as a central personality in the resurgent conservatism lamented by Britton. Rocky often seemed a parody of the punch drunk, inarticulate but loveable proletarian hero, characteristics which were utilised in a variety of increasingly ludicrous situations as the series developed. The progression from working class hero in **Rocky** to the vengeful cold warrior of **Rocky IV** (1985) serves as a useful career context against which the Rambo figure eventually emerged. With the release of both **Rocky IV** and **Rambo: First Blood Part II** in 1985, Stallone completed a triumphant double in which he both defeated an entire army of Soviet-assisted, oriental cannon fodder in the jungles of Vietnam, and pulverised a monstrous communist superman on his own doorstep before extolling the virtues of universal brotherhood to the oppressed Soviet masses and sinister Politburo officials. Thus, by the middle of the decade, the image of Stallone as the preferred action hero of the new right was effectively secured. These Stallone films (I use this phrase in order to stress his varied but pivotal role as writer, director and star in much of his work) actively sought to correct the uncertainties of the post-Vietnam age by confronting them head on, both in the metaphorical arena of the boxing ring and the literal terrain of South-East Asia[3].

Despite the trend for ideological re-assertion outlined by Britton, the declining popularity of the western genre was perhaps symptomatic of a brief disillusionment with popular American mythology. The figure of the lone, instinctive male hero is central to the western but the generic frameworks within which he could function had been significantly dismantled in the wake of the Vietnam conflict. Therefore, the problem arose as to how such hero figures could be re-imagined in the altered socio-cultural context. For those filmmakers interested in a radical overhaul, the hero emerged often as disillusioned, confused and psychotic (see, for example, **Pat Garret And Billy The Kid** [1973], **Taxi Driver** [1976], **The Deer Hunter** [1978], **Apocalypse Now** [1979] and **Cruising** [1980]). Yet, for all of their impact (or lack thereof), these films often merely represented counter-currents, never becaming the dominant voice of popular Hollywood cinema. The Rambo figure thus became the apotheosis of the mythic hero figure as imagined through a reactionary, mid-80s conservative consensus. His emergence in the wake of the critical examination of the hero in the 1970s signals the extent to which the popular culture increasingly followed revisionist impulses.

For all their iconic resonance and quasi-mythic allusions, the films featuring the character of John Rambo (**First Blood** [1982], **Rambo: First Blood Part II** [1985], and **Rambo III** [1988]) underwent a rapid rise and fall in cultural capital. Rambo was the figurehead of a substantial group of '80s action heroes (in films such as the Nam MIA drama **Uncommon Valour** [1983, and directed by **First Blood** helmer Ted Kotcheff], **Missing In Action** [1984], **Red Dawn** [1984] and **Top Gun** [1986]), running the gamut of post-Vietnam fallout as an embodiment of war veteran disillusionment, the personification of a new militarist zeitgeist and winding up a curious anomaly in the face of a rapidly thawing cold war. With its almost wilfully wrong headed idealism, the Rambo series nevertheless represents a radical contrast to many of the action films that followed in its wake. Where titles such as **Commando** (1985), **Die Hard** (1988) and **True Lies** (1994) use post-modern "irony" and pastiche to mask their xenophobia and rampant conservatism, the second and third instalments of the **Rambo** trilogy foreground and actively celebrate these attributes without any irony whatsoever, rendering them easy targets for critics intent on consigning the series to the ideological dustbin. Such reactions might be justified to a point but do not begin to address the contradictions and tensions which the **Rambo** films actually express when examined individually. The triumphant fantasy figure of the second and third films in the series has overshadowed the disturbed, near psychotic character outlined in the first film.

The value of popular cultural icons is often measured by the extent to which they either endorse or contradict the dominant ideological impulses of their time. Therefore, there is little doubting the extent to which Rambo drew from the revisionist, and often covert cold war adventures of the Reagan administration. Rambo's secret missions in foreign territories mirror a decade in which American involvement in El Salvador, Nicaragua and Grenada confirmed the White House's commitment to a new anti-communist polemic. Reagan himself was recorded after viewing **Rambo: First Blood Part II** as stating that should he ever face a hostage situation, "we'd know what to do next time".[4] However, there is a certain anomaly in the Rambo films wherein the imposition of a mythic archetype runs in parallel to an attack upon some of the institutional foundations upon which such figures may be legitimized. In other words, Rambo may have come to embody much of what many found so loathsome about the re-imposition of military authority (through presidential endorsement) in the 1980s, but the character's attacks (both physical and verbal) upon the bureaucratic machinations of government serve to partly estrange him from the hawkish administration he seemed to personify. In this sense, the Rambo films also reflect the tensions inherent in notions of a great American democracy, which has historically floundered between an almost imperial Presidential authority and a constitution which enshrines the fundamental principle of government of the people, for the people, by the people. Across the series, Rambo undertakes unilateral decisions to pursue seemingly personal missions of recuperation, be they in the mountains of Oregon, the jungles of Vietnam or the deserts of Afghanistan. These actions question the extent to which Rambo can legitimately represent both the veterans of the Vietnam war and the American people in general, waging battles that are as much enactments of individual frustration and vendetta as genuine expressions of war grievance.

The embodiment of Rambo as the ultimate avenger of the Vietnam war is a far cry from the figure conceived in the early seventies by novelist David Morrel. *His* "First Blood" presents a character just six months out of the war, alone and adrift in an indifferent American landscape. The use of the archetypal lone drifter immediately invokes the western hero but positions him in a world where individualism is met with institutional oppression. This theme expands across the series as Rambo's personal war is developed into a global crusade, pitting him against the police, sadistic, sub-human orientals, power crazed Soviet officers and lily-livered government bureaucrats. The best part of a decade separates the war from the events of the film version, which does little to expound upon how Rambo re-integrated back "into the world" during that time. Morrel stresses from the outset that, by appearence, Rambo was "just some nothing kid", his long hair and beard redolent of the hippie image fresh in the cultural consciousness at the time of writing. This evocation of the non-descript is the antithesis of the physicality eventually embodied by the films. While the vaguely hippiesque persona is partly carried over into Stallone's interpretation, the films make striking use of his increasingly muscular physique and the various cultural connotations that such an appearence suggest. By **Rambo III**, far from being "just some nothing kid", the character has seemingly developed into a fusion of labourer, hippie, mountain man, body builder and Native American warrior, partaking in organized martial arts contests in order to fund the monastery in which he now resides. This conflation of spiritual being and iron pumping gym freak seeks to reconcile Rambo with the Eastern people he so mercilessly slaughtered in the previous film. With the baying crowd of a Bangkok warehouse ritually repeating his name (just as the soviet people did in **Rocky IV**), **Rambo III** somehow contrives to have its hero gratify the blood lust of a foreign nation. Rambo's own ethnicity places him in a direct line of descent from a race methodically slaughtered by a previous generation of American militarism. In

Rambo is harassed by Sheriff Teasle; *First Blood*

Rambo: First Blood Part II, his heritage is revealed as "German-Indian", a combination that manages to conflate the indigenous American and intimations of the Aryan superman. David Morrel has stated that he chose the name of his character while reading the work of the French symbolist Arthur Rimbaud and noticing that an apple in his wife's grocery bag was labelled 'Rambo'. While this serendipitous event might suggest a figure conceived in terms of a fusion of natural and literary reference points, Morrel felt simply he had hit upon "the sound of force". As far as the films were concerned, it was a sound that reverberated internationally, representing a confused notion of an international democratic ideal embodied in the figure of one man.

At least in relative terms, there is an attempt to problematise the heroic status of Rambo in **First Blood**. The film is marked by the unsteady negotiation of a variety of thematic and formal oppositions, pitting Rambo against community, against the police, against the environment and ultimately, against himself. He is informed by Sheriff Teasle (Brian Dennehy) that "wearing that flag [the stars and stripes] and looking the way you do is just asking for trouble" and the notion of a war re-staged against his own people marks Rambo as at once removed from, yet inextricably bound by, the social structures of the post-Vietnam free world. The film frequently depicts Rambo isolated against the open road, the forest and the mountains and apart from his final monologue to his only ally, Col. Trautman (Richard Crenna), he is in a constant state of isolation and antagonism. While his flight into the mountains demonstrates an ability to utilise

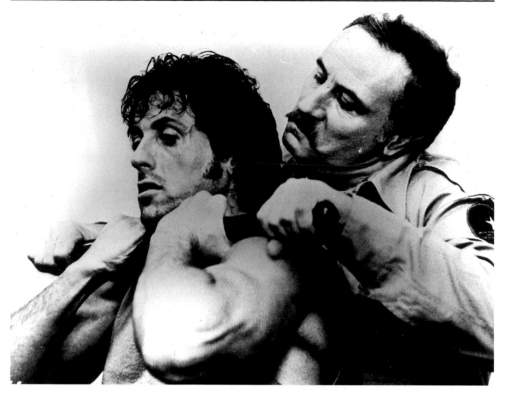

Rambo is brutally restrained by Galt (Jack Starrett); *First Blood*

the environment for his own purposes, he is reduced to the level of human prey, albeit one that proceeds to disable its attackers one by one. This situation is exacerbated by the refusal of the town's chief lawman to allow him to pass through peacefully. The peacetime function of the trained combat veteran is defined explicitly as somehow contrary to the insular demands of small town American life.

Rambo's prohibition from the community is contrasted by his mastery of the surrounding wild terrain. However, this also serves to further define the nominal 'home' country as oppressive and inhospitable. Rambo is mocked by the police when he informs them that his fearsome knife is used for hunting, a claim that appears eccentric and fanciful without the knowledge of his military background. This division between individual and community is itself an extension of a masculine and generational suspicion initiated by the police chief. The role of Teasle, attired in the traditional stetson of the western hero, is undermined to the point where his mistrust and harrasment of the younger generation sparks a conflict that will eventually see his institutional authority severely undermined. His initial antipathy to Rambo is sparked by accusations of vagrancy and uncleanliness, characteristics which potentially soil the town's social fabric. The police department itself evinces various levels of contempt, an attitude summed up by the reaction of Galt (Jack Starrett) to Rambo's bodily scarring – "who gives a shit?". The line seems designed to evoke a deeper public

First Blood

intimately bound with what appears to be an acute manifestation of post-traumatic stress disorder. Trautman stresses another paradox of a figure like Rambo, whereby his gravestone might inform the world that despite his congressional medal of honour for countless missions beyond enemy lines, he was ultimately "killed for vagrancy in Jerkwater, USA". Such is the lot of the Vietnam veteran in the world envisaged by **First Blood**. While the war itself came to negate the traditions of heroism established in previous conflicts, the film re-instates the heroic dimension of the combat soldier, his status partially upheld through adherence to codes of honour and duty which seemingly no longer apply. There is no suggestion of a My Lai in Rambo's military précis, just as there is no implication of insubordination and neglect. His loyalty to country is therefore seen to be futile in the face of his betrayal by the very countrymen his military actions supposedly protected.

Rambo's "private war" eventually concludes back in the urban heartland of the town which has hitherto accomodated his oppression and rejection. His use of sticks, rocks, knives and booby traps is supplanted by his appropriation and mastery of a giant M-60 machine gun. His assault upon the town is marked by the systematic decimation of lines of communication, electricity supplies, ammunition outlets and fuel provisions. Teasle's declaration that "this is my town" sets up a variation on the classic final showdown between sheriff and outlaw, a confrontation which Rambo inevitably wins by blasting his foe through on overhead skylight. However, the futility of Rambo's actions are finally demonstrated through his final surrounding by dozens of armed pursuers. The personal conflict with Teasle is resolved by the Sheriff's maiming and hospitalisation but this does nothing to answer Rambo's own disillusionment with the authority that Teasle represents. The vanquishing of the bad father is therefore complemented by the reconciliation and confession to the good father. The Colonel serves throughout the film as the only character to truly comprehend Rambo, an understanding that also allows him to see the personal motivations that have driven his protégé's flight from captivity. Trautman, the career soldier, has seemingly come to terms with the loss in south-east Asia and his stabilty contrasts the latent psychosis represented by Rambo. Accusing his protégé of doing enough "to make this private war happen", Trautman's declaration that the war is "over" precipitates Rambo's final despairing monologue, a recollection which encapsulates the inner motivations for his destructive acts;

"Nothing is over! Nothing! You just don't turn it off. It wasn't my war. You asked me, I didn't ask you. And I did what I had to do to win but somebody wouldn't let us win. And then I come back to the world and I see all those maggots at the airport, protesting me and spitting. Calling me babykiller and all kinds of vile crap. Who are they to protest me? Who are they unless they've been there and been me and know what the hell they're yelling about?... For me civilian life is nothing. In the field we had a code of honour – you watch my back, I'll watch yours. Back here there is nothing... Back there I could fly a gunship, I could drive a tank. I was in charge of million dollar equipment, back here I can't even hold down a job."

Rambo's tirade reveals a confusion of betrayed patriotism and redundant ethics compounded by a sense of personal worthlessness. The re-enactment of the war at home is shown partly as a result of his inability to 'switch off', to transfer the skills for which he was trained into a world *without* war. He is the redundant tool of an imperialistic ethos, cast aside and pitted against his fellow Americans. 'Blame' is re-directed toward a nameless, faceless "somebody", a bureaucratic shadow that lacked the will to follow through and get the job done. This high level, official impotence is coupled with the protests of the peace movement which greeted Rambo's return home. There seems to be a hint of an unspoken, perhaps unwitting alliance between the war protestors and the unidentified "somebody" whom Rambo sees as responsible for the loss in Vietnam. The 'weakness' of these civilian and bureaucratic figures is contrasted to the honour of the soldier, which seeks to preserve unity and brotherhood in the face of death. Rambo's sense of betrayal is bound by his feeling that his personal worth is linked with the failings of the system that moulded him. This confusion of personal and mass responsibility laments loss on a national scale while identifying the tangible effects on an individual whose personality has been shaped by his experience of that loss. Rambo's ensuing tale of a friend, dismembered by a bomb in the streets of Saigon, is marked by a further fusion of sentimentality and rage. He recalls his friend's fantasy to go cruising in a Chevrolet upon the return home, an image redolent of the '50s consumer idealism shattered by the unrest of the following decade. This dream is broken by the devastating effect of the bomb and the refusal of anybody to help his dying friend. Rambo recalls his friend's cries of "I wanna go home, I wanna go home", a dying wish which **First Blood**, with its bleak definition of home, defines as hollow and doomed. Weeping and embracing his surrogate father, Rambo's personal war ends with his apprehension and imminent incarceration, a fate that the film appears to suggest outwardly reflects the psychological cell within.

Rambo's final speech in **First Blood** effectively acts as the blueprint from which the series' ensuing mission of redemption is drawn, using it to develop a revisionist ideal taken to fantastical, grotesque extremes. In **Rambo: First Blood Part II**, punishment for his previous transgression is revealed from the outset as hard labour in a military prison. In contrast to his isolation in the first film, Rambo is re-introduced in the midst of concentrated masculinity. Visual intimations of the tamed, caged beast are soon allayed by promises of a new mission and a pardon from the president himself. The mission, to locate veterans believed to be still alive in Vietnamese labour camps, immediately transforms Rambo from the forgotten, despised veteran to a figure capable of personally carrying out the president's work. Moreover, the film expands the gloriously mythic character traits that **First Blood** merely hinted at. The pre-title sequence poses the question that essentially serves to shape the character for the rest of the series – "Do we get to win this time?" asks Rambo. "This time it's up to you", Trautman assures him. Immediately, the mission is engaged both in terms of conflict resolution and personal vengeance, defining the war as a clear cut east-west antagonism decisively at odds with the initially stated aim of reconnaissance. In taking the personal war back whence it came, the film allows Rambo to confront the communist enemy but also supplies a face to the treacherous bureaucratic "somebody" previously referenced by Rambo's final monologue in **First Blood**. "While I'm still alive' *it's* still alive" asserts Rambo and the confirmation of American MIAs in the jungles of Vietnam gives full justification to his belief that "nothing is over". Indeed, the retention of such prisoners by communist forces seems to suggest that the war has never really ended at all.

Rambo's mission is immediately tainted by intimations of the indecision and lack of will that he believes lost the war first time around. The mission leader, Murdock (Charles Napier) refers obliquely to the "committee" to which he belongs, and becomes the personification of the bureaucratic pussy footing so despised by Rambo. However, Murdock also functions to shift blame for such reluctance away from the president into the realm of congressional politics. The "somebody" that Rambo holds responsible is not the commander in chief himself but the cynical, lying inhabitants of Capitol Hill. The briefing sequence is marked by Rambo and Trautman's suspicious glances at each other and great emphasis is placed upon the technological apparatus utilised by Murdock's team. Rambo's physicality and instinctual persona is contrasted to the dehumanising, impersonal effect of the literal machinations of military technology. Furthermore, the cool, aloof demeanour of Rambo is the opposite of Murdock's rapid fire chatter and copious sweating – this is a man who, quite literally, cannot stand the heat. Rambo also knows instantly, through his capacity for information recall, that Murdock is lying about his war service. The technology seems to function as much for its own symbolic value as for any practical purpose, suggesting that technology is somehow antithetical to modes of combat as represented by its hero. Murdock's assurances about the reliability of his state of the art hardware are met by Rambo's response that "I always thought the mind was the best weapon". The mission is to be non-confrontational and Rambo is instructed to take photographs that might justify further inquiry into the plight of the MIAs. This refusal to engage in combat or active attempts to free the prisoners frustrates Rambo's personal mission and he instantly becomes suspicious of once more being subject to "somebody" else's political agenda. Ultimately, the MIAs are merely the pretence upon which the film justifies its xenophobia and paranoia. The ensuing narrative, through Murdock's inevitable betrayal of Rambo, seeks a corrective replay of the hero's view of the war in which his sense of duty and honour was neutralized by the treachery of his superiors.

The film is explicit in its fetishization of both Rambo's physique and the weaponry which he deploys. The antipathy towards technology is tempered by the suggestion that it is only useful when used as an active, practical extension of the body. This is spelled out visually just before Rambo embarks on the mission – a slow pan down his arm is lit to emphasise every sinew, artery and muscle before halting on the giant knife which he methodically sharpens. It is almost as if the blade is an extension of the body, an endorsement of the primitive hunter impulse which was so mocked by the police officers of **First Blood**. The arm shot is intercut with short images of Rambo loading rifles and packing equipment, all accompanied on the soundtrack by heightened metallic clanks and clicks. The body *becomes* a weapon despite Rambo's stated belief in the mind's superior power, his half-naked form yielding contrasts with not only the uniformed enemy but also the emaciated MIAs he has come to rescue. His actions and postures privilege a physical, instinctual American masculinity while lamenting the waste and emaciation of lost forgotten men (or "ghosts" as Murdock calls them). Rambo is shown to master a range of military equipment, from assault rifles to Soviet helicopters, abilities which effect a new level of potency in conjunction with the instinctual qualities he demonstrates. In **First Blood**, he escapes the pusuing police on a motorcycle, while **Rambo III** demonstrates his horsemanship. Over the course of the three films, this combination demonstrates a mastery of both the natural world and the mechanical. In his final, enraged assault upon Murdock's computers, the recoil of Rambo's giant machine gun causes his physique to ripple and shudder, almost as if the gun itself is bio-mechanically fused with his arm. This final symbolic, but devastatingly destructive act utilises state of the art firepower but affirms the instinctual and the primitive over the modern.

The film still insists on Rambo's estrangement from the hardware with which he is supplied, confirmed during the near disastrous parachute drop where he is forced to cut away his cumbersome equipment in order to save his life.

Rambo: First Blood II

When we next see Rambo he is running deep in the jungle, clad in a headband and armed only with his trusty knife and a back pack which is soon revealed to contain a deadly bow. Again alluding to the Native American warrior archetype, the arrows of this weapon are tipped with explosives, a feature which reconciles the incongruities of primitive and modern warfare. Silhouetted against the shafts of early morning sun which break through the trees, the film re-affirms Rambo's affinity with seemingly alien, inhospitable terrains as he effortlessly navigates his

Rambo: First Blood II

surroundings. This initiates the almost mystical relationship Rambo holds with the jungle, an ability to master and conquer foreign landscapes where even indigenous people prove incapable. Over the course of the film, Rambo utilises the elements in order to entice, foil and slay his enemies. Fire, earth and water become Rambo's natural allies as he immerses and camouflages his body in mud, leaps unnaturally from below the surface of a river and creates huge infernos in his wrath. The body is thus shown in a kind of destructive harmony with the natural world, an ability which furthers Rambo's mission to reinstate dominion over the sadistic, sub-human Soviets and Vietnamese.

Indeed, all of the enemy is defined partly in terms of their deviance (the Vietnamese officers are shown dealing in prostitution) and moral derangement. Barely characterised, the Vietnamese military enemy is strictly uniformed, unlike the classic image of the guerilla Vietcong. This defines the enemy in terms of villainous Japenese stereotypes of countless World War II films and thus constitutes a suspicion of the east that stretches back beyond the dawn of the cold war. The enemy is seen to be strictly in collusion with the Soviet military, embodied by the leeringly sadistic Col. Pudovsky (Steven Berkoff). Rambo's decimation of a force equipped with modern military hardware confirms the film's affirmation of his methods over the deployment of technology. Rambo's brief alliance and romantic flirtation (his only one in the series) with Co (Julia Nickson) ends almost as soon as it started and her role as the one "good" oriental

Rambo: First Blood II

suggests that the film's mistrust of eastern masculinity is total. Moreover, Co's death serves a purely functional narrative purpose, allowing Rambo's mission to extend to his avenging of a slain lover. Her dying words ("you're not expendable") merely justify Rambo's sense of his personal mission and the pendant which he takes from her body remains around his neck for the rest of the series.

Rambo's physical resilience is underlined by the tortures he withstands upon capture by his enemies. His role as imperial messiah is visually affirmed by the crucifix like postures he adopts as he is bound, suspended and chained to a variety of torture instruments. His dousing in a swamp and torture by electrocution assumes sado-erotic dimensions as leeches attach themselves to his skin and his tensed, naked muscular form is gleefully mutilated by his captors as he writhes and screams in agony. While Rambo suffers for the sins of non-believers, his survival of such punishment ensures a fearful day of judgement, his moral authority affirmed by the quasi-religious connotations of his suffering. As with his mastery of the elements, Rambo's capacity to withstand intense pain alludes to a mystical ability over the physical self, a trait which also provides further contrast to the cowardly, sadistic characteristics of his captors. In perhaps the film's most infamous scene, a Vietnamese officer is shown fleeing terrified from the rampaging Rambo, freezing in fear atop a rock formation just in time to see an explosive tipped arrow hurling towards him before his entire body explodes in a shower of flame and gore. The officer's bodily disintegration literally reduces him to nothing, a grotesque metaphor for the film's extreme view of the essential worthlessness of eastern masculinity.

By its conclusion, Rambo is confirmed as the triumphant superman of a new cold war that has expanded into full blown, covert conflict. Yet the film still seeks to identify him as somehow representative of the common war veteran's experience. Trautman goes so far as to admit that the war "might have been wrong" but pleads with him not to "hate his country". This is a highly curious assertion given the preceding 90 minutes. The correction of history attained by Rambo seems to wholly endorse the 'rightness' of the war, his discovery of American prisoners a confirmation that the conflict of interests with the red menace goes on. What the film actually suggests is that if the war was in fact "wrong", it was even more wrong that America should proceed to lose it. The moral conundrum of the unjust conflict proves secondary to the maintenance of personal and national dignity as achieved through global dominion. Rambo's individualism and hyper-masculine heroics are seen as the natural extension of a combat veteran's desire to belong to their country. His final plea that his country should love he and his fellow veterans "as much as we love *it*" seeks an acceptance that seems hollow in the context of the betrayal and deceit he has once more encountered. He spares Murdock's life upon his return to the mission base, if only to demonstrate that for all of his purging of the communist threat, he is also capable of mercy. He demands that Murdock find the other MIAs still in Vietnam, a hint that Rambo may also have gone some way to affecting a turnaround in the despised bureaucrat. Burying his fearsome knife in the table inches away from Murdock's face, Rambo demonstrates in his wrath that, in this instance, the sword is truly mightier than the pen.

Rambo's ongoing estrangement points to the difficulty in constructing heroes from the remnants of a war that should never have happened. By the release of **Rambo III**, the film's attempts to displace guilt over civilian atrocities and murder onto the Soviet occupation of Afghanistan appeared vaguely ridiculous, given that Mikail Gorbachev had ordered withdrawal that very year. Afghanistan is posited as the Soviet Union's own Vietnam, in which it is doomed to replicate the mistakes made by America. Of course, Rambo is sided with the oppressed rebels in order to further his revision of the history books and there is a vaguely embarrassing climax in which he and the Colonel are rescued from the Soviets by a stampeding Afghan cavalry. Rather than missing American soldiers, it is the rescue of Trautman that proves the foundation for Rambo's final war, allowing the Colonel himself to demonstrate his own resilience in the face of torture and skill in the battlefield. But it is the least interesting film of the series, not least because its geographical setting seems somehow less fundamental to the revisionist hysteria of the earlier instalments. Afghanistan may provide an opportunity for Rambo to waste more reds but this is distinctly somebody else's war, unlike the unfinished business central to **Part II**. In the face of collapsing world communism, Rambo was running out of battles to wage. America had a new middle-eastern enemy in waiting and the smart bombing and stealth technology of the Gulf War seem infinitely more antithetical to the Rambo persona than the technological gadgetry of Murdock's command centre. Rumours circulated in the film press several years ago that Rambo would return as a kind of militarized eco-warrior, a seemingly ridiculous concept that in fact appears to have grown out of the series' frequent marrying of Rambo's survivalist

CHAPTER 11
VIETNAM:
THE TRANSPARENT WAR

Vietnam has famously been described as the first "Media War" – the first war to play out in real time in the living-rooms of middle America where televisions brought the stench of death itself into those carpeted suburban sanctums that normally smelled more of new leather upholstery and gin and tonics mixed from alcove bars... televisions that carried the images of atrocities that horrified a nation at what it was sending its sons to do.

So goes the popular wisdom. The nightly network news was never, in fact, an agent of the "anti war" movement and became even more squeamish about dealing with the controversial realities as the War worn on. The turning of America against the War was a slow and complex process and even today the conflict polarizes and divides the Nation. In the late '90s, for example, a Vietnamese shop owner from Los Angeles was boycotted and later beaten for having a picture of Ho Chi Minh in his store. A judge begrudgingly upheld his legal right to keep the portrait of a man who symbolized "hatred and violence" up. Conversely to many, Ho Chi Minh, never an autocratic dictator, is perhaps the last communist patriarch left in the world whoses honor remains intact. During President Clinton's historic 3-day visit to Vietnam in mid-November, 2000, he was obliged at one point to appear on stage in front of a giant portrait of Uncle Ho.

Nevertheless, despite the unsettled issues the war left in its wake, no conflict before or since has ever been so heavily or passionately documented from so many sides. The War was the "story" of its day, and gave birth to the modern variant of investigative journalism and field reportage which differed in virtually all essentials from WW2 or the Korean War.

Documentation on the War was hardly confined to the nightly news, and the aim of this text is to survey the vast range of genres and approaches that formed the spectrum of documentary reportage on "The American War", as the Vietnamese refer to it. This inventory is not intended to be definitive but to sample a representative portion from each genre[1].

UNREPENTANT ADVOCACY – RADICAL/POLITICAL FILMS FROM THE AMERICAN UNDERGROUND AND INDEPENDENT SPHERES
"I was Angry about Vietnam and wanted to do something."
    – Emile de Antonio

The Vietnam War had a greater impact on media than any other war in history. It virtually invented political film-making and gave birth to the occupation of the renegade photo-journalist, where the photographer was much more than just a picture taker. The previous conventions of war reportage, established and strictly enforced during WW2, discouraged the media from broaching problematic social issues that might cast our nation in a poor light and give propagandistic ammunition to our enemy – and were now shattered. Suddenly the very basis of our Country's involvement was being attacked!

By the mid-60s the unquestioned sway and credibility that TV had in the '50s was starting to ebb. People who did not believe the mainstream media, and who saw film as a way to the truth, set out to be heard.

But this position of unrepentant advocacy also ran counter to the dogma of documentary that demanded *objectivity* – an "objectivity" that some claimed excluded analysis or political content. An objectivity that was a chimera. An objectivity that, said many leftists, was tantamount to passivity and even complicity. Or, as Alan Rosenthal, editor of *The Documentary Conscience* (1980), expressed it specifically in regard to Vietnam:

"The American networks never stopped talking about the War and examining the issues. The coverage was immense. Every night pictures of bombing and fighting from Vietnam. Every night Huntley, Brinkley and Cronkite with the latest reports. It was all being told, wasn't it? What more could one want? The answer was, everything... The problem of course is that 'hard news' reporting does not deal with history, context or analysis, but with chronicling events – and encasing them in a reassuring consensus perspective... But where was the report putting the War in a political context? Analysis was needed... When Saigon fell, none of the network footage could explain why."

The tenor of the times in this respect, from an underground perspective, is encapsulated in the April 21st, 1966 *Village Voice* column by New American Cinema spokesman, Jonas Mekas.

"With all the new techniques and equipment available to us, with almost weightless and invisible 8mm and 16mm sound cameras, we can go today into any place we want and put everything on film ...8mm movies should be shipped from Vietnam and from the [American] South, 8mm movies [should be] taken by 10 year old Harlem kids armed not with guns but with 8mm cameras – let's flash them on our theater screens, our home screens; 8mm movies smuggled out of prisons, out of insane asylums, everywhere.

"Why should we leave all the reporting to the press and TV?... let's swamp the Cinematheque [A NYC underground screening venue] with newsreels, home movie newsreels, not the Pathe Brothers newsreels, not the Walter Cronkite reports!... The time is here to change the ways of journalism on this planet Earth. The schools of journalism will soon replace their writing classes with 8mm movie-making classes... nothing should be left unshown or unseen."

If Mekas seemed to be calling for a virtual revolution in reportage, there was in fact an aspect of insurrection to this struggle for information, inasmuch as films could be, and routinely were, seized by the Customs and police for "aiding and

Year Of The Pig

abetting the enemy".

It was in this atmosphere of increasing radicalization that Mekas' compatriot, Emile de Antonio, made perhaps the best known film from an unapologetically leftist perspective, YEAR OF THE PIG, in 1969. A WW2 veteran, one-time member of The Young Communist League, ex-professor of philosophy and bohemian dilettante who hobnobbed with the likes of Warhol and John Cage, de Antonio's reasons for making the film were simple: "I was angry about

Vietnam and wanted to do something."

YEAR OF THE PIG is a mixture of footage which de Antonio culled from Czech, East German, and Soviet sources, among others, and interviews with a range of Vietnam experts such as journalists, politicians, philosophers and Buddhist historians. There is no omniscient commentary or voice over. At times situations and editing sequences are manipulated to make US officials appear villains or fools, but there is also much truth and poignancy in the film. Whatever it was, it certainly wasn't *cinéma vérité*, which de Antonio saw as a joke and a lie.

As de Antonio explained to Rosenthal in a 1980 interview; "The (mainstream) media never did anything substantial or critical. That was part of the greatest hype that the American people have ever suffered from the media. Every day we saw the War. Every day we saw dead Americans, dead Vietnamese, bombings... but never one program on why; never one program on the history of it; never one program attempting to place it in context. I wanted do do an intellectual and historical overview of the whole thing going back to WW2 and just before, then through the French experience down to the Tet offensive, which was where I finished the film."

Emile de Antonio despised the so-called "objectivity" of TV network reportage. "[They are] objective enough to be mindless, so that no sponsor or his grandchild should be offended...Life is bleached out."

YEAR OF THE PIG played widely on college campuses and in its own small way helped spark and fuel the anti-war movement. By 1970–1971 films were being made that would have been inconceivable a couple years before. Two films that represent this sharp anti-war shift, both from 1971, were INTERVIEWS WITH MY LAI VETERANS and THE SELLING OF THE PENTAGON.

The *cinéma vérité* style INTERVIEW WITH MY LAI VETERANS by Joseph Strick, presents uncensored interviews with American veterans of the My Lai massacre. Here images of clean-cut American boys talking with plaintive and uncoached directness about the notorious massacre was as shocking as any battlefield atrocity footage, and had an immediacy about it that transcended propaganda. It went on to win an Oscar for Best Documentary Short.

THE SELLING OF THE PENTAGON which Peter Davis made for CBS, was about the battle going on back home – the battle for public opinion. It dealt with the various types of pro-war spin the Pentagon was selling to the American public to keep them "on board".

WINTER SOLDIER (1972) was made by the Winter Film Collective and documents The Winter Soldier Investigation that took place in 1971 in Detroit. The WSI was a look into atrocities committed by American troops in Vietnam, and uses a range of techniques to document its findings. Images of intense, anguished, now long-haired young men are intercut with photos of them "before"; in crew-cuts and uniforms.

"Authenticity and horror", writes Amos Vogel in his 1974 book, *Film As A Subversive Art*, *"are built with small precise details. An American officer advises his men not to count prisoners at the beginning of their removal in American planes, only upon arrival. A woman is split open from vagina to neck. A small child is stoned to death for taunting the Americans... The effect of the testimonials is enhanced by the cross-cutting of color slides and live footage of*

Winter Soldier (and following page)

tortures, killings, bombings and burnings... far from being a horror show or propagandistic exercise, however, the film, by the very enormity of what it portrays, becomes a philosophical set piece..."

HEARTS AND MINDS, 1975, was Peter Davis's second film on the War. It was also posed from a clearly leftist perspective, although with a budget of $900,000-USD and studio backing from Columbia Pictures, it was certainly no underground film.

A central theme in the picture is how the virulent strain of Nationalism/Patriotism that had its roots in the Second World War led America into Vietnam and sustained its participation in the conflict. The film inter-cuts fighting and flag waving pageantry and maintains they are part and parcel, and that this aggressive form of patriotism has worked its way into the very fibre of civic and sporting life.

One key sequence bears upon a high school football game where machismo flies fast and thick and the coach of the losing team tells his boys to "keep fighting". The film follows up on such sequences with scenes of American-caused destruction in Vietnam.

Hearts And MInds

The final scene of a patriotic parade, in which a group of War protesters are jeered and attacked by the spectators, pounds its message home. The film, at least in parts, seemed heavy-handed and manipulative – and hence ineffective – to many, including de Antonio from whom Davis lifted some footage.

However heavy-handed and perhaps bombastic the film might have been, its linkage of patriotism to this aggressive machismo was prophetic, as the 1984 Los Angeles Olympics would prove. Here, at a sporting event supposedly dedicated to global fellowship, this virulent strain of American patriotism resurfaced in the form of a nationalistic frenzy or hysteria, an almost blind aggression.

HEARTS AND MINDS was distributed theatrically, but not by Columbia, which got queasy after a look at the final cut, although it ended up playing wide on college campuses.

SHAPING THE LEGACY OF THE WAR – DUELLING TV DOCUMENTARIES FROM THE EIGHTIES

"....This was a war we should have fought to win"
–Charlton Heston

As noted, television coverage of the War through the '60s and early '70s was immense but usually lacked the will to tackle controversial issues and grapple with unpalatable truths. Films like Eugene Jones' A FACE OF WAR from 1967 and others were good (if imperfect) films, but focused on the fighting men rather than the larger historical issues.

One notable exception was Felix Greene's INSIDE NORTH VIETNAM (1968), in which Greene largely avoided stock battle scenes to focus on the peasants who toiled ceaselessly to rebuild their homeland, only pausing when US aircraft fly overhead threatening new destruction. Girls working the fields one moment, the next firing machine-gun rounds into the sky, cut haunting figures.

By the early '70s a new kind of drug addict was turning up in large numbers on American streets – war vets hooked on heroin in Nam. Today the addicted, traumatized Viet Vet has become a crashing B-movie cliché, but then the situation was a shock to middle America, and the few films which addressed the issue – like the ABC-produced HEROES AND HEROIN (1971) – were highly controversial.

The more analytical programs that would place the War in a historical context – the kind of programs that so many complained were lacking in the '60s and '70s – finally began to arrive in the '80s with the ambitious, PBS-produced 13-part series entitled VIETNAM (1983). After all, the War had been over for years, the dust had settled and now it was time to get to the truth of it all, right?

The trouble was that Vietnam seemed to be one subject no one could be objective about, with conservatives and liberals even divided over where to locate the War's origins. As Thomas J. Slater writes in "Teaching Vietnam", a chapter in Michael Anderegg's *Inventing Vietnam – The War In Film And Television*: "conservatives locate the origin of the War in America's desire to protect South Vietnam from communism, while liberals tend to emphasize America's continuation of the failed imperialist efforts of The French."

These two interpretations were manifest respectively in VIETNAM, and in the two hour rebuttal, TELEVISION'S VIETNAM: THE REAL STORY produced by the conservative Accuracy In Media group and aired on June 26th, 1985, also on PBS.

VIETNAM, although thoroughly researched and seemingly objective, did tend to present a view of the War that conformed more to leftist perspectives: that the War was a quagmire inherited from the French, that the Tet Offensive was a disaster and that American forces were in chaos. An unflattering if not to say disturbing impression of William Westmoreland, commander of American forces, is presented. Appearing nervous and confused in front of microphones, he at one point unconvincingly laughs off an audible explosion in the background as a "test firing". That it probably was, but one gets the impression that the VC are at that very moment over-running the Army's main headquarters!

TELEVISION'S VIETNAM; THE REAL STORY, produced by Peter C. Rollins for AIM, also presented Westmoreland, but in an (postwar) interview looking

Girl soldier; *Inside North Vietnam*

comfortable, relaxed, in-charge and knowledgeable as he reclines in a leather-upholstered easy chair. A completely different impression emerges.

Charlton Heston, *aka* Moses and Ben Hur and today patron saint of arch conservative causes like the National Rife Association (NRA), etc., is employed as an on-screen narrator in TELEVISION'S VIETNAM as well as in AIM's companion follow-up program, TELEVISION'S VIETNAM: THE IMPACT OF MEDIA, which focused on reportage of the Tet offensive. He claims that Tet was a major defeat for VC forces, which by any standard it was, but other assertions challenge credibility. At one point, over footage of the evacuation of Saigon in 1975 and subsequent images of "North Vietnamese brutality", Heston asserts that "After seeing the horrible consequences of communist rule in Indochina – the holocaust in Cambodia and the flights of the Boat People from Vietnam – Americans came to recognize that this was a war we should have fought to win." Heston recites some stock conservative wisdoms here; that there was a military victory there to be had in the first place, and that America was fighting a War "with one hand tied behind its back".

As Rollins himself stated in a prologue to VIETNAM: THE REAL STORY, the truth about Vietnam probably resided somewhere between the original PBS and AIM accounts, and viewers would have to make up their own minds.

FILMS FROM THIRD PARTY COUNTRIES
"Vietnam is positive it will win the War, for it is a People's struggle"
-THE THREATENING SKY by Joris Ivens

The Vietnam War not only affected America and Southeast Asia, but virtually the whole world in a way that no regionally contained war ever has or ever will. It was the cold war flash-point that caught fire, pitting America against the Communist world for whom it became an agent of unification. It was used to demonize the US around the world and instilled a generation of young Western Europeans with a reflexive anti-Americanism that is still in evidence today. And it affected other third party countries, like Australia and Canada, who contributed troops back in the early '60s when it was still officially a UN "police action".

The War simply dominated all discourse for a decade.

WW2 has been called the last "good war", the last clear struggle between good and bad, between right and wrong. But for many of the foreign journalists, film-makers and photographers who covered Vietnam, there was nothing particularly complex or ambiguous about it – they had no doubt this was a struggle between good and evil. But even though the variety of films produced abroad often predicably took a critical stance on American involvement, they do represent a multiplicity of approaches and perspectives, from radical leftist polemics and atrocity-filled front line reports to diary-style coverage of the lives of the men in the field, and to the eventual journeys back a quarter century later in search of closure.

France already had a long history of bloody conflict with Vietnam, and while it was now in the '60s officially an American alley and NATO member, it did have large leftist and student movements which were energized to action by the War. Films were made.

Two films of French origin from 1966, THE ANDERSON PLATOON and VIETNAM, LAND OF FIRE, are notable.

THE ANDERSON PLATOON, a French and US co-production by Pierre Schoendoerffer was a highly regarded documentary that, like other documentaries such as the previously mentioned A FACE OF WAR, focused on the soldiers themselves, portraying them both as heroes and victims of forces beyond

Far From North Vietnam

their control. We see the troops of the Anderson platoon living, fighting and dying. The film won the Oscar for "Best Documentary".

VIETNAM, LAND OF FIRE (creditless) was a mix of newsreel and documentary footage that portrayed the War as hell itself. One sees villages ablaze, charred corpses, grievously injured children and the effects of Napalm and other poisonous chemicals. VC resistance is also shown.

An avowedly political film from the French left was FAR FROM NORTH VIETNAM (LOIN DU VIETNAM), 1967, a composite anti-war invective made by Alain Resnais, Agnes Varda, Jean-Luc Godard, William Klein, Joris Ivens and Claude Lelouch. It was produced by Chris Marker through the film cooperative he founded in 1967 to make political films, SLON (Société pour le Lancement des Oeuvres Nouvelles).

In 1972 Jean-Luc Godard and Jean-Pierre Gorin made the spartan LETTER TO JANE in response to the famous photograph taken of the actress during her controversial visit to North Vietnam. The photo shows her expressing concern as she stands amid a group of North Vietnamese.

Godard and Gorin criticize her attempts to serve The Cause. This "revolutionary statement" of hers, in their eyes, is suspect. The screen simply shows a series of still photographs moved about by hand, while in conversational tones, Godard and Gorin utter monotone criticisms and observations. They continue to speak when the screen goes blank, apparently now speaking directly to the viewer. There is no camera movement, no actors, no other action.

They comment on formalist aspects of the photograph; the composition of the figures, the focus and the expression on Jane Fonda's face. Stills from old war movies starring John Wayne and Henry Fonda are displayed and the film-makers point out the remarkably similar expressions of concern on the faces of

Jane Fonda in *Vietnam Journey: Introduction To The Enemy*

the two actors. Is Jane's expression a manifestation of genuine concern, or is it merely another enacted scene in the litany of Hollywood moviestar set-ups that all three have made their lives' work?

Undeterred, Fonda returned to the States and co-directed the documentary VIETNAM JOURNEY: INTRODUCTION TO THE ENEMY (1974), in collaboration with Haskell Wexler[2] and Tom Hayden.

Joris Ivens, the highly respected and very political Dutch documentarian (a committed leftist since the '50s) who collaborated on FAR FROM NORTH VIETNAM and traveled extensively behind the Iron Curtain, made a number of films about the War. THE THREATENING SKY, from 1965, was his first and was intended as a pure piece of agitation. In his own words, "This film shows how the Vietnamese people resist with heroic strength against the criminal aggression of the Americans. Vietnam is positive that it will finally win the War, since it is a People's struggle."

He made two other films about the War in 1968, THE PEOPLE AND THEIR GUNS and THE 17TH PARALLEL. THE PEOPLE AND THEIR GUNS, made with the French SLON collective, is described by Amos Vogel as "perhaps the purest Western example of a Maoist film, a heavily didactic 'agitprop' portrayal of Laos' struggle against American imperialism." THE 17TH PARALLEL was perhaps his best known film on the Vietnam War and came with a predictably anti-American slant intact. Other films made by Ivens about the War include LA GUERRE POPULAIRE AU LAOS and RECONTRE AVEC LE PRÉSIDENT HO CHI MINH, both from 1970.

Canada, for its part, had an activist documentary tradition, a government at odds with (and supposedly independent from) America policy – and a growing expatriate community of American draft dodgers. The topic was ripe for examination.

MILLS OF THE GODS, made in 1965 by a Canadian documentarian, Beryl Fox, for CBC (Canadian Broadcasting Company) was one of the boldest and most insightful early reports on the War and one of the very few helmed by a woman.

Fox, who came from a working-class socialist background in North Winnipeg, expressed a desire to go to Vietnam at a time when it was almost unthinkable for a woman to infringe on the exclusively male domain of war reportage. She had read about the conflict and became interested in how civilizations were effected by wars.

Initially she was accompanied by photographer Eric Durchmed, until he was called away on another assignment, and from there-on-in she shot the film by herself or with the occasional "pick up" cameraman. She found herself largely free to go out on small forward patrols beyond the reach of PR liaisons. She placed herself in danger, but she got "the story".

The result was a movingly photographed film about the harrowing nature of war, an objective yet committed indictment of its senselessness. In one particularly disturbing scene we see an American pilot gleefully describing one of his napalm attacks. He glories in his hits as he looks down from his plane at "the running ants below and the toy grass houses going up in flames".

MILLS OF THE GODS was broadcast on public television, but only after being prefaced by a disclaimer that it did not reflect the views of NET (National Educational Television).

"Some years later," Fox would relate in a 1980 interview with Alan Rosenthal, "I met an American woman who told me she'd seen MILLS OF THE GODS at a time when she was trying to figure out how to relate to her own country. After seeing the film, she and her husband decided to move to Canada. When I heard that, I thought, 'my gosh...to have that kind of effect on people's lives is the ultimate. That's what people make films for. That's what it's all about.'"

Fox would go on to make two more films about the War: SAIGON, for CBS in 1967, and LAST REFLECTIONS ON A WAR in 1968, which was about Bernard Fall, a noted war correspondent who was a good friend and guide to Fox in her first days in Vietnam and who died there.

Although he was born in Australia and educated in the US, at Stanford, Michael Rubbo made two outstanding films about the War for The National Film Board of Canada, SAD SONG OF YELLOW SKIN, in 1970, and STREETS OF SAIGON in 1973.

SAD SONG OF YELLOW SKIN, shot in Vietnam in 1969, eschews familiar battlefield footage of patrols, helicopter attacks and devastated villages and instead aims to present a more textured picture of everyday life in Saigon. We see the back streets, dingy rooms, crowded markets and pitiable street children of a city in upheaval. In one scene we view a young Vietnamese soldier visiting his family on leave. A watchful Army minder hovers nearby, listening to every word. With quiet but telling human moments like this, Rubbo avoids overt politicking or the shocks delivered by atrocity footage. Although he was adamantly against what the US was doing in Vietnam, he also met Vietnamese in Saigon who "really feared being regimented into some society that might be like Czechoslovakia after 1968". He found "the truth" was a complicated proposition. Much of the radicalized Left didn't much like the film though, thinking it was too soft, but it played widely.

The Left liked THE DEMONSTRATION, shot by the respected World In Action film group in 1968, a lot more – but the American Networks didn't, and despite its quite straightforward treatment of an anti-war demonstration outside the American embassy in London, refused to broadcast it. As the War progressed, the American Networks became increasingly more conservative in what they would show and how they would depict the War, hence some of the most interesting documentaries were the earliest.

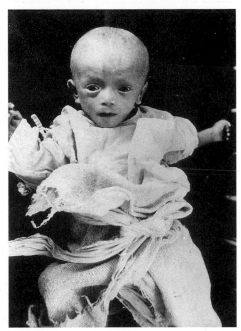

Vietnam And Kampuchea 79

After the War ended in 1975, documentarians were freer to explore it in a less politically charged environment. One example of this was VIETNAM AND KAMPUCHEA 79, a Danish production directed by Ib Markwarth for Telefilm Company. It surveyed the state of things four years after the Americans were forced to push choppers off their battleships.

Using some exceptional and often startling Vietnamese archive footage, the Danish team also filmed in Hanoi, Saigon and Phnom Penh, interviewing prostitutes and addicts off the street as well as high ranking government officials. They also filmed in the border areas by China and Thailand where armed rebel groups continued to destabilize the region. Films like this showed that Vietnam's social and political fabric had been damaged by the War just as badly as the land itself. (The popular wisdom goes that Vietnam "Won the War but lost the peace", yet how many countries could survive the instability wrought by ten years of pummeling by the World's greatest super-power, let alone immediately thereafter transform themselves into any kind of prosperous model democracy? Accusations that Vietnam had not succeeded to do this, and that it somehow impinged on the legitimacy of their victory, can only be considered disingenuous at best.)

The British film, VIETNAM AFTER THE FIRE, directed by J. Edward Milner in 1988 for Channel Four, was another such look at the grievous postwar situation. The film surveys the awesome destruction visited upon the land and the toxic poisoning that still lingered 20 years later. Mines, unexploded bombs, dioxins... one is left to wonder whether the Vietnamese flora and fauna will ever recover. The human tragedy is no less overwhelming: 1 in 5 Vietnamese babies are born deformed or handicapped due to the residual effects of Agent Orange and other teratogens.

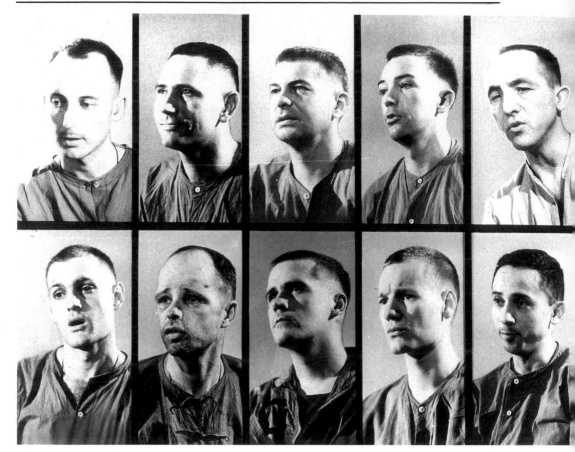

Pilots In Pyjamas

East block countries, East Germany in particular, produced plenty of films on Vietnam. East German film-makers, Gerhard Scheumann and Walter Heynowski, were responsible for quite a few documentaries about the War, the best known of these being PILOTS IN PYJAMAS from 1968. Their other films include THE DEVIL'S ISLAND (1976), about a famous NV prison Island, THE FIRST RICE AFTER (1977), I SINCERELY REGRET (1977) and THE IRON FORTRESS (1977). Another East German film-maker, von Richard Cohn-Vossen, made two pertinent titles in the mid-60s; THE BALLAD OF THE GREEN BERETS and ROBERT JACKSON ACCUSES.

In 1984 Wolf-Eckhart Bühler made AMERASIA about black American vet, John Scott, who attempts to return to Vietnam for closure. While waiting in Bangkok for his visa to come through, he ends up at a Christmas party in a small bar in the City's red light district. To his amazement he discovers his fellow patrons are all Americans; mercenaries, CIA-agents, ex-GIs. Scott becomes intrigued by these men who chose to never return to America. Disturbed and curious, he seeks them out in the bars and brothels of Thailand, on the beaches, in the slums and in the rice paddies, to get their stories.

In 1987 von Günter Giesenfeld shot HAI TAM RELATES (HAI TAM ERZÄHLT), a docu-portrait of the peasant, Hai Tham, and his home province of Thai Ninh in the South – perhaps the area most intensely targeted by American chemical weapons. A district of fallow rice paddies, erosion, contaminated rivers as well as record rates of stillborn births and deformed babies is revealed.

Two recent films from (now unified) Germany show how the residual effects of the War are still being felt. GOODBYE VIETNAM, from 1999, traces the journey of the director, Phan Van Sylviane, back to Vietnam where she was born, and confronts issues of culture and identity so often faced by those of mixed race parentage.

DO SAHN – THE LAST FILM, (1999) by Hans-Dieter Grabe is the story of the Vietnamese man, Do Sahn, who in 1970, at eight years of age, was seriously injured in the War and brought aboard the German hospital ship, Hegoland. After undergoing various treatments over the next five years in different German hospitals, Do Sahn returned to Vietnam. For the next twenty years he led an existence as a rickshaw driver, a junkie, an odd-job laborer and a beggar – to eventually die of AIDS on April 30th, 1996, one more innocent victim of the War.

As noted, many of the recent documentaries about Vietnam are journeys back in time and memory by those seeking answers, meaning, closure. SHELL-SHOCKED, by Australian, Stephen Ramsey, is one such film.

In this hour-long documentary that includes much old home movie footage of the War, Ramsey follows four Australian veterans as they travel back to Vietnam in an attempt to heal old psychic wounds. Their arrival back in Vietnam, a place that had such a devastating impact on their lives, causes an extreme range of emotions. A reunion with some their old enemies concludes the film, and we realize that they too are suffering from post traumatic stress syndrome.

FILMS BY THE AMERICAN MILITARY
"The highest survival and return-to-duty rate of any war in history"
–ARMY MEDICINE IN VIETNAM, 1967

While the American military would seem to lack objectivity when it came to Vietnam (to say the least), the films they themselves made on the War possess an inadvertent documentary quality if only because they accurately depict the official thinking and approaches of the day. In many ways, in fact, military films might be the most revealing of all *due* to the absence of any pretense of objectivity. And the passing of time has only rendered them all that much more transparent. The many hundreds of military films made about Vietnam divide up into those "restricted" films shown to specific groups of relevant military personnel, and those shown to general audiences in the cause of influencing wider public opinion. Of the five broadly representative films I shall examine here, WHY VIETNAM? and VIETNAM, VIETNAM belong to the latter category.

WHY VIETNAM? produced in 1965 by The Department Of Defense, was intended to make the escalation of the War in Vietnam acceptable to the American public. It based its arguments on "the Domino Theory", which was popular at the time. The theory was predicated on the assumption that if one country in a region "fell" to communism, others would fall.

VIETNAM, VIETNAM, in turn was produced about the same time by The United States Information Agency (UISA) exclusively for screenings outside North America, and was directed by an elderly John Ford. Alan Rosenthal writes in *The Documentary Conscience*, that it was "so highly distorted and extreme in its views that it became an object of ridicule and was eventually withdrawn from circulation."

If most films about the Vietnam War were horror stories full of death and destruction, VIETNAM VILLAGE REBORN was a happy and upbeat exception that even came complete with clowns and ice cream.

Produced for The Office of The Chief of Information by The Army Pictorial Center in 1967, this 28-minute film focused on the problem of so-called "infected" villages – villages that might be harboring or aiding VC.

An officious narrator in suit and tie explains the need to win over these villages, or to use the famous expression, to win the "hearts and minds" of the villagers. The viewer proceeds to witness how special psychological units of the First Infantry Division "secure" the village of Lam Son II.

First we see the village secured by troops. All the men except young boys and the elderly are loaded into a truck to be interrogated. The truck drives away. Then the villagers are given free health check-ups and inoculations (doling out free medical care was seen as a standard issue tactic in winning over the confidence and sympathy of villagers). After that, a food tent is erected and it's time to eat.

Later the troops set up a circus in the village. Kids get ice-cream. There's a clown...and even a rock band. Lots of probably coached shots of grinning if somewhat bewildered kids and villagers, as canned up-tempo music plays. But this only enhances the vague forboding the viewer might well feel at this point, since the truck load of men never comes back. And seen today, through the prism of what we know transpired in other isolated, rural villages like May Lai, the feeling one gets from this film is hardly comforting.

ARMY MEDICINE IN VIETNAM, a 27-minute film made in 1967 by The Department Of Defense and the Army's Walter Reed Hospital, had the same up-tempo sense of "can do", but was a very different side of the coin. The film was only to be viewed by medical personnel, particularly those on their way to Vietnam, and to prepare them for things they would never see in a modern, Western country. Things they would only see in a primitive, impoverished, "backward" country with health standards from The Middle Ages, as narration intones, a country caught up in an intense war. Not until the Afghanistan war in the '80s, when Kabul itself came under intense rocket attack, would doctors see the quantity and variety of injuries that Vietnam offered. To the dispassionate medical professional, then, Vietnam was a kind of horrible wonderland or museum exhibit, and at the end of the film we even take a detour into a leper colony that has nothing to do with the War. Here we see advanced leprosy victims, one of whom is a man with a hole in his head where his nose once was.

Modern American emergency medical technology is praised as something that's enabled the Army to achieve "the highest survival and return-to-duty rate of any war in history", the narrator brags as we see a soldier receive

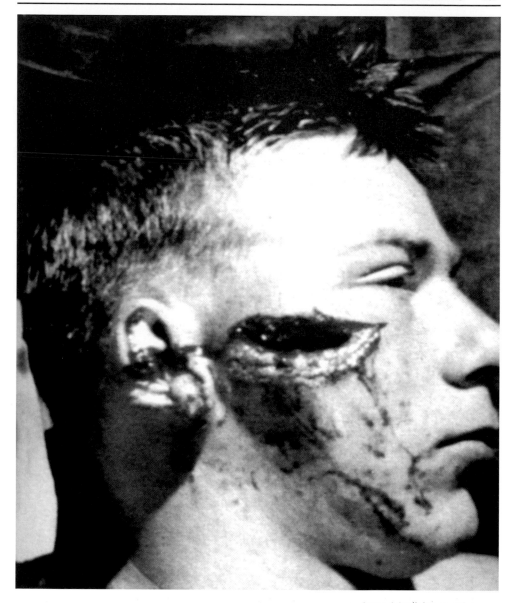

Army Medicine In Vietnam

treatment for a vicious gash across his face and hear that within a week he'll be back on the front lines.

The optimism exuded by the happy background music and the boastful narration is set in brutal counterpoint to the close-up Technicolor images of shattered, burned and bleeding bodies. We are treated to unwatchable scenes of skin being peeled off a severe burn victim, a bullet being extracted from an eye, a completely shattered face being rebuilt and the bloody stump of a leg being amputated. And if the somewhat eerie monotone narration is to be believed, this

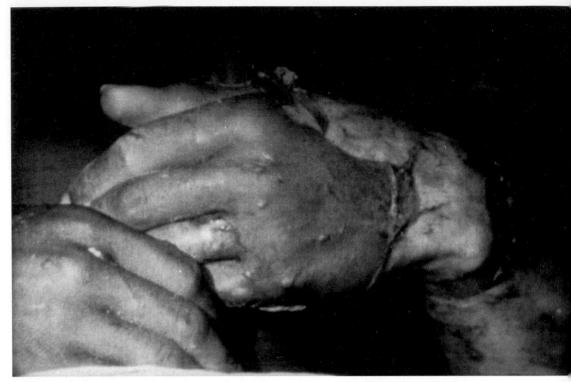

Army Medicine In Vietnam

is a *success* story we're watching.

The film was circulated to other NATO countries and continues to be shown today. This writer has encountered many Danes who saw the film while doing their compulsory military service. Amos Vogel, the author of *Film As Subversive Art*, called it "unquestionably one of the goriest, bloodiest, most explicit films ever made". And according to a German who served as a medic in his country's military in 1974, it turned his whole platoon into committed pacifists. In fact, it might just be the best anti-war film ever made.

KNOW YOUR ENEMY – THE VIET CONG, from 1968, was an 18-minute installment of the KNOW YOUR ENEMY Series initiated during WW2, and comes the closest to orthodox documentary form of any of the films discussed in this chapter.

A man sits in a projection room surrounded by spools of film, giving us the impression he is in a film archive, and prepares to roll a film as he tells us we are about to meet the VC. The production is almost exclusively composed of captured VC footage. We see VC in the field, on patrols, standing over dead Americans recently caught in an ambush... as our narrator describes what we are seeing. We see an underground hospital, a clandestine printing press, Vietnamese saboteurs damaging train tracks and blowing up a bridge. And we see beautiful Vietnamese girls in traditional dress perform a welcoming dance for high ranking officials who have come to their village. Our narrator describes "the

Know Your Enemy – The Viet Cong

enemy" as resourceful, stubborn and committed, but they also appear to be quite human and the viewer is perhaps just as likely to feel admiration for them. It's an unintentionally sympathetic look look at a people fighting a guerrilla war. Possibly it was intended to give GIs a sense of respect for their adversaries, to give them the sense that they were fighting a worthy opponent. More likely, however, the intent was probably to highlight the dangerous cunning of the VC whose acts of sabotage and frequent ambushes are portrayed as "cheating" against Americans trying to fight a real war.

MADE IN VIETNAM – THE VIEW FROM THE OTHER SIDE
"A tribute to those who had fought for the hard earned victory in war..."
–Kong Kam Yoke on THE GIRLS OF NGU THUY

It often seems that the country that contributed the least to debate and reportage on the War was Vietnam itself, that other countries made films *about* Vietnam but that the country itself was voiceless. Postwar issues, for example, seem to be framed exclusively in an American context. The secondary effects of Agent Orange on American troops is an issue that has dominated the news in the West for over a decade, and one is left to wonder what happened to the people we were dropping Agent Orange directly *onto*. And while America makes better relations with Vietnam contingent upon the resolution of the 1,400 MIA cases still unsolved, little is said – or done – about the 300,000 Vietnamese MIA cases. 58,000 Americans died. Three million Vietnamese died. Even today over 2,000 Vietnamese are wounded or killed by unexploded ordinance from the War. Yet the American MIA cases still dominate news reports and have taken on an almost mythical significance.

If Vietnam "lost the peace", it also appears to have lost the postwar media spin. In fact, Vietnam produced a significant number of films about the various consequences of the War, through few of them have ever been seen in the West.

Vietnam's French colonial overlords introduced film to the country early on, but most of the movies were titles imported from the West. In 1938 a group of students and intellectuals called for more native films to be made in the Vietnamese language. In 1945 when war broke out with the French, Ho Chi Minh – recognizing the power of cinema as a tool of propaganda – actively began to promote the development of film. In March of 1953 he officially signed a decree declaring the establishment of a national cinema.

Throughout the course of the War with the French, which culminated in 1954 with victory at Dien Bien Phu, only war documentaries were made. Soldiers with photographic experience were recruited as cameramen and shot live-action reports from the front – processing the film right there in the jungles. A renowned Soviet film-maker by the name of Karman came to Vietnam during this period and collaborated with the Vietnamese on a 6-minute, color battlefield documentary entitled VIETNAM ON THE WAY TO VICTORY (VIETNAM TREN DUONG THANG LOI). It's considered to be the best film about the war of resistance against the French.

Over the course of the next two decades, as the UN "police action" turned into a war against America in 1964 and escalated, film production grew and diversified. Young Vietnamese were sent to film schools in Czechoslovakia, East Germany, China and The Soviet Union. In 1963 Vietnam established its own film school.

Film production was entirely State funded, quantity was regulated and subject matter was confined to agriculture, industry and the War. Documentaries, feature films and even animation films for children were produced. War films became the most popular due to their inherent drama and the strong sense of patriotism the Vietnamese felt at the time.

The Trees Of Miss Tham

Such patriotism was the subject of the beautifully photographed (black and white) melodrama based in reality, THE TREES OF MISS THAM, from 1967. The film tells the story of a beautiful and courageous young patriot who is assigned by village administrators to watch over the roads and supply routes of her home province. During an air-raid, the main road is cratered with bombs. Yet there is no alternative, the trucks must get through, and Miss Tham leads them forward – at one point even standing upon an unexploded, half-buried bomb to dampen vibrations so the rumble of passing trucks doesn't set it off. However overwrought its theme of patriotic self-sacrifice is, THE TREES OF MISS THAM exhibits a technical polish and commitment to dramatic narrative that few other North Vietnamese films possessed – and in any case, very few dramatic features were as yet being made.[3]

The death of Ho Chi Minh on September 3rd, 1969, led to a number of films about the revered Vietnamese leader, one of the best of them entitled simply HO CHI MINH, produced in Vietnam in 1970.

In 1971, one of North Vietnam's leading documentarians, Le Minh Thich, filmed GIRLS OF NGU THUY. A portrait of 37 girls from the coastal village of Ngu Thuy and their courageous participation in the War, the film took the top prizes at the North Vietnam Film Festival (The Golden Lotus) and the Leipzig International Film Festival.

A number of very tough and very poignant battlefield reports were made by the Vietnamese in the early '70s. THE BOMBARDMENT OF HANOI DECEMBER (1972) documents the Christmas bombing of the Northern Capital City. The bombardment was supposedly only directed at outlying industrial and strategic sites, but at least a couple of bombs fell on densely populated neighborhoods. BATTLE FOR THE HO CHI MINH TRAIL (1973) pictures in newsreel style the struggle to keep by-pass roads open so the heavily bombed Ho Chi Minh trail could stay in use. Several cameramen were killed in the making of this picture. Another film, RICE GRAIN IN THE BELT, was probably the first documentary shot in the trenches and tunnels of the South.

Despite the growth of cinema in the North, there were precious few films that did not somehow involve the War. In sharp contrast, films made in Saigon at this point were more influenced by the kind of films being made in Hong Kong, and were of a more superficially entertaining or escapist nature. They showed no trace of the War and usually dealt with the lifestyles of the wealthy city dwellers. War related documentaries were, moreover, handled by the American Military.

After the War and reunification of the North and South, film production was consolidated into two production centers; Giai Phong Films in Ho Chi Minh City (formally Saigon), and Vietnam Feature Film Company in Hanoi. Together they achieved an annual production of about 10 to 15 feature films, 12 cartoons and 50 documentaries.

This immediate postwar period was an interesting moment in Vietnamese cinema, for while the industry was still State supported, something called The Renewal Policy (Doimoi Policy) was instituted to give new freedom to film-makers and all artists in general. Films were no longer restricted to themes of economic production or war.

A kind of social realism came into vogue as film-makers were given the latitude to make pictures critical of the government and society. Issues of daily life were treated and the social ills of the day were depicted and occasionally criticized. A film like TO CONQUER THE PAIN (aka DIE QUALEN BERWINDEN), from 1979, for example, documented the plight of drug-addicted Vietnamese war veterans with a brutal if clinical realism and had no propagandistic thrust. Many of these addicts are plastered with tattoos of violent imagery which in the main consists of Nazi swastikas and symbols. It's a shocking, bizarre and not totally comprehensible glimpse into hardcore Vietnamese vet drug culture, and such a film would have been unthinkable in earlier times. Audiences felt that their concerns and realities were now being addressed up on the screen, and they responded enthusiastically. The documentary HANOI THROUGH ONE'S EYES (HANOI TRONG MAT AI) was another example of this new candour.

But the harsh realities of the War could not be erased, and films like THE LATE HERITAGE (1983), which documented the devastating consequences of American chemical warfare in the South, continued to be produced.

Despite the desire of the Vietnamese people (60% of whom weren't even born when the war ended) to get on with their lives and integrate into the global economy, the memory of the War still looms large, and calls forth mixed emotions that include sadness, solidarity and even nostalgia. Director Le Manh Thich, for his part, went back to the village of Ngu Thuy in 1997 and shot the 30-minute RETURNING TO NGU THUY, an emotional reunion with the surviving women of THE GIRLS OF NGU THUY which he had filmed almost three decades earlier. As Kong Kam Yoke, a critic & festival programmer from Singapore, writes, "It is a tribute to those who had fought for the hard earned victory in war and a reminder to all about the humanitarian values that helped to sustain the Vietnamese through all the pain and suffering."

CONCLUSION

The Vietnam War showed as no other conflict ever had the power of the modern electronic media. After all this, it seemed impossible that American could ever again fight a war "in secret".

By logical extension, that should be even more true today in our modern world of total access where every guerrilla group has its own web page, where rebel commanders give interviews over cell phones in the heat of battle, and where video camcorders have brought the concept of "no more secret spaces" a quantum leap forward.

It's not true, of course. The Gulf War showed us that. There reporters were, for the most part quite happily, relegated to cheerleader status. A war where it was frequently observed that the American military showed that it had "learned the lessons of Vietnam" and denied journalists access every step of the way.

Technology, by making the Vietnam War visible, also helped make the anti-war movement possible, but ultimately the Movement was the result of social and political forces. Technology alone guarantees nothing, and in fact the widespread tendency to assume that it makes "the truth" easier to obtain and understand is dangerous in and of itself. This attitude creates a more passive and gullible public, willing to believe the official news media outlets and hence prone to manipulation. The "official lines" swallowed wholesale during The Gulf War and Nato's attack on Yugoslavia bear witness to that. Back in the '50s people actually assumed it was illegal to "lie" on television. We've hardly grown more discerning.

Technology alone is not the answer. The human element remains paramount, and the activist role *film-makers* played in Vietnam and the effect they had in provoking the public to react stands as one of the main achievements of the era.

Was Vietnam the last transparent war? As more "secret wars" than ever dot the globe today (secret because we can not "get to" them or because we are indifferent to them), one has to think, maybe it was.

NOTES

1.   I would like to thank Erich Wagner of The Werkstattkino in Munich for research assistance and for extending an invitation to attend his pioneering series on Vietnam War documentaries, held at the theater in November of 1992. It was a glimpse at a body of film

CHAPTER 12
NO CIVIL
DISOBEDIENCE

The latter part of the 1960s saw the advent of a smaller, shorter-lived genre of Vietnam War-related cinema – the "peacenik/draft-dodger" movie, in which student anti-war demonstrations and ruses used by America's youth to avoid conscription were used as plot devices in films ranging from the underground to teen exploitation and arthouse productions.

Images of protest had first emanated from outside the States, in films such as **Far From Vietnam**, the 1967 French documentary production featuring work by Alain Resnais, Jean-Luc Godard and others (see previous chapter). Ingmar Bergman's **Persona** (1966) was also notable for featuring scenes (seen on a TV set) of the Vietnam conflict as a visual corollary to an actress's psychic collapse. But perhaps the most powerful and shocking single image yet to infiltrate the world's media had come in 1963 from Saigon itself, when a Buddhist monk named Thich Quang Duc made the ultimate statement – the taking of his own life. And this was no ordinary suicide – Thich Quang Duc killed himself by self-immolation, his cross-legged body soaked in gasoline and set ablaze. As he burned alive, the terrible scene was recorded on camera. Though not strictly a war protest – the monk was actually protesting about the ill-treatment of Buddhists by the then pro-Catholic governrnent in Saigon – this action served its purpose, drawing world attention to the troubled region. The Italian pseudo-documentary **Mondo Cane 2** (1963) includes a reconstruction of Thich Quang Duc's suicide (presented as actual footage). The suicide is also alluded to in another Italian production, Paolo Cavara's **The Wild Eye** (1967). This fictional film tells the story of a cameraman who travels the world looking for provocative subject matter to film; much of the movie is set in Vietnam and in Saigon. Here we witness scenes of terrorism and murder. One incident in particular – the police execution of a Viet Cong suspect – anticipates a real-life event from the following year which would prove to be the most shocking real-life image from Vietnam so far when it was broadcast on US TV. In Saigon in 1968, a VC suspect was shot in the head at point blank range, in the street, by South Vietnamese Police Chief Nguyen Ngoc Loan. The horrific news footage of the suspect collapsing dead with arterial blood arcing from his temple would become a recurring image of the horrors of the Vietnam conflict.

When the Monkees decided to feature an anti-war episode in their confused movie vehicle **Head** in 1968, they elected to include this footage in the sequence – thus establishing their desire to escape their pre-packed/clean teen origins and become "serious artists". Of course, this signalled the beginning of the end of their career. The rest of the "anti-war" sequence in **Head** briefly shows the band in Nam battle-dress, coming under fire before they emerge from a

Self-immolation of Thich Quang Duc [Associated Press]

bunker to find themselves onstage at a concert filled with screaming girls.

Meanwhile, World Boxing Champion Muhammed Ali had become America's most famous anti-war protester and "draft dodger". Ali refused induction into the army on the grounds that he was a black muslim and a pacifist, and therefore obliged to be a conscientious objector. When pressured, he gave the notorious retort: "No Vietcong ever called me nigger". In May 1967 Ali was stripped of his title and sentenced to 5 years in prison for draft evasion. David L Weiss, filming a documentary on the legendary boxer, titled it after Ali's quote; **No Vietcong Ever Called Me Nigger** was released in 1968.

The first American films to feature protest elements had emerged in 1967. Andy Warhol's **Nude Restaurant** was a typical production of the Warhol Factory in the mid-'60s. With cast regulars including Taylor Mead, Viva and Ingrid superstar, this slow-paced and overlong film features various situations, including some sexual action. The lead role of a young draft-dodger is taken by Julian Burroughs, who professes his anti-war sentiments in New York's Greenwich Village. Production assistant was Paul Morrissey, who the same year received a directorial credit for Warhol's **Bike Boy** and **Lonesome Cowboys**.

The same year saw an early, award-winning short (6-minute) film from Martin Scorsese, **The Big Shave**. A man goes into his bathroom to shave, and ends up slicing off the entire skin from his face and cutting his own throat in an avalanche of blood. End. This film is traditionally construed as Scorsese's negative comment on the Vietnam war – although it's not entirely clear why.

Another underground film-maker based in New York, Adolphas Mekas

Street execution of Viet Cong suspect [Associated Press]

(whose other notable films include **Hallelujah The Hills**), made **Windflowers** in 1967. Released in 1968, this tells the story of a young draft-dodger on the run from the FBI. The man is finally shot and killed by a rookie agent, showing that sudden death and snuffed-out youth were not only conferred upon those who actually shipped to Nam; the war also had its deadly effect on those back home, pervading every echelon of American society. **Windflowers** remains a bleak anti-war statement.

By 1968, student protests all across America were gathering momentum and mass, as draft-dodging gave way to a more militant form of anti-war activism, as mirrored by such hard-hitting independent films as Robert Kramer's **The Edge** (1968) and Art Napoleon's **The Activist** (1969), and also in the burgeoning, rock-driven "youthsploitation" market serviced by the likes of Roger Corman's **The Trip** (1967). This new intensified protest peaked at the Washington Peace Rally of October '68, the largest of its kind. A reconstruction of this rally features in the hideous **Forrest Gump** [see also chapter 7]. Furthermore – and much to the U.S. government's dismay –

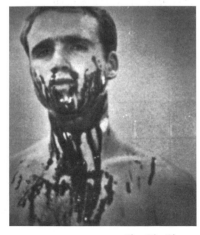

The Big Shave

Protest in Washington; *Winter Soldier*

many disgruntled, disillusioned and disabled Vietnam veterans were now joining in with protests of their own. These protests were recorded and later shown in documentaries such as **Winter Soldier** [see previous chapter]. Anti-war student protest footage was already being used in "mondo"-type films, such as **Mondo Hollywood** (1967).

1968 also saw the release of the first of two Vietnam-related films by a young Brian De Palma, future director of **Carrie**, **Scarface** et al. Both **Greetings** (1968) and its sequel, **Hi Mom!** (1969) feature early appearances by Robert De Niro, whose cinematic Nam connection would go on to encompass **Taxi Driver**, **The Deer Hunter**, and the later **Jacknife** (1989), in which he played an older vet still trying to come to terms with the war all those years later. In **Greetings**, De Niro plays Jon Rubin, a young film-maker living in New York. He and his two friends, played by Jonathan Warden and Gerritt Graham, are involved in draft-dodging – Warden's character has had his Army call-up, and is desperate to get out of it. Various ways include getting beaten up in a black bar, pretending to be gay, and pretending to be an ultra-fascist lunatic. We never actually find out whether he succeeds or not, because the film veers off in manic other directions. There are discussions of political assassination (more shades of **Taxi Driver**), scenes of drug-pushing (ditto), and several scenes of voyeurism and nudity; De Niro's character seems obsessed with getting girls to strip for his camera. Finally, De Niro is called up himself and tries the "right-wing lunatic" scam; it evidently fails, as we next see him in Vietnam, dressed in combat gear. At one point he comes under enemy fire. Old habits die hard though, and when he comes across a Vietnamese girl hiding in the bush, he immediately offers to film her naked.

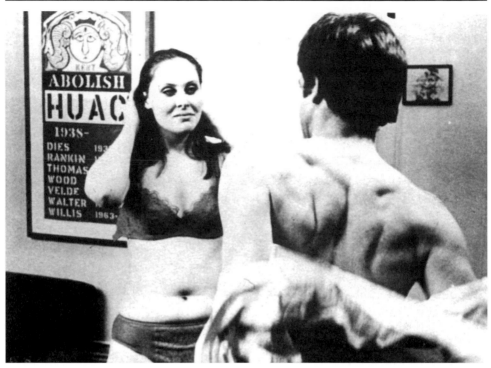

Greetings

The films ends with footage of Lyndon Johnson delivering a pro-war speech on TV. **Greetings** was one of three notable films released that year to include "in-country" scenes of the war (the others being **The Green Berets** and **Head**). De Palma and De Niro soon resurrected the character of Jon Rubin as a Viet vet in **Hi, Mom!**, a year later [see chapter 7].

Draft-dodgers feigning homosexuality was also the subject of Bruce Kessler's self-explanatory **The Gay Deceivers** (1969), which featured Jack Starrett as a hypocritical Army Colonel. Starrett, a key actor/director on the Hollywood B-movie scene, also directed the Viet vet/biker conflation **The Losers** and the Viet vet/blaxploitationer **Slaughter**; he acted in both **Born Losers** and **Angels From Hell**, and later appeared in **First Blood** as an antagonistic lawman who gets blasted out of the sky by John Rambo. As a call for gay rights, **The Gay Deceivers** was somewhat ahead of its time, and subsequently failed to receive due recognition.

Meanwhile, underground film-maker Kenneth Anger was another visible anti-war spokesman. He publicly expressed disdain for the war in a 1967 interview – dismissing it as "the establishment's way of masturbating young boys' violence" – and in 1968 was a noted presence at the huge Washington peace rally. In 1969 he finally conveyed these feelings in one of his films – **Invocation Of My Demon Brother**.[2] Compiled largely from cutting-room fragments of Anger's lost/stolen/aborted 1966 project **Lucifer Rising, Invocation** is a complex work with many strands and motifs, one of which comprises repeated footage of some young US marines jumping from a helicopter into Nam (other motifs

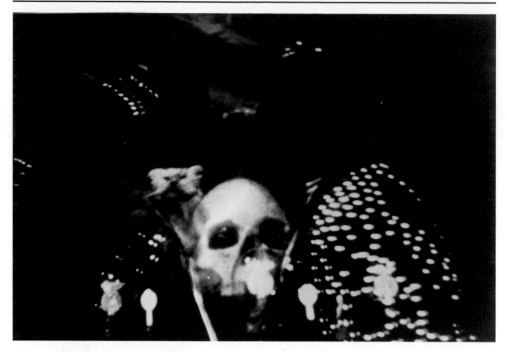

Invocation Of My Demon Brother

include the Rolling Stones playing live at Hyde Park, and Anger himself as a magus involved in a magickal ritual). The Nam footage is clearly seen only two or three times, but is actually present, subliminally, throughout the 10-minute duration of the film.

Driven remorselessly by an abrasive, repetitive moog synthesiser motif (by Mick Jagger), **Invocation Of My Demon Brother** resonates with an atmosphere of violence, negative energy and potential death. Its looped images of young Americans leaping to almost certain annihilation purvey abject futility, an endless cycle of waste and destruction. Through this, its dark charnel imagery and its other connotations of murder (the Stones remind us of the Altamont Festival, where a spectator was stabbed to death by Hell's Angels, while the presence of Bobby Beausoleil – Lucifer in the original **Lucifer Rising**, and Anger's former housemate – evokes the grim spectre of Charles Manson), Anger's film remains a haunting epitaph for the '60s.

Student activism came to the fore in variable quality 1970 feature films such as **Getting Straight**, **The Strawberry Statement**, **RPM**, and Jack Nicholson's directorial debut **Drive, He Said**, reaching a delirious, obscure and explosive artistic zenith with Michelangelo Antonioni's **Zabriskie Point**. Protest also featured in much of the rock music of the late '60s, and the film of 1969's festival **Woodstock** features two outstanding examples; Country Joe and The Fish peforming their anti-war "Feel Like I'm Fixin' To Die Rag" and, most poignantly of all, Jimi Hendrix giving his legendary, ironic electric feedback rendition of America's National Anthem, the "Star-Spangled Banner". But the most high-profile protesters of 1969 were, without a doubt, the newly-married

Jimi Hendrix in *Woodstock*

John Lennon and Yoko Ono, whose series of anti-war "bed-ins" grabbed the world headlines. **Bed-In** (1969) is Lennon's own film record of the protests, which included week-long bed sessions/political discussions in Montreal and Amsterdam. The film also features the Plastic Ono Band performing Lennon's seminal anti-war song "Give Peace A Chance", and other numbers.

It was Dennis Hopper who had first grasped the full potential of annealing a psychedelic/revolutionary rock soundtrack onto populist counter-culture cinema in **Easy Rider** (although his precursor was Kenneth Anger who, in 1963, had tracked his homoerotic underground biker classic **Scorpio Rising** with contemporary pop hits). Hendrix, the Byrds, Steppenwolf and The Electric Prunes were just a few of acts to feature in Hopper's biker classic, and this trend continued in the likes of Richard Crawford's **Captain Milkshake** (1970, in which a GI on leave from Nam experiences dope-smoking, free love and protest before returning to die in battle) and **The Strawberry Statement**, finding its apogee in **Apocalypse Now**'s stunning deployment of the Doors' "The End" before descending into cliché (cf. **Forrest Gump**). Meanwhile student anti-war activism in the States – and elsewhere in the world – had gradually increased to the point where violent riots, in which a number of students were killed by police, were becoming a common occurrence[1]. Scenes of extreme police brutality against protesters would be used to shock in such films as Sheldon Renan's **The Killing Of America** (1981). This documentary on US violence and murder also utilised, once again, the by now infamous Vietnam street execution footage from 1968 – which by then had become, along with the Zapruder Kennedy assassination reel, probably the most widely viewed real death – or "snuff" – sequence of all time.

Unflattering footage from Vietnam cropped up in a variety of similar documentaries, ranging from the relatively harmless (scenes of US combat troops getting stoned on marijuana in the porn-sprinkled pro-dope compilation **Aphrodisiac!** [1971]), to the hideous (burnt and napalm-disfigured Viet women and children in the notorious snuff compendium **Faces Of Death 2** [1981]). **Love** (aka **Mondo De Amore Cruel**, 1985) went one stage further, featuring a XXX segment in which returning Viet vets were shown as dog-fuckers, performing acts of unspeakable bestiality with their canine friends. Rosa von Praunheim's **Death Magazine** (1979), a compendium of images of death, also included scenes of barbarity from Vietnam such as severed heads impaled on stakes.

Considered even more heinous than draft-dodging or anti-war demonstrating, was the act of army desertion. Whether viewed as cowardice or the ultimate form of protest, this issue was generally deemed too sensitive to be covered in films of the early '70s, only surfacing in low-key entries like **Parades** (1972) or **AWOL** (also 1972). That same year, a Japanese director, Hiroshi Teshigahara – more famous for his outré SF-tinged films such as **Woman Of The Dunes** or **The Face Of Another** – broached the subject in **Summer Soldiers**, the story of American GI deserters living in Kyoto. Teshigahara examines the alienation of the soldiers, who struggle with a foreign language and culture. When one of the deserters is unable to have sex with a prostitute, his isolation and crisis of identity reach a nadir[3].

Back in the States, while draft issues continued to be covered in such worthy but sometimes dull feature vehicles as **Hail, Hero!** (1969), **Cowards** (1970), **Summertree** (1971), **Outside In** (aka **Red, White And Busted**, 1971), **Prism** (1971) and **The Trial Of The Catonsville Nine** (1972), 1970's **Explosion** was a more interesting proposition. A nihilistic exploitation picture, **Explosion** (original title: **The Blast**) starts with the tale of a would-be draft-dodger who is finally persuaded by his father to stay, enlist, and ship to Vietnam. He is very quickly killed in action. The man's younger brother flips out and runs away from home before he too can be drafted and blown to pieces in a strange country. On his travels he hooks up with a drifter (played by Don Stroud); they steal a car and head to Canada. The young kid starts to display symptoms of delusional

Explosion

psychosis, and it turns out that he was in any case exempt from the draft, due to mental problems. When a pair of cops catch the drifter stealing petrol, the young psycho flips again and blows the law officers away. The violence escalates to a bleak, detonative climax as the two rebels are finally killed in a hail of bullets. Freeze-frame. End.

It seems probable that daily TV exposure to the absolute violence and horror of war in Vietnam, gradually inured the sensibilities of late '60s America to the point where film audiences and censors alike could now endure much more graphic and realistic depictions of screen violence, as evidenced by the blood-drenched, bullet-riddled, almost orgasmic slow-motion climaxes to such "period pieces" as Arthur Penn's **Bonnie And Clyde** (1967) and Sam Peckinpah's **The Wild Bunch** (1969 – once described as "the **Citizen Kane** of the Vietnam era"). As this trend continued into the '70s, the horrifying massacre of Native Americans by white American soldiers shown in **Soldier Blue** (1970) was, for many, too close for comfort to the recent, real-life atrocities committed by US troops in My Lai. This, and similar films such as Robert Aldrich's **Ulzana's Raid** (1971) – another bloody tale of the white soldier's clashes with the American Indian – had suddenly acquired a new, disturbing allegorical resonance in the light of the Vietnam conflict. While not exactly protest films, these works had a lot to say about the rights and (mostly) wrongs of US foreign and domestic policy towards peoples of "other" ethnicity.

Last House On The Left

The first film to really transpose this new gruelling violence from a "historic" to a modern-day setting, was Wes Craven's ground-breaking **Last House On The Left**, in 1972. Based on Ingmar Bergman's **The Virgin Spring** but played out in an all-too-familiar contemporary American milieu, **Last House On The Left** was a landmark in visceral film-making. Eschewing the cartoon gore of **Blood Feast** and other '60s slashers, Craven's film was a bleak, terrifying study of rape, revenge and mutilation rooted in grim reality. The director later commented: "**Last House** was really a reaction on my part to the violence around us, specifically to the Vietnam War. I spent a lot of time on the streets protesting the war, and I wanted to show how violence affects people. It blew away all the clichés of handling violence. Before that, violence had been neat and tidy: I made it painful and protracted and shocking and very human. And I made the people who were doing the killing very human." In this sense, Craven's film can be seen as his own kind of protest movie.

But the protest movie to end all protest movies came not from America, but from Belgium. Burr Jerger's **General Massacre** (1972) is a rabid, bloody and perverted beast which resulted in Jerger being investigated by the CIA due to the sheer vitriol of its anti-USA, anti-militarist, and anti-Vietnam War sentiments. Jerger himself plays the General, a fascistic, racist, homicidal monster who makes Colonel Kurtz in **Apocalypse Now** seem like a boy scout. We soon see the General murdering his wife (in flashback), seducing and sleeping with his teenage daughter, and using live animals for target practice. Shockingly, real animals are killed in the movie, mondo-style, including a cow which is mercilessly riddled with bullets. Other shocking footage includes inserts of atrocity images from Vietnam, with shots of maimed or killed Viet Cong soldiers; also used is the

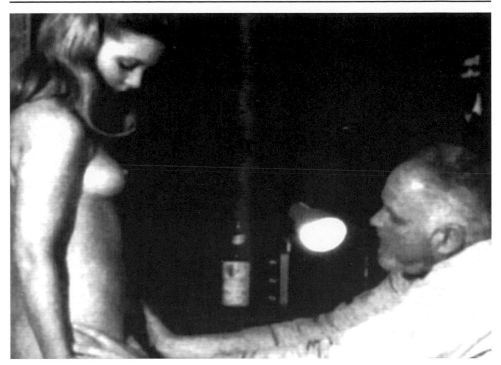

General Massacre

harrowing "bullet-in-the-brain" street execution sequence previously deployed by the Monkees in **Head**. Scenes of the General under interrogation reveal that he is a top ranking war criminal, guilty of butchering and raping Vietnamese women and children as well as annihilating scores of enemy soldiers. He sneers at the questioning of his black interrogator, calling him "nigger" and proclaiming that Vietnam should be levelled in a nuclear holocaust. It is hard to imagine a more hateful and extreme character, and Jerger's portrayal of him as typical of the US military was just too much to swallow. For this, as well as its animal cruelty, incest and bloodlust, **General Massacre** was long banned in France and fiercely proscribed by the US government.

1973 to 1975 saw, finally, the winding down of the Vietnam War. By the time Robert Kramer's anti-war **Milestones** (1975) – dedicated "to Ho Chi Minh and the heroic Vietnamese people" – was released, it was a dying gesture[4]. The short era of the protest movie, which had peaked with the unmatchable atrocities and blasphemies of **General Massacre**, was over, and the floodgates were about to open on a new deluge of movies both about the combat itself and about its physically maimed or psychologically damaged veterans.

NOTES

1.   One of the most notorious of these violent riots occurred at Kent State University, Ohio, on May 4, 1970. Four students were killed by police. The incident was exhumed and a political post-mortem performed in **Kent State** (1981), a powerful and disturbing film which shunned nostalgia in its direct reconstruction of events which had traumatized a

nation. Police brutality to protesters also spurred film activist Peter Watkins – whose **The War Game** (1965) had been a stark warning of nuclear war – to make **Punishment Park** (1971), in which he posited the US government setting up a vast concentration camp in the desert for the internment of dissidents, and in particular anti-war protesters.

2.   Other underground/experimental/avant-garde filmmakers aside from Kenneth Anger also dealt with Vietnam. Their works range from crude home-made "how to" films that show, for example, how to escape the draft on medical grounds by shooting yourself in the leg, to structuralist texts that deconstruct image and perception instead of bone and flesh. **Viet-Flakes**, an 11-minute film made by noted avant-gardist, Carolee Schneemann in 1966, belongs in the latter category. It was, in her own words, *"composed from an obsessive collection of Vietnam atrocity images I collected from foreign magazines and newspapers over a five year period.*

"Magnifying glasses from the 'Five and Dime' store were taped onto a borrowed 16mm bolex in order to physically 'travel' within the photograph – producing a rough animation. Images in and out of focus, broken rhythms and pans, the abstracted shapes and motions, speeding perceptual contradictions. For instance, a pointillism of falling black specs in focus becomes bombs dropping through the sky; an impressionistic swirl of tones translates as faces of US soldiers leading barefoot villagers from a gas-filled tunnel; a 'Rembrandt ink drawing' focuses in as a tank dragging a roped body..."

Stan Brakhage's **Song XXIII** (aka **23rd Psalm**, 1966/67), was his reaction to the advent of the Vietnam War, a film made up of TV news reports and footage, stock WW2 images, and poignant scenes of children playing war games.

War Stories, a 45-minute film made by Richard Levine in 1983, was, as critic J. Hoberman wrote in his January 24th, 1984 *Village Voice* column, "A War documentary unlike any other".

"Using footage supplied by both the American and Vietnamese governments, WAR STORIES could be called sumptuous were it not for the fact that its material successfully resists easy consumption. Levine's images resemble the Warhol or Rauschenberg silk-screens of 20 years ago (but even less slick), or maybe a color TV with a bad concussion. Every motion is looped at least a dozen times and submerged in a swirl of multiple superimpositions, with every layer tinted a separate color. Representation is pushed to its breaking point and yet nothing really obscures the iconography of stretchers and body bags, death and degradation that you read less with your eyes than with your gut..."

Far from the abstractionism and structuralism of the above-mentioned films are the reports on the War and its aftermath from very personal perspectives, but these films also very much belong to independent or "underground" film traditions. **Regret To Inform**, a first feature film made by American photographer, Barbara Sonneborn, in 1998, is one such example. Via a mixture of archival footage and interviews, Sonneborn seeks to examine the War's impact from a woman's perspective, introducing us to both American and Vietnamese War widows. She is herself one – her first husband having been killed in the War. Such documentations of personal journeys back to seek closure or understanding are numerous at the turn of the millennium [for other examples see Chapter 11].

(note by Jack Stevenson)

3.   One of the most popular destinations for US army deserters was Sweden. Several Swedish films were made which examined the problems faced by these fugitives living in a strange land, such as **Terry Whitmore For Example** (1969) or the docudrama **Deserter USA** (also 1969).

4.   A few nostalgia movies about the draft and protest era have appeared since – for example **Purple Haze** (1982), **Fandango** (1985), or **1969** (1988) – but seem pretty pointless. And films dealing with "grown up" draft-dodgers 20 years on – **Running On Empty** (1988), **Rude Awakening** (1989) – are equally out-moded.

APPENDIX 3

HARDWARE

CHAPTER 13
STICKS AND BONES:
WEAPONS TRAINING

1.

It has been stated that the cost of the United States' involvement in the Vietnam conflict was $159.42 billion. In radical contrast to this massive economic expenditure, the North Vietnamese peasant / soldier received monthly pay of $1 in 1964[1]. Such disparity gives an indication into the economics behind the conflict. The war was a confrontation between the might of the United States' industrial military machine and economic poverty of third world North Vietnam.

The American military, which represented a nation at the zenith of industrial-technological military power, was able to call on a vast range of weapons. During the early years of the war the soldier in the field was generally supplied with the M14 rifle capable of automatic and semi-automatic fire, but this was replaced by the M16. Initially designed for air-base security, the M16 gained a degree of notoriety amongst grunts as it was not suited to the field of combat; as one soldier stated, they "would jam if you looked at them wrong"[2]. They were eventually replaced by the M16-A1 rifles. Although both weapons were lightweight the extra ammunition the troops were required to carry in order to feed the rifles' powerful demands negated this advantage. Although outlawed by the Geneva Accord, many battalions also carried shotguns; as Mason wrote in his autobiographical account of the war: "The accords don't allow shotguns, either, but I know we have crates of them at our company for perimeter defense"[3].

But beyond the heavily armed and highly trained grunts, the military was also able to rely on numerous helicopters used to deliver squads to the combat zone and support them in the field. The US forces also relied upon B52 bombers, which throughout the war dropped nearly 8 million tons of bombs[4] on Vietnam. Somewhat notoriously, the military also used the incendiary Napalm, and the defoliant Agent Orange.

The People's Army of Vietnam (*aka* North Vietnamese Army) and guerrilla groups the National Liberation Front and the People's Liberation Armed Forces (*aka* the Viet Cong) were superficially less powerfully armed, generally using a combination of Soviet weapons (the AK47 and the Simonov SKS) and older weapons from World War 2, as well as captured American arms. However, the real strength of these guerrilla forces lay in their ability to devise home-made weapons and vicious booby traps. These ranged from simple mines (frequently constructed from abandoned American ammunition and undetonated bombs) through to trip-activated crossbow traps, heavy bamboo spiked balls, and Punji stakes – sharpened shit-smeared bamboo spears. These traps were responsible for

11% of US combat deaths and 17% of injuries between 1965 and 1970, and also had the added psychological effect on the morale of grunts who would not only have to contend with the dense forests but also with the knowledge that a misplaced step could be their last.

The primary strategy employed by the US military involved search and destroy missions whose aim was to "locate... pin down... then annihilate enemy units"[5]. The target would be bombed, the troops flown in by helicopter to secure an LZ (Landing Zone). The noise and mayhem would alert the guerrillas who would retreat – effectively vanishing into the thick foliage – leaving the American military frequently unable to locate the enemy. Worse for the American soldiers, was that the country, much of which was covered in dense rain forest, provided the guerrilla forces with the ideal terrain from which to mount ambushes – killing troops then fleeing back into the dense foliage, and often back into the networks of tunnels excavated beneath its mossy floor. Whilst the American military imagined the NVA and Viet Cong would – or could be forced to – stand and fight, the North Vietnamese forces had different plans and largely fought a secretive, guerrilla war.

American bombing missions – such as the massive Rolling Thunder campaign (1965–1968) which attempted to level key targets and the NVA's supply routes – were largely redundant, with few easily defined targets and with an increasingly well armed North Vietnamese population (who, as the war progressed, were provided with anti-aircraft weaponry by the USSR). Further, with many of the North Vietnamese peasants given light weapons and instructed to fire at aircraft, it could be argued that the bombing campaigns actually helped morale rather than break it[6]. As civilian casualties mounted it could even be argued that the US Military inadvertently encouraged the rural population to embrace the Communist North. Moreover, the excesses of the bombing sorties began to create negative propaganda in America, where television footage actually assisted in the growth of the anti-draft and peace movements[7].

The American military machine (and that of the South Vietnamese Army) relied upon skilled men working with highly sophisticated machines in an alien territory, and as a result forces were dependent on the movement of large quantities of ammunition, spares, machines and, of course, fuel. Here was a military machine that was, by necessity, beaurocratic, with clearly defined chains of command reaching back to the Pentagon. The military organizational structure was "designed for concentrated, mass, linear operations run from the top down"[8], which eventually "proved the self-defeating nature of centralization"[9]. Further, the young American grunts were, especially as the war dragged on, less interested in fighting a war that increasingly appeared unwinnable than in surviving the year-long tour of duty they were required to do[10]. This was in radical contrast to the ideologically motivated guerrilla force, which had literally nothing to lose. The North Vietnamese Army and the "Viet Cong" were fighting a true guerrilla war – using mines, traps, and spears as well as direct confrontation – in largely familiar terrain, and using that landscape to their advantage. Whilst still organized, the underground nature of the guerrilla groups allowed for a degree of autonomy that the American grunts did not have.

It was this cultural disparity between the ideologically driven guerrillas and NVA on one side, and the American army on the other side, that ended the war. Quite simply the American people would not tolerate the high number of casualties, both those sustained by the US military and, as evidenced by increasingly harrowing news coverage, those endured by the indigenous civilian population. In this war of attrition the North Vietnamese would not give up; the war had its roots in colonialism, and would continue until the country was liberated. What the American public initially believed would be a short winnable war was dragging into a decade-long apocalyptic quagmire. In the final analysis the cost – both in human lives and politically – was ultimately not worth America fighting for.

2.
*"The horror... the horror" – Kurtz, **Apocalypse Now***

In those films set within the Vietnam War (such as Francis Ford Coppola's **Apocalypse Now** [1979], Oliver Stone's **Platoon** [1986] and Stanley Kubrick's **Full Metal Jacket** [1987]); those set within a metaphorical Vietnam (such as Walter Hill's **Southern Comfort** [1981]); and those based around Nam vets in the years following the war (e.g. Ted Kotcheff's **First Blood** [1982], Steven Hillard Stern's **The Park Is Mine** [Canadian TV, 1986], James Maro's **Street Trash** [1987] and TV's *The A-Team* [series, various directors, 1983–87]), the depiction of weapons, and the relationship of the narrative protagonist and the cinematic audience to those weapons, is by necessity a complex one. Weapons and their use are portrayed with increasing degrees of symbolism and levels of metaphor not commonly seen within films located in the milieu of other wars[11]. The complex representation of weapons must be located within the apparent failure of a high-tech military in the face of the comparatively low-tech guerrilla forces; further, the relationship between the protagonists and their weapons reflects the crisis and dissolution experienced by many Americans in the post-war years.

In those films that locate their narrative directly within the grunts' experience of the conflict – most clearly **Platoon** – the weapons are largely presented naturalistically. The guns and ammunition are heavy, things can go wrong with rifles, and being shot at – and shooting – is shit-your-pants scary. The film seeks to emphasize a degree of authenticity, and succeeds in conveying this largely because of its basis in a form of autobiographical experience – the metanarrative around the film informed audiences that the director Oliver Stone was a combatant. **Platoon** also presents the use of an M16 barrel as a pipe for smoking marijuana; whilst certainly rooted in real events, this image suggests other uses of weapons, and the dope-smoking image can be seen as an oblique reference to the anti-war protests and hippies back in the USA (a flower placed in a gun barrel, for example). The image also serves to symbolise the 'moral' choice faced by the combatants.

Full Metal Jacket – like **Platoon** – focuses on the daily routine of grunts and appeals to a degree of authenticity, largely as a result of its lack of clear narrative flow and disregard for satisfactory closure – following a lengthy depiction of basic training the film ostensibly follows a day's fighting. There are no secret missions or special adventures here, it is not even clear if anybody within the narrative has "learned anything" from their experiences. However, **Full Metal Jacket** articulates a fetishistic relationship with the supremely phallic M16, especially during the training sequences where the recruits are told to sleep with their weapons and give them a female name: "You will give your rifle a girl's

Platoon

name because this is the only pussy you people are going to get. Your days of finger-banging ol' Mary J. Rottencrotch through her pretty pink panties are over!" The relationship with these weapons becomes increasingly muddy, as one of the recruits who has been bullied by the Drill Sergeant, uses his gun to kill his victimiser before turning it on himself – thus proving that there is a limit to the degradation that a grunt will endure during training. At the film's climax the gun-as-phallus becomes actualised, as the soldiers turn their weapons on a wounded female Vietcong guerrilla.

It is in an allegorical Vietnam War movie that the symbolism of weapons becomes most clear. In Walter Hill's brilliant **Southern Comfort** a group of National Guards spend an autumn weekend training in the Louisiana bayou. As the part-time soldiers walk through the countryside they jokingly open fire on a group of local Cajun fishermen, who dive into the water. What the locals are unaware of is that the squad are armed only with blanks; it is, after all, a training exercise. For the rest of the film the guardsmen are picked off one by one, hunted in the increasingly unfamiliar, alien landscape, and are slain by a variety of lacerating booby traps (which are based on actual traps used in Vietnam) by the locals, who clearly do not want the arrogant and bullish guardsmen invading their terrain.

    Southern Comfort's Vietnam allegories are emphasised by the presentation of weapons within the film – the guardsmen's guns are useless, firing only blanks – and the guardsmen are emotionally ill-equipped to deal with the guerrilla conflict being waged upon them by the Cajuns. Moreover, the bayou's residents clearly understand the terrain and the power of booby traps, both as killing devices and as a way in which to fragment the morale of the

Southern Comfort

troops. **Southern Comfort** also articulates the fear of patrol into the unknown – when it becomes apparent that they are being hunted the company begin to argue amongst themselves and their fear becomes increasingly palpable[12].

In the epic **Apocalypse Now** (which, like **Full Metal Jacket** used *Dispatches* author Michael Herr as one of its script writers) the representation of weapons and men-as-killing-machines take on a far more radical trajectory. The film locates its narrative less in the authentic experience of grunts than within a re-working of Joseph Conrad's novel *Heart Of Darkness* – the socio-political experience of the soldier in the combat zone is replaced by a secret mission that explores the very nature of humanity, man-in-conflict, and war. Whilst undoubtedly some scenes do evoke the actual experience of grunts and conflict, the film's battle sequences – some of the most remarkable ever filmed – evoke a glorious visual excess beyond the chaotic and terrifying claustrophobia of autobiographical experience. Moreover, as the film progresses the narrative increasingly emphasizes the descent into atavism of the protagonists. As the journey up-river progresses and "civilization" is left behind, so the protagonists embrace an increasing primitivism, the survival instinct igniting an increase in communication failure and social breakdown between the crew on the boat.

When the crew reach Kurtz's compound deep within the Cambodian rainforest, they witness a rag-tag group of soldiers who – under Kurtz's command

Colonel KIlgore; *Apocalypse Now*

– have become modern savages. The jungle fortress is littered with corpses and human heads piled on the stone ruins that form the encampment; Kurtz's troops stand in silence, their faces masked by mud and paint, and in their hands they hold spears and bows and arrows as much as military-issued weaponry. They have erased their training (and their humanity?), instead becoming pure atavistic savages. How else to fight the Vietcong? In a war in which hands are tied by rules and regulations it is only through the negation of these rules that survival can be guaranteed and the war can be won. The niceties of accords, conventions and rules of engagement make no sense when you are fighting an all-but invisible enemy knee deep in shit in the middle of the rain forest. Kurtz has become a target for the American Military precisely because he has embraced the darkness that lies at the heart of man.

Early in the film Captain Willard witnesses the apparently semi-crazed Air Mobile cavalry commander Lieutenant Colonel Kilgore and comments: "If that's how Kilgore fought the war, I began to wonder what they had against Kurtz... it wasn't just insanity and murder, there was enough to go around for everyone" – but there is a crucial difference between Kilgore and Kurtz. Kilgore has embraced war but he has embraced it from the perspective of the American military. He can call in the air-strikes, he may state he "loves the smell of napalm", but he also cares for his men and follows orders – the film shows his troops 'evacuating'

Colonel Kurtz; *Apocalypse Now*

Vietnamese peasants, a standard military manoeuvre. Kurtz however has no relationship with any objective other than pure war – his corpse-littered compound testifies to that. Kurtz has recognised that to win a war one must embrace "the horror". Indeed, Kurtz himself draws attention to the distinction between his own pure war and that experienced by the established order by describing the US top brass as "grocery clerks" and Willard as a "delivery boy".

To defeat Kurtz, Willard must also embrace this pure primal violence, this darkness. At the film's climax, when he finally goes to kill Kurtz, he rises from the river, his face dirty with camouflaging grease, born-again through his experiences in the war, on the journey up-river and, most of all, whilst imprisoned at Kurtz's compound. To kill the rogue commander, Willard descends into the same black miasma as Kurtz, and it is notable that his final method of execution is with a machete. Finally, guns are just too sanitized; they kill too clean; the killer too removed from the flesh of the killed to be a suitable bearer of the heart of darkness. The stabbing of Kurtz is mirrored in the cross-editing of the film with the bloody ritualised slaying of a cow: this is a method of destruction as old as humanity itself.

If the Vietnam War was lost because of the American unwillingness to accept massive casualties, and because the American military sought to fight a war of direct engagement rather than a guerrilla war, then Kurtz represents the

The Park Is Mine

possibility of a way in which the war could have been won – through transforming young men into an ultimate guerrilla force defined by unflinching cruelty and the embracing of a savage primitivism. To this end the use of spears, bows and arrows, knives, garrotting tools, torture and savagery represents the ultimate manifestation of the war in Vietnam – if you want to win, you have to go the whole way, and embrace savagery. This – the film suggests – is what war

– all war – finally is.

Whilst **Apocalypse Now** depicts a *becoming-atavistic* as the logical outcome of war pursed by all means necessary, it clearly locates this within a narrative that – in the end analysis – is largely liberal. In many subsequent movies the need to become a savage, and to embrace feral fighting techniques, and even creating Vietcong style booby traps has emerged as a recurring trope – as if through recreating the war, or conflicts based around the war, in which the American protagonists can utilise the guerrilla fighting techniques historically employed by the Vietcong, a new fantasy in which a victory emerges from defeat is possible. This is most clearly articulated in films such as **First Blood**, in which Vietnam veteran John Rambo, hiding in the American forests of the Pacific Northwest, employs vicious booby traps and the brutal combat techniques of guerrilla warfare against the American police force, still fighting a war "somebody would not let us win"[13].

The ability of the soldier to embrace his own savagery and to utilize the homemade weapons skills attributed to the Vietcong also emerged in the popular eighties television series *The A-Team*. The protagonists are a group of rogue American soldiers who have escaped an American prison (echoing John Rambo's crass sentiments that the soldier in the field was not allowed to win) in order to become 'morally centred' mercenaries nominally engaged in fighting criminals. With an entertainingly monotonous regularity the heroes would each week be captured by their foes and left locked in a garage or factory, and each week they would use their special forces-derived skills to create guerrilla style weapons and even rudimentary vehicles from the convenient 'scraps' that littered their temporary prisons. Whilst eschewing the overt right-wing politics of **First Blood**, and clearly aimed at a school-aged audience, *The A-Team* nevertheless embraced a similar cinematic pleasure in the presentation of heroes engaged in becoming a guerrilla fighting force.

Survival skills enabling the post-**First Blood** vets to turn even the most innocuous device or object into a lethal weapon becomes an almost satirical trait in exploitation films such as **The Park Is Mine** – in which a vet takes over New York's Central Park – and the gleefully lurid low-budget shocker **Street Trash** which features a *vet-turned-wino-king,* who is shown trapped behind enemy lines in a Vietnam flashback making knives from human bones.

If **Apocalypse Now** recognises the potential for violence as an absurd tragedy – the heart of darkness at the centre of man-in-conflict – then in **First Blood** and its ilk this ability to embrace cruelty becomes the way in which to win. It is not the failure of weapons or incommensurable fighting strategies, but the weak-willed liberals back home with no taste for cruelty that lost the war. **First Blood** et al create a universe in which victory emerges from becoming more-violent, more-cruel, more-cunning than the enemy. Although such uncritical fantasies were absurd, they fed directly into the political climate of the early eighties and Reaganism.

In these films – and others – weapons emerge as signifiers of the relationship between culture and conflict. Failing guns, carcinogenic Agent Orange, the difficulty of jungle combat, bobby traps, and the continual voyeuristic presence of television crews and photographs covering the whole grim scenario: it is no wonder that the Vietnam War becomes identified with a return to a dark, brutal, feral past in which the engines of modern military

Street Trash

technology are dinosaurs brinking on obsolescence and extinction. The atavistic nature of narrative protagonists is a way in which to address the dehumanising brutality of war. Emerging as a statement of humanity's potential for savage primitivism in the arena of war in **Apocalypse Now**, such violent atavism becomes, in subsequent heroic-vet movies, a way in which the war can finally be won by America.

NOTES

1.   The US Department of Defense estimate of $159.42 billion in 1975 has been subsequently challenged, not least by the American Friends Service Committee who suggested in 1979 that the cost could be as much as $274.7 billion (source: James Pinckney Harrison, *The Endless War: Fifty Years Of Struggle In Vietnam*, Free Press, Collier Macmillan Publishers, London, 1982).

2.   Gerard J. DeGroot, *A Nobel Cause? America And The Vietnam War*, Longman / Pearspon Education Limited, Harlow, 2000, p.282.

3.   Robert Mason, *Chickenhawk*, Corgi Books, London, 1984 (1983), p.147.

4.   See Gerard J. DeGroot, *A Nobel Cause? America And the Vietnam War*, p.183.

5.   Gerard J. DeGroot, *A Nobel Cause? America And the Vietnam War*, p. 146.

6.   The German bombing of Britain, for example, in the Second World War actually served to increase the morale of the public, and is now constructed as one of the defining moments of 'Britishness'. The relationship between the rural peasant population and the guerrilla forces is defined in graphic detail in Mason's *Chickenhawk* (see p.223–225).

7.   Whilst there were numerous acts of violence presented on television news it is notable that the atrocities documented are those practiced by the American military on those suspected of being VC; however it should be observed that the American troops could also become victims to torture at the hands of the guerrillas – this relentless cycle of atrocity is detailed in *Chickenhawk*, where the narrator describes the shooting of bound VC prisoners as a form of retaliation to the discovery of the torture / castration of a group of grunts (p.363–364).

8.   Alvin and Heidi Toffler, *War And Anti-War, Survival At The Dawn Of The 21st Century*, Little, Brown and Company: London, 1994 (1993), p.45.

9.   Manuel De Landa, *War In The Age of Intelligent Machines*, Zone Books, Swerve Editions, New York, 1991, p.79.

10.   Amongst the slogans painted on soldier's helmets (such as "hell sucks") was the phrase UUUU – which stood for "the unwilling, led by the unqualified, doing the unnecessary, for the ungrateful" (Gerard J. DeGroot, *A Nobel Cause*, p.290) and "Eat The Apple, Fuck The Corps" (Michael Herr, *Dispatches*, Pan Books, London, 1979 [1977], p.87). While Mason observed that "maybe the only people who wanted us around were the Saigon politicians who were getting rich by having the Americans here." (Robert Mason, *Chickenhawk*, p.261).

11.   One notable exception to this is the Gulf War movie **Three Kings** (David O Russell, 1999).

12.   Many of Walter Hill's films deal with people trapped in an increasingly unfamiliar territory under threat from dangerous locals (see **The Warriors** [1979] and **Trespass** [1992], for example), but it is **Southern Comfort** – a more ferocious update of John Boorman's **Deliverance** (1972) – that represents the clearest Vietnam allegory. Violent "redneck psycho" exploitationers such as **Mother's Day** (1980), **Just Before Dawn** (1980), or **Hunters' Blood** (1987) might also be considered in this light.
            In another film which might be read as a Nam allegory, James Cameron's **Aliens** (1986), the same psychological fragmentation and dislocation occurs, as the heavily armed space Marine Corps are attacked and killed by an almost endless flow of aliens armed only with teeth and acid blood. This is especially so in the first encounter with the xenomorphs, which transpires at the very edges of the alien's hive located within a gigantic industrial structure – the terrain, increasingly unfamiliar having been constructed by aliens, actually camouflages the creatures who unexpectedly emerge from the walls and ceiling of their fleshy nest. The troops open fire with flamethrowers but are unable to use many of their ballistic weapons due to the proximity of the nuclear reactor; their weapons rendered useless they are unable to fully defend themselves. The techno-hard-bodies of the grunts are emasculated against the terrifying savagery of the 'monsters'. Moreover, whilst the troops are unwilling to die the aliens pour forward in a murderous rush apparently willing to risk death in order to shield the Queen (metaphorically, their motherland). As the film progresses so the troops realise that only complete withdrawal will guarantee their survival, even as they run-out of ammunition.
            Paul Verhoeven's **Starship Troopers** (1997) continues this xenophobic SF thematic, as the eponymous heroes invade a star-system of giant tunnel-dwelling arachnids (to get the full pseudo-Nam effect, replace the word "bug" with "gook" as it proliferates the script). The other SF film to register here is Schwarzenegger's jungle

Predator

nightmare **Predator** (1987), in which a group of crack US troops are mercilessly picked off and slaughtered by an unseen enemy, who butchers their bodies and keeps their polished skulls as trophies.

13.   If **First Blood** – and subsequent Rambo movies – appear as right wing fantasies of victory then these pale into insignificance when compared to the reactionary cinematic output featuring Chuck Norris, whose martial arts-infused Nam Vet "epics" include **Missing In Action** (Joseph Zito, 1984), **Missing In Action 2: The Beginning** (Lance Hool, 1985), and **Braddock: Missing In Action 3** (Aaron Norris, 1988), all of which focus on a disgruntled vet who returns to the Nam to search for prisoners kept hostage by the NVA long after the war ends. The enemy in these films is not just the stereotypical "gooks", but also the liberal political system back home. Norris also appeared in numerous other films as the 'heroic' Nam Vet, including **Good Guys Wear Black** (Ted Post, 1979), **A Force Of One** (Paul Aaron, 1979), and **Forced Vengeance** (1982).

CHAPTER 14
HELICOPTERS
IN THE MIST

Helicopter. A flying machine designed to rise vertically by one or more lifting screws revolving horizontally.

Revolution. I.4. The action...of turning or whirling round, or of moving round some point. *III.2.* A complete overthrow of the established government in any country or state by those who were previously subject to it; a forcible substitution of a new ruler or a form of government.

It seems almost redundant to point out that helicopters are a significant part of the iconography of the Vietnam War film. While perhaps not an absolutely essential feature of the genre (if we accept that the "Vietnam War film" is indeed a genre), it is difficult to think of any narrative, filmic or otherwise, dealing with this particular war that does not feature, directly or indirectly, some reference to this ubiquitous means of transport and attack. It is, however, worth noting briefly that there has been a tendency in theorising film genres to reduce categorisations to a listing of iconographic elements, but, as Peter Brunette and David Wills argue, the icon always exceeds the boundaries of any single genre since its very status as icon depends on extra-generic information. In their discussion of the Western, for instance, they write:

The presence of six-guns, cowboys, and a Western locale may be the marks of the genre "Western" but will, unlike the texts in which they appear, themselves never belong to the genre of the Western. They also "belong", respectively, to a historical practice of law enforcement or law breaking, a sociological category, and a geographical region, all of which, larger than the text in which they appear, come to inhabit it. (p.48)

The helicopter, then, while marking a particular film as a member of the genre, "Vietnam War film", always remains outside of that genre itself, just as quotation marks are never part of the quotation as such. In order to be less reductive in a discussion of the helicopter, it is necessary then to explore the figure of the helicopter not only in its manifestation within the films themselves but within a broader history of technology and its development.

    Unsurprisingly, **Apocalypse Now** (Francis Ford Coppola, 1979) looms large in the background of any such discussion, but in an attempt to add as little as possible to the enormous amount of verbiage steadily accreting to this title, this may be an opportune moment to resurrect one of the less well know forebears of this canonic film.[1] Joseph Losey is probably most well know for his

Apocalypse Now

examinations of constipated desire in **The Servant** (1963), **Accident** (1967) and **The Go-Between** (1971) or for his exile from the USA during the HUAC investigations of the late 1940s (explored in his less than subtle allegory, **The Boy With The Green Hair** [1948]). Almost forgotten now is his paranoiac escape thriller, **Figures In A Landscape** (1970) (released as **The Hunted** in the UK), in which two men flee from a pursuing helicopter across a mysterious and unspecified countryside. The very stark nature of this film is useful in identifying some of the main negative tropes associated with the helicopter in cinema.

Just as it seems pointless, and even possibly foolish, to try and make absolute generalisations about *all* Vietnam War films featuring helicopters, so it seems to make sense to concentrate on a couple of examples that are hardly considered to be "classics" of the genre. John Woo's **Bullet In The Head/Die Xue Jie Tou** (1990) and Oliver Stone's **Heaven & Earth** (1993) do not put the helicopter at the centre of their narratives and so provide an opportunity to examine the use of the helicopter as peripheral image while also being two of the few films about this period that are not told primarily from the Americans' point of view. Since both films are also historically distant from the Vietnamese conflict, they offer some measure of the stability of the image of the helicopter within the genre.

Using the helicopter as a representative of technology as such, this article will also deal with the odd relationship that technology has to the human body, perhaps best expressed in the Comte de Lautréamont's infamous description in *Les Chants de Maldoror* (1869): "He is as handsome…as the fortuitous encounter on a dissecting table of a sewing machine and an umbrella". This image of fascination, desire and dread, which seems to anachronistically evoke the blades of the helicopter as it ferries blasted and bloody bodies from battlefield to hospital, is strangely apt as an epitaph for an exploration of technology as a figure of both utopian progress and destructive potential. One the one hand, technology is the source of civilisation while on the other it is a destroyer of the natural and of the essentially human. The problematic boundary between that which is machine and that which is human will be a central concern here. The metaphor of the machine is used in the films discussed in a politically and ideologically ambiguous manner in which the machine is curiously sexed: the helicopter as masculine war-machine *and* as feminine saviour-machine (although crude, this binary opposition seems fruitful at this point). It is the former reading of technology which is perhaps most prevalent in this sexing of the machine. In her study of feminism and technology, Judy Wajcman writes:

"Conceiving of technology as a culture reveals the extent to which an affinity with technology has been and is integral to the constitution of male gender identity." (Feminism Confronts Technology, p.158)

Clearly, the American helicopter in Vietnam represents a certain potency, often contrasted to the "primitively" equipped Vietcong, with the machine idealised as a sign of progress, invulnerability, masculinity and, even, capitalism itself. In this context, the image of the machine easily translates into a metaphor of colonial power, a metaphor which is so clearly marked in **Apocalypse Now** with the helicopter squadron of the Cavalry Division. Although there is here the implication that the Cavalry have swapped their natural horses for mechanical helicopters (just as Billy and Wyatt ride motorcycles instead of horses in their search for the American dream in **Easy Rider** [Dennis Hopper, 1969]), it is a trifle misleading to consider that the colonisation of the West in America was entirely pre-technological. In *The Pilot And The Passenger*, Leo Marx comments on the 19th century drive into the West:

"In America machines were pre-eminently conquerors of nature – nature conceived as space. They blazed across a raw landscape of wilderness and farm."[2]

The machine is thus both the harbinger of civilisation and also the right to civilise. The perception of being in possession of advanced technology is one that is used to justify the use of that technology in establishing the dominance of the culture which wields it. In *The Body Electric*, Jeremy Benthall asks, "Why do we get excited or inspired by technology?" The answer:

"Because it opens new possibilities for human action, and in turn these technical possibilities can lead to an enrichment of moral, cultural and social life." (p.21)

This triumphalist attitude towards technology is, however, in no way stable. Although strongly associated with progress, the machine is as often, and sometimes simultaneously, seen as both utopian and dystopian. It is this ambiguity which underlies the helicopter, both as machine and as image, in particular, of technology as such.

TECHNOLOGY/PROGRESS/FEAR

In Samuel Butler's bizarre 1872 novel, *Erewhon*, a world is imagined in which criminals are treated as patients in need of medical attention and sympathy, while the sick require strict discipline, imprisonment and even capital punishment. It is world in which technology is viewed with great distrust and the story of the growth of this disillusion is chronicled in a section entitled, "The Book of the Machines":

"So that even now the machines will only serve on condition of being served, and that too upon their own terms; the moment their terms are not complied with, they jib, and either smash themselves and all whom they can reach, or turn churlish and refuse to work at all. How many men at this hour are living in a state of bondage to the machines?" (p.208)

Benthall goes on to show that there is a profound mistrust of technology: "It is a common pattern to find a critique of technocracy embedded in a glorification of the potential of technology, so that the discourse carries a double message" while Leo Marx finds a similar manifestation in what he terms "covert culture":

"When we analyze the imagery employed even by those who professed approval of technological change, we discover evidence of widespread if largely unacknowledged doubt, fear, and hostility."[3]

This is the fear that we find in Butler's *Erewhon*; the fear that the machine will eventually usurp the human and be in a position to subject its very inventors. In a borader metaphoric move, the power of technology is transformed into the technology of power when Leo Marx recalls the speech of a student activist, speaking out against the Vietnam War in 1964:

"There is a time when the operation of the machine becomes so odious, makes you so sick at heart, that you can't take part; you can't even tacitly take part, and you've got to put your bodies upon the gears and upon the wheels, upon the levers, upon all the apparatus and you've got to make it stop. And you've got to indicate to the people who run it, to the people who own it, that unless you're free, the machines will be prevented from working at all."[4]

Political power is now seen as a metaphor of machinery and the fragile human body is set up in opposition to that power. Thus in the context of Vietnam the U.S. government is associated with the machine and, in the war itself, the machine quintessentially associated with U.S. forces is the helicopter. Before going on to consider some of the films in more detail, it may be instructive to take a detour through the annals of helicopter history.

HISTORY AND THE HELICOPTER

The principle of the helicopter, it is generally agreed, was first formulated by Leonardo da Vinci at the turn of the sixteenth century.[5] Its most serious proponent was Igor Sikorsky who started to develop a working helicopter in 1908.[6] This attempt was unsuccessful and Sikorsky turned his attention to large, multi-engined aeroplanes and to "flying boats".[7] He returned to helicopter design only in 1938, although he had been following the various advances in helicopter aviation since 1928.[8]

The story of this development is documented by the first helicopter test-pilot, Charles Lester Morris, in his *Pioneering The Helicopter* (1945). This narrative provides a fascinating description of the heady excitement involved in testing this new invention: the increasingly longer periods aloft, the refinement of movement control, the greater distances travelled and so on. Much of the funding at this time, not surprisingly, came from the U.S. Army, although very little of Morris' tale involves itself with the war. He does however regret not being able to pit his skills and machinery against those of German researchers:

"I was deeply sorry that wartime restrictions prevented us from officially going after the world speed record for helicopters established by the German FW-61." (p.88)

Morris (and Sikorsky[9]) constantly highlight the beneficent utility of the new helicopter:

"This rope-ladder idea may have ramifications in lifesaving, including the transportation of doctors or workers into restricted areas where trees or other obstacles might prevent a landing and also the lowering or raising of life rafts, materials, tools, food, and medicine." (p.87)

There is, however, an area of their research (touched on very briefly) which Morris finds particularly enjoyable:

"One of the most interesting projects was bombing....Gregory would hover two or three hundred high, and when he thought he was over the target, he would give Kilpatrick a poke and the bomb would be heaved overboard" (p.115).

This aspect of the research is not elaborated on by Morris.

Sikorsky is also fascinated by the process of bombing. In fact, he begins his experiments early on when he becomes interested in chemicals at the age of twelve, around 1901, and manufactures many "evil-smelling concoctions". Sikorsky's biographer then provides us with this interesting fact:

"Later, Igor found a pamphlet written by anarchists which described how to make a bomb. He made several, exploding them in the garden some distance from the house."[10]

The young Igor's fascination with technology begins where it ends, with bombs being dropped. The helicopter, developed during the second world war (and purportedly used by the Germans in the invasion of Holland[11]) is from its inception involved in a contradictory discourse of technical destruction and salvation. Morris relates the following anecdote concerning Igor Sikorsky (this will have ramifications for our future discussion of the apocalypse):

"[The discussion] pertained to the pronunciation of the word helicopter. Mr. Sikorsky used a long e – "heel-i-copter". He liked to call the ship the heely

Platoon

(spelled heli), and it would have bordered on the profane with a short e as in "hell". (p.26)

A mere slip of the tongue, then, turns the saviour into the anti-Christ. This contradictory position occupied by the technology of the helicopter is exacerbated unbelievably in the Vietnam War.

Only Sikorsky's biographer, Frank J. Delear, seems to think that the helicopter had an unambiguous role in the War. He implies that the helicopters were *only* used on rescue missions:

"The crews of this service's Sikorsky "Jolly Green Giant" helicopters wrote new chapters in selfless heroism in Southeast Asia by snatching hundreds of downed airmen from jungles, valleys, and mountaintops, defying capture and death themselves on almost every flight." (Igor Sikorsky: His 3 Careers In Aviation, p.190)

This gung-ho description belies the very great importance of the helicopter to the American project in Vietnam[12]. In his excellent "Flight Controls: The Social History Of The Helicopter As A Symbol Of Vietnam", Alasdair Spark writes that "in a very real sense the helicopter made the Vietnam War possible". He quotes Lt.Gen. J.Tolson in an official army study (1974):

"No other machine could have possibly accomplished the job...those scores of missions ranging from an insertion of a long range patrol to the vertical assault of an entire division; it alone could place artillery on the mountain tops and resupply these isolated bases; it alone could evacuate the wounded out of a chimney landing zone..." (p.87)

The helicopter is seen by the army as only secondarily a life-machine. Spark quotes a crewman describing loaches, Huey Hogs, and Huey Cobras as "never intended to carry troops or supplies, or letters. They were just these pieces of death machine that flew around, and that's all they did".[13]

The helicopter both saved soldiers from death, delivered them to it and dealt it out to the Vietcong. The soldier developed an extremely ambiguous love/hate relationship with the helicopter; "the fundamental authority of the helicopter lay precisely in this disturbing power to insert them into and extract them from the war".[14] Even being *inside* the helicopter is a traumatic business. On the one hand, you are in flight and on a small piece of American territory, while on the other you are helpless and completely exposed to enemy fire. Spark quotes William Willson's description of soldiers feeling "helpless prisoners in this tin trap" and Tim O'Brien noting "how perfectly exposed you are. Nowhere to hide your head. You are in a fragile machine. No foxholes, no rocks, no gullies".[15] In *The Helicopter And The Punji Stick*, H. Palmer Hall writes: "The helicopter is the great friend and the great enemy of the American soldier in the novels and the films of the war" (p.151).

The manic schizophrenia of the helicopter experience, its confusion of love and hate, is captured in Michael Herr's journalistic novel, *Dispatches*, often cited as an important influence on **Apocalypse Now**:

"In the months after I got back the hundreds of helicopters I'd flown in began to draw together until they'd formed a collective meta-chopper, and in my mind it was the sexiest thing going; saver-destroyer, provider-waster, right hand-left hand, nimble, fluent, canny and human; hot steel, grease, jungle-saturated

canvas webbing, sweat cooling and warming up again, cassette rock and roll in one ear and door-gun fire in the other, fuel, heat, vitality and death, death itself, hardly an intruder....

"*Helicopters and people jumping out of helicopters, people so in love they'd run to get on even when there wasn't any pressure. Choppers rising straight out of small cleared jungle spaces, wobbling down on to city rooftops, cartons of rations and ammunition thrown off, dead and wounded loaded on.*" (pp.15-16)

Apropos this particular passage in Herr's book, Fredric Jameson comments that this "new machine" does not "represent motion" like the locomotive or machinery, but can "only be represented *in motion*".[16] The helicopter is the machine that is completely mobile "giving not just independence from the ground but total independence in the air....Helicopters could ascend vertically, stop in mid-air, hover, pirouette and fly backward....".[17] The helicopter is both the promise of freedom and the threat of destruction or abandonment.

It is interesting to note that even the very *representations* of the helicopter in films and novels are described by H. Palmer Hall in similar dizzying terms: "After spending a few years reading hundreds of books and viewing dozens of films based on the experiences of soldiers in the Vietnam War, I must confess that images begin to blur. A helicopter in book number one hundred and three seems the reincarnation of a Huey I met back in books number two and seven and in numbers ten through seventeen and so on. A chopper flies out of **Platoon** and in a moment of bizarre discongruity lands in the midst of **The Green Berets**" (p.150).

THE SURVEILLANCE/DISCIPLINE MACHINE: DEATH FROM ABOVE

In the very first pages of George Orwell's *Nineteen Eighty-Four*, the slogan "BIG BROTHER IS WATCHING YOU" is introduced. Is it a coincidence that the helicopter is not too distant?

"*In the far distance a helicopter skimmed down between the roofs, hovered for an instant like a bluebottle, and darted away again with a curving flight. It was the police patrol, snooping into people's windows.*" (p.6)

Only eight years after the first successful trials, Orwell already sees the importance of the helicopter's mobility in terms of social control. Spark shows how the helicopter's use in Vietnam resulted in their use in crowd control back home.

"*With spotlight, observing camera and a megaphone issuing orders to those below, the helicopter henceforth became the technologically extended arm of state authority, and US citizens the target of its interest.*" (p.103)

Spark's description of the surveillance helicopters "as autonomous agents of state authority, apparently pilotless or anonymously crewed"; as the "`hermetic helicopter'... sleek and dark-canopied, self-contained and sealed, with no openings to the world, as if it were an alien spacecraft" (p.104) would seem to

Figures In A Landscape

make the helicopter the ideal modern inheritor of Michel Foucault's analysis of the Panopticon which "is a machine for dissociating the see/being seen dyad: in the peripheric ring, one is totally seen, without ever seeing; in the central tower, one sees everything without ever being seen".[18] The helicopter seems to be the "perfect disciplinary apparatus" which makes "it possible for a single gaze to see everything constantly" (p.173). This is the position the helicopter inhabits in Joseph Losey's **Figures In A Landscape**.

The plot of the film is almost that of a crudely distilled Kafka story: two men, whose crimes are unknown, escape from imprisonment into an unnamed country and are pursued by a helicopter until they reach the mountain border where one of the men is killed by the helicopter while the other finds presumed safety. Based on the 1968 novel by Barry England, Losey was brought in after the first director refused to change the ending of the book in which both men are killed. The very simplicity of the story clearly focuses the men's struggle for freedom on their relationship with the implacable presence of the helicopter. In the very first shots of the film, Ansell (Malcolm McDowell) and MacConnachie (Robert Shaw, who also rewrote the screenplay on set) are seen in silhouette, hands fastened behind their backs, running along a beach at sunset. The helicopter appears outlined against the sky and the camera cuts to behind the two pilots' heads giving a point-of-view shot of the escapees. The pilots themselves, with their black jumpsuits and smoothly opaque full-face helmets,

The Deer Hunter

are never humanised and strongly resemble the slick appearance of the helicopter. They are not human beings, merely interchangeable parts of a greater machine.

It is now that a rather heavy-handed metaphor, which is invoked throughout the film, first appears: in a montage sequence the helicopter is associated with the flight of an eagle, while Ansell and Mac are linked, none to subtly, to galloping horses. Later the men are compared to goats being herded or pigs being shot, while the helicopter is constantly connected to the flight of birds. The ease and grace of flight (in its aerial sense) is clearly contrasted to the sheer physical effort required in moving across the ground and, of course, the omniscient view afforded by the helicopter's superior position puts the easily visible men at a massive disadvantage. As Ansell and Mac continue their journey, stealing food supplies and even a gun from a country village, it is their physical deterioration through contact with the ground that is continually stressed. Towards the end of the film, Mac melodramatically bursts into tears:

"I can see the bones of my fingers. Lips are salty...smell like animals. Filthy. Christ. Jesus. What have we done to ourselves? Not living. We're dead. We should never have tried it...Oh God! Oh Jesus! Oh Christ! We're worse than animals."

Their metaphoric connection with land animals eventually saps them of their humanity and, in Mac's case, of life itself. Throughout the chase it is Mac who most vociferously resents the constant presence of the helicopter and he develops an almost irrational desire to kill the pilots inside. Mac persuades Ansell to expose himself in order to lure the helicopter closer to the ground and when it does so, manages to shoot one of the pilots who falls out of the machine. Mac and Ansell ransack the body and find a machine gun and a watch ("4:22, July 17th" – but it is broken) as well as some cigarettes. Their moment of triumph is, however, short-lived and soon they are being hunted by ground troops through lush vegetation and cultivated fields. The helicopter returns to drop fire-bombs and napalm until the two eventual reach the comparative safety of the mountains.

Eventually reaching a snow-covered border point guarded by soldiers of what appears to be a less hostile, but still inscrutable, military faction, the two men are within yards of safety when Mac decides to attack the still-following helicopter with the machine gun. Ansell moves towards the safety of the border while the deranged Mac stands his ground and is unsurprisingly shot down in slow-motion by the helicopter. There is a helicopter point-of-view shot of the body which tracks back in an echo of the beginning of the film.

While the film was shot in Spain, there is never any mention of geographical place or of any specific time. The landscape is often seen in wide-shot and reduced to a geometric abstraction. The appalling vulnerability of the human body is always emphasised: even in Mac's rather tiresome stories about his wife who was disfigured horribly by a friend's Alsatian. During their escape, Mac and Ansell are constantly defined by their relationship to the helicopter and while there is never any explicit mention of Vietnam in the film, it is clear that a strong analogy is being suggested. As Paul Virilio points out in his elegant commentary on the film:

"Combat here is a game in which all the instruments take part in the saturation of space. Those who conduct the hunt visually are concerned to annul distance, first on board their means of transport, then with their guns. As for the escapees, they use their weapons not so much to destroy as to establish a distance: they live only in what separates them from their pursuers, they can survive only through pure distance, their ultimate protection is the continuity of nature as a whole. Avoiding roads, houses and anything that points to human uses, the two men coil up in creases of the land, seek out the cover of grass and trees, atmospheric disturbances, and darkness. It is useful to recall that **Figures In A Landscape** *was made at the height of the Vietnam War, when the First Cavalry Division – the same that once chased Indians across the Great Plains – was carrying out its traditional missions in combat helicopters. Ten years later, Coppola drew extensively on Losey's film to stage the helicopter ballets of* **Apocalypse Now***, following the rhythm of a Western and using a bugle call to sound the charge of a cavalry squadron."* (War And Cinema, p.18-19)

It is not necessary, here, to provide any further commentary on **Apocalypse Now** other than to note Virilio's explicit link between the camera and the gun, where the technology of perception is inextricably linked to the technology of destruction. It is this logic of the helicopter as surveillance/annihilation machine that is almost unavoidably linked to the machinery of the camera itself. In answer to the question: "But what shall we dream of when everything becomes visible?", Virilio answers: "We'll dream of being blind".[19]

Whereas **Figures In A Landscape** puts the helicopter at the centre of its narrative, it is more usual for the helicopter to feature as an uncanny atmospheric image hovering eerily in slow motion and often heralded by the distinctive sound of its rotor blades. The helicopter's ambiguous denotation as death and life machine is clearly delineated in **Bullet In The Head** and **Heaven & Earth**.

Beginning in Hong Kong in 1967 during the communist protests against the current regime, John Woo's[20] **Bullet In The Head** (almost invariably referred to as the "Eastern **Deerhunter**" but which seems to have more than a touch of **Rebel Without A Cause** to it) follows the story of three friends (improbably called Ben [Tony Leung], Frank [Jacky Cheung] and Paul [Waise Lee] in the English translation) who are forced to leave Hong Kong when they become involved in a murder. Saigon seems the obvious place to go and they smuggle goods there to pay for their passage. In a complex concatenation of events, they attack a Saigon gangster's establishment, stealing a crate filled with gold (and, unknown to them, containing documents detailing the names and locations of CIA agents in Saigon) as well as a Hong Kong singer, Sally Yen (Yolinda Yam), who had been a virtual slave to the gangster. Leaving Saigon by car to meet a boat at a river rendezvous, the group is ambushed by the Vietcong and Sally is killed with much attendant melodrama. Paul becomes increasingly obsessed with the gold and will not let his friends dump it in order to make good their escape and they are captured by the Vietcong and held prisoner alongside American soldiers.

The prisoners are tortured and forced to shoot each other for the sadistic delight of their caricatured captors until Frank and Ben manage to turn the guns on the Vietcong and attempt a seemingly doomed escape. Opportunely, it is exactly at this moment that American helicopters, as literal *dei ex machina*, come chugging down the river with radio cries of "Reds everywhere! Watch your ass!". In an explosion-heavy sequence the VC camp is annihilated by the helicopters while Ben, Frank and Paul manage to escape (although Paul does shoot Frank in the head, hence the title, to prevent his cries of pain revealing them to the VC). The remainder of the film details Frank's transformation into a brain-damaged, heroin-addicted assassin-for-hire in Saigon and his mercy killing by Ben who then returns to Hong Kong to confront Paul, who is now a respected member of the yakuza, with Ben's bullet-fractured skull.

While the plot of **Bullet In The Head** is as vertiginous as any of its many action sequences, it is clear that the helicopter appears fairly unproblematically in its role as saviour-machine[21].

The third instalment in Oliver Stone's Vietnam Trilogy, **Heaven & Earth**, tells the story of a Vietnamese woman's experience of the conflict, presenting an idyllic rural life ("And I lived in the most beautiful village on earth" accompanied by perhaps the crassest use ever of swelling orchestral pomposity) beset by the corrupt Vietnamese government in cahoots with the equally corrupt American forces on one side and the probably justified but equally inhuman communist army of the Vietcong on the other. The peasants are strongly associated with the lushness of the land and it is while walking through the impossibly green fields that our protagonist, Le Ley (Hiep Thi Le) is overwhelmed by a US helicopter descending from out of the sky, leading a ground reconnaissance of the area. It is the very power of the American technology itself that emphasises the vulnerability of the humans within. As one of her friends says to Le Ly later:

"They say that [the American soldiers] *all have blind blue eyes behind their glasses and if you take their shoes off, they have sore feet and cry in pain. Take away their glasses, their boots, they can't fight."*

Heaven & Earth

The paradox of technology is here very clear. While making one invulnerable it simultaneously makes one weak and soft. The helicopter as the ultimate emblem of this dual strength and weakness of the nature of technology is here exemplary.

Starring Tommy Lee Jones – who had previously appeared as a trigger-happy Viet vet in **Rolling Thunder** (1977) and the TV productions **The Park Is Mine** (1986) and **Stranger On My Land** (1988) – **Heaven & Earth** provides a sentimental human drama that emphasises the frailty of the individual in the face of immeasurably powerful political and military forces. Although clearly not intended to be so, it is ironic that Le Ly eventually makes her fortune in the US of A by becoming a real estate agent and trading in land presumably originally wrested from the indigenous American population. Thus the very commodity, land, that the film romanticises in its beginning as belonging in some essential way to its Vietnamese peasant population is that which, on another continent, provides access to the capitalist dreams of that peasant. Perhaps it is no coincidence that when Le Ly encounters the helicopter in the fields of Vietnam, the wind from its rotors sends her straight hair into disarray, while the mark of her Westernisation is an elaborate hairstyle requiring the use of an electric blow dryer. **Heaven & Earth** dreams of an impossibly pre-technological world without hair dryers, helicopters or governments but it also presents a world in which the destructive potential of military and colonial technology is transformed into the harmless luxuries of hair products and, more problematically, of wealth itself.

MACHINE IDEOLOGY

Can the helicopter-in-operation be seen as liberation in and of itself? That in the very action of running (the ever-present/ce of being "in motion") this machine provides a freedom not available otherwise? Morris recalls a demonstration of the new helicopter attended by Helen Keller: "who, though deprived of sight and hearing throughout her entire life, `sees' more deeply and enjoys living more fully than almost anyone else I know". He writes:

"The engine was started, and the breeze from the rotor blew on her face. The average person would have thought no more of it – there was a wind – that was all. But not Miss Keller. She stood and <u>felt</u> it, with all the senses at her command. It seemed as though she almost absorbed it through her pores, until she had built up her detailed mental images of what was going on. After it was over, she said, 'It was buoyant! I could feel the lifting force of the machine. It was in some ways like Dr. Alexander Graham Bell's kite.'" (p.142)

Thus we are reminded of the importance of the helicopter as an avenue of flight rather than one of discipline or violence. Wajcman writes that it "is important not to underestimate women's capacity to subvert the intended purposes of technology and turn it to their collective advantage" (p.163). The machine that would seem to be wholly in the hands of men may be taken in hand and used as a trajectory of escape and freedom. Perhaps it is time to turn our helicopters into hair dryers.

NOTES

1.   Michael Ondaatje has recently referred to **Apocalypse Now** as "a film that has entered the mythology of film-making, and become a part of our subconscious". For similarly enthusiastic responses to the film see Peter Cowie's *The Apocalypse Now Book* (Faber and Faber, 2000) and Karl French's *Apocalypse Now* (Bloomsbury, 2000). **Apocalypse Now Redux**, Walter Murch's re-edit of the film, is appraised in this very volume.

2.   "The Machine In The Garden" (1956), p.118.

3.	"Literature, Technology, And Covert Culture" (1957) , p.136.

4.	Mario Savio, "a graduate student at the University of California at Berkeley", quoted in "The Pilot And The Passenger", p.198.

5.	Ivor Hart "The Mechanical Investigations Of Leonardo da Vinci", p.192.

6.	Frank J. Delear "Igor Sikorsky", pp.17-18.

7.	Ibid., chapters 4-10.

8.	Ibid., pp.167-171.

9.	Delear, pp. 165-166.

10.	Ibid., p.12.

11.	Morris, pp.40-41.

12.	For a detailed chronology of the deployment of the helicopter in the Vietnam War see Jonathan van Nortwick and Alan Barbour's "Chronology" at the USMC/Vietnam Helicopter Association website <http://www.popasmoke.com>.

13.	This is cited in Ron Glasser's *365 Days* (1972), p.96-97.

14.	Spark, p.92.

15.	*The LBJ Brigade* (1967) and *If I Die In A Combat Zone* (1980) respectively, pp.92-93.

16.	"Postmodernism, or, The Cultural Logic Of Late Capitalism", p.85.

17.	Spark, pp.96-97.

18.	"Discipline And Punish", pp.201-202.

19.	Louise Wilson in "Cyberwar, God And Television: Interview With Paul Virilio". *CTHEORY*. 21 October 1994 (www.ctheory.com).

20.	John Woo also directed **Heroes Shed No Tears/Ying Xiong Wei Lei** (1986), which fringes on the Vietnam War film genre in its tale of mercenaries hired by the Thai government to capture a rebel general who is hiding out in the Vietnamese jungle. This remarkable film features sadism and cruelty, dismembered bodies, eye trauma and sick violence in a "bullet ballet" of search and destroy. Woo's first American movie, **Hard Target** (1993), is an update of **The Most Dangerous Game** (1932), in which a group of rich killers in New Orleans hunt homeless Vietnam vets as human prey.
	Other Chinese films relating to the Vietnam conflict include Tsui Hark's nihilistic but exhilarating **Don't Play With Fire/Diyi Leixing Weixian** (1980), which features arms-dealing Viet vets alongside Triad gangsters and student terrorists. But Hong Lu Wong's maniac **Cannibal Mercenary** (1983) is probably the most violent gore movie to be associated with the Vietnam War genre. The film concerns a band of Thai mercenaries sent

John Woo's *Heroes Shed No Tears*

into the jungle to rescue a woman from the Viet Cong. After a series of bloody battles with the VC, in which decapitation is the preferred method of dispatch, they meet up with the woman only to have their mission changed – they must now assassinate a renegade general who is trafficking drugs and who commands a savage band of human flesh-eating tribesmen.

Captured by this renegade, two of the mercenaries are butchered and eaten alive in a blood-spurting, brain-smearing cannibal orgy, before the others escape. After a bloody climactic battle, only the mercenary leader survives. The film ends with him in a military hospital, tortured by flashbacks which conveniently reprise every ultra-violent moment from the movie – including castration, blinding, and lynching – in one concentrated sequence. A crazed concoction of martial arts, gore and cannibal mayhem, **Cannibal Mercenary** truly takes the Vietnam jungle trip to "the end".

More recent is Yang Chin Cong's **Legendary Frog Women** (1989), which focuses on a group of female POWs who escape their Viet Cong captors to engage in revolutionary guerilla warfare.

21.   A view very much put across in such US documentaries as **Chopper Wars** (1988). In **Chopper Wars**, we see both original and recreated footage of US helicopters in Nam, including both rescue work and such gung-ho sequences as "Recon by Fire", in which choppers draw enemy anti-aircraft fire so that jet fighters can scream in and destroy the VC in devastating napalm attacks. **Alone, Unarmed And Unafraid** (1968) was a similar film documenting recon missions over Nam flown by US Air Force pilots.

INDEX OF FILMS

Page number in bold indicates an illustration; entry in italic denotes TV series

WWW.CREATIONBOOKS.COM